*revive*DAILY

A Devotional Journey
from Genesis to Revelation

Year One

Laura Kim Martin

Revive me, O Lord, according to Your word.
—Psalm 119:107 NASB

time to
revive
Richardson, Texas

Time to Revive
Published in conjunction with Iron Stream Media
100 Missionary Ridge
Birmingham, AL 35242
IronStreamMedia.com

New Hope Publishers serves its authors as they express their views, which may not express the views of the publisher.

Library of Congress Control Number: 2020908093.

Cover art © 2015 by Mindi Oaten Art.

ISBN-13: 978-1-63204-090-9
Ebook ISBN: 978-1-63204-091-6

1 2 3 4 5—23 22 21 20 19

I dedicate this book to my husband, Kyle Lance Martin, my best friend and partner for life! Your unconditional love for me, your challenge and encouragement to live obediently to the voice of the Lord as we walk by faith, and your ability to have fun and make me laugh carried me along this writing journey. I love you.

I also dedicate this book to my four kiddos: Maya Joy, Nadia Grace, Selah Raye, and Jude Alexander. You fill my life with joy and adventure as we seek the Lord together as a family! You are loved so much!

Delight yourself in the Lord;
And He will give you the desires of your heart.
—Psalm 37:4 NASB

About the Cover

I sought the Lord for His will regarding the cover for *revive*DAILY. One day, I found myself standing in our guest room, looking at a framed painting by prophetic artist Mindi Oaten. In that moment, something in me leaped! This guest room had hosted many of the reviveSCHOOL teachers over the course of the two years we taught, studied, and wrote through the Bible. In addition, this room, with this one painting on all the walls, served as a source of refuge for me when I needed to rest or dig into the Word and write. And in that reflective moment, I knew this painting was to be the cover for *revive*DAILY!

Mindi painted this particular piece, *Tree of Life,* on Day 185 of reviveINDIANA, while in Fort Wayne, Indiana. Mindi wrote this description of the piece:

> Positioned along the glistening Living Waters, life is found in the tree that is planted and rooted in the Lord. These trees are unlike any other tree. Their fruit is so uncontainable and of every variety. It's leaf glimmer and sparkle in the light of the Lord's love and righteousness. This tree of life when rooted and established in favorable soil will bring healing to every corner of the earth. For God covers and longs to heal the nations.

Then he showed me a river of the water of life, clear as crystal, coming from the throne of God and of the Lamb, in the middle of its street. On either side of the river was the tree of life, bearing twelve kinds of fruit, yielding its fruit every month; and the leaves of the tree were for the healing of the nations.
—Revelation 22:1–2 NASB

I am grateful for this artwork as the cover of *revive*DAILY, *Year One* and *Year Two,* because the message portrays my hope and prayer for each reader of this devotional. This one painting is divided in half between

Year One and *Year Two* book covers to portray the image of life transformation and growth in Christ as you spend time in His Word. As you study the Bible day by day and journey from Genesis through Revelation, I pray you will become like this tree of life: planted and rooted in the Lord, bearing uncontainable fruit and sparkling in the light of the Lord's love and righteousness!

> *Instead, his delight is in the Lord's instruction,*
> *and he meditates on it day and night.*
> *He is like a tree planted beside streams of water*
> *that bears its fruit in season*
> *and whose leaf does not wither.*
> *Whatever he does prospers.*
> —Psalm 1:2–3

Mindi Oaten has ministered with the Time to Revive team since 2015 as a prophetic artist working in acrylic on canvas. Mindi lives with her family in Alberta, Canada. As part of the curriculum for reviveSCHOOL, Mindi painted a prophetic painting for each book of the Bible. You can view her artwork biblical at www.reviveSCHOOL .org. You can view and order prints of all her prophetic artwork at www.mindioaten.com.

On the front cover and throughout each devotional page, you will see the shape of a double diamond. A diamond can symbolize: light, commitment, faithfulness, promise, victory, and treasures and riches. As you read through the Bible and this devotional, I pray your life becomes transformed by the light of Christ found in the rich treasures of His Word.

Contents

A Devotional Journey from Genesis to Revelation

This is the first year of a devotional journey walking you through the Word of God from Genesis to Revelation. You will read all sixty-six books of the Bible in two years, alternating between sections of the Old and New Testaments, while recognizing the Messiah in each book. Imagine Paul discussing the Scriptures with disciples in the Hall of Tyrannus daily for two years, so that all of Asia heard the message of the Lord (Acts 19). The purpose for *revive*DAILY is for life transformation through the power of reading God's Word!

The Daily Reading Plan: Year One

Pentateuch

The Gospels

The Historical Books

You are half way through this two-year journey! The Lord has even more for you! Press on and continue through the Word of God with *revive*DAILY: *Year Two*, featuring devotions walking you through the remaining books of the Bible:

The Poetic Books

Paul's Letters

The Major Prophets

Other Letters in the New Testament

The Minor Prophets

Revelation

Acknowledgments

When Moses' hands grew heavy, they took a stone and put it under him, and he sat down on it. Then Aaron and Hur supported his hands, one on one side and one on the other so that his hands remained steady until the sun went down.
—Exodus 17:12

As believers walking out our calling, we face a spiritual battle every day. I love how the Lord revealed Moses' reality during a physical battle he faced against the Amalekites. Moses grew weary, and Aaron and Hur found a stone for him to sit on and then helped lift up each of his arms to help Moses remain steady.

In a similar way, the Lord brought teammates, friends, and family alongside me during this writing process. They "lifted my arms" and kept me steady on this journey.

I'm grateful for the Time to Revive team—your help in the many details, casting vision, prayer, and support! Thank you for walking out the vision and calling for reviveSCHOOL, and by faith, believing in the greatness and power of God.

I'm grateful for every reviveSCHOOL student, pastor and leader. What a journey we went on studying the Word of God! Thanks for your words of encouragement and displaying love to our family.

I'm grateful to all of the Time to Revive ministry partners walking along this journey with me, my family, and our team. I believe the Lord continues to answer your prayers as He moves in ways beyond what we'd ever imagined as Time to Revive equips the saints for the return of Christ.

I'm grateful to Ada Garrison-Disinger for saying "Yes" to helping with *revive*DAILY. The beauty that came from your heart as you studied the Word of God encouraged me along the way!

I'm grateful to Amy Revels, who week after week, volunteered to read through each *revive*DAILY lesson, editing, formatting, fine tuning, and speaking truth into me. Amy, you demonstrated grace, love, patience, and perseverance. I treasure our connection in this work and in our friendship. I could not have done this without you. Period.

I'm grateful for publisher, John Herring, who sat down with Kyle and me and said "Yes" to publishing *revive*DAILY at a McDonald's in Indiana. Thank you for the expertise and the hearts behind the mission at Iron Stream Media. I'm grateful for the team's excellence, encouragement, and grace along this publishing process.

I'm grateful to my early Saturday morning reviveSCHOOL Bible study girls meeting week after week throughout this entire writing process. You made this study come to life, as we not only read through the Bible together, but also shared our lives together. The Lord knit our hearts together in a special way.

I'm grateful to my friend, Wendy, who consistently prayed for me, talked with me, read *revive*DAILY, and encouraged me to keep going. You pursue Christ, you love people, and you ran this race with me, helping me press on, fixing my eyes on Jesus while writing through the Word.

I'm grateful to Mandy, for your friendship, but also for helping me with the vision for the book cover! Thanks for listening to my honest thoughts in critical moments and for celebrating life along the way!

I'm grateful to a handful of girlfriends who individually pursued me to have coffee, called me, and periodically checked in. You didn't go away, even though I felt as if I hid in a cave for two years. Thanks for being present and pouring into my life. Thanks for praying for me.

I'm grateful for the Martin family supporting Kyle and me. I believe your commitment to prayer will have a forever impact on our family. Thanks for always having the table set and an open door of gracious hospitality for our family and our team. And thanks for intentionally adding a coffee maker, as it displayed your understanding of my early morning writing routines when we came to Indiana!

I'm grateful to my mom and dad. You love the Lord with all your hearts and faithfully pray for Kyle and me. You raised me up in the Lord and were with me when I prayed to receive Christ. You have given me unconditional love and security in a way that mirrored my heavenly Father's love in my life. Thanks for encouraging me to keep writing through the hard times, visiting Dallas to help when needed, and welcoming me to write lakeside in Minnesota anytime.

I'm grateful for my children, Maya, Nadia, Selah, and Jude. You all have grown up during this season of reviveSCHOOL. You each teach me so much about God's sacrificial love, sufficient grace, and never-ending faithfulness. Above all, I love being your mom!

I'm grateful for my husband, Kyle Lance Martin. We've always said we are buddies for life. We just love doing life together, don't we? During this season, thanks for your vision for *revive*DAILY and for encouraging me to press on and stay focused. I'm grateful to run this race together, studying together through the Bible. Hang on—we know there's more to this journey ahead!

I'm grateful to my Savior, Jesus Christ, for salvation through faith and all sufficient grace. I'm grateful for every promise in His Word and His faithfulness. I will praise the name of the Lord forever! His love endures forever and ever, Amen!

But seek first the kingdom of God and His righteousness,
and all these things will be provided for you.
—Matthew 6:33

Welcome to *revive*DAILY

This is the day the LORD has made; let us rejoice and be glad in it!
—Psalm 118:24

Dear friend,

Our lives may look different from one another. Even so, I imagine you are much like me—*You desire to know Jesus more intimately. You want to learn more about the Bible. You are searching for something deeper to satisfy your soul.*

The Lord has a heart for you. He knows you. He loves you. He has called you by name. You are His child. I love the heart of the Lord for His children.

> *LORD, You have searched me and known me.*
> *You know when I sit down and when I stand up;*
> *You understand my thoughts from far away.*
> —Psalm 139:1–2

The book you hold is a the first of a two-volume collection of daily messages the Lord spoke to my heart as I read through the Bible over the span of two years. Every day, I read a section of Scripture and asked the Lord to reveal what He wanted for me to understand. I asked how I could apply the truth of His love and grace to my life. I asked the Lord to make it real to me. I asked Him to help me understand the storyline of the Messiah throughout Scripture. I asked the Lord to help me see His heart as I journeyed through the Word, just like you are getting ready to do.

How This Came About

Ever since I was a young child, I have trusted the Lord with my life. As a teenager, I began to really read His Word and followed where He led me by faith. When I became a young wife and then eventually a mom to four, I fully surrendered my life to Him, enduring trials, testing, and discipline. I watched the Lord work miraculously in my marriage, in the lives of my kids, and through the Time to Revive (TTR) ministry, which the Lord led my husband Kyle and me to begin. With a heart for reviving the Church, TTR carries out its calling to equip the saints through evangelism and discipleship to be ready for the return of Christ.

In 2010, TTR began traveling to cities and counties across America as the Spirit led, gathering believers to go out and share the Gospel with a focus to love, listen, discern, and respond to others. We would pour into these communities for a short period of time and leave an equipped and unified remnant to go out, to disciple, and to grow in the Lord.

For we walk by faith, not by sight.
—2 Corinthians 5:7

One of these communities was Elkhart County, Indiana. After a season of equipping in 2015, TTR moved on to other communities, but the Lord had a different plan. In 2017, the team felt led to go back to Elkhart County and reengage, similar to what Paul did when he traveled for the Gospel. In October 2017, Kyle sensed the Spirit lead him to pause his travel from city to city and spend two years studying the Scriptures with a group of believers, focusing on where the Messiah is found from Genesis to Revelation. And so, a new journey began and reviveSCHOOL was born.

He withdrew from them and met separately with the disciples, conducting discussions every day in the lecture hall of Tyrannus. And this went on for two years, so that all the inhabitants of Asia, both Jews and Greeks, heard the message about the Lord.
—Acts 19:9–10

From the beginning of reviveSCHOOL, a group of students gathered in Indiana, and then others around America began to join online, and even in a few groups in Liberia, Africa. Kyle began recording daily teachings in a studio in Texas, a team created study questions, and another team wrote study notes. Shortly after a unique time of prayer, Kyle said to me, "Laura, I think you should write every day through the Bible." As Kyle said this, the Lord spoke to my heart the words from Peter:

Humble yourselves, therefore, under the mighty hand of God,
so that He may exalt you at the proper time,
casting all your cares on Him, because He cares for you.
—1 Peter 5:6–7

Out of obedience I said, "Yes, I will write every day as You, Lord, lead me!" You see, I had always wanted to read through the entire Bible. I would start in Genesis, or in Matthew or the book of John, but I never made it all the way through. I'd engage in a specific Bible study, or I'd read a Psalm and Proverb each day. I read engaging devotional books. There were even years when my kids were small, I would lay the Bible on my kitchen table and read a sentence or two as I walked by just to sustain my soul. But I could not deny this growing desire to sit in the presence of the Lord all day and meditate on His Word.

Take delight in the LORD, and He will give you your hearts' desires.
—Psalm 37:4

The Lord has the best plans for us and wants to grant our hearts' desires. But we must say *yes* to Him! In His sovereignty and timing, the year I began reading, studying, and writing for two years was the same year all four kids went to school. For the first time in twelve busy, crazy years, I had time at home alone. The Lord granted me the desire of my heart in such a sweet, personal way.

And so, my journey writing through the Word of God began. I worked a few weeks ahead of the reviveSCHOOL students so they could read the *revive*DAILY devotional as they studied through the Scripture. Thus, many of the titles of the devotions match the reviveSCHOOL lessons they are entwined with (you can find them at www.reviveSCHOOL .org and in the separate printed volumes). I asked the Lord for His power to work within me, not in strife or performance, but that the words would be drawn from His heart.

Now we have this treasure in clay jars,
so that this extraordinary power may be from God and not from us.
—2 Corinthians 4:7

I asked the Lord to anchor my heart in Him, that I would not be tossed around or lose focus on my assignment from Him to write. So many things in this world can demand our attention, even great things, but I knew my eyes, heart, and mind had to be fixed on Jesus, anchored in His hope alone.

We have this hope as an anchor for our lives, safe and secure.
—Hebrews 6:19a

I began every day by reading His word, then, I listened to the daily *revive*SCHOOL teaching and asked the Lord to reveal His heart each day from the daily Scripture reading.

How happy is the man who does not follow the advice of the wicked or take the path of sinners or join a group of mockers! Instead, his delight is in the LORD's instruction, and he meditates on it day and night. He is like a tree planted beside streams of water that bears its fruit in season and whose leaf does not wither.
Whatever he does prospers.
—Psalm 1:1–3

After two years studying the Word of God, this psalm became true in my marriage, in my parenting, and in the entirety of my life. When you keep your hands to the plow and read His Word day after day, night after night, delighting in the Lord's love for you, He strengthens you. You become like a tree planted beside the water. Jesus is the living water your soul craves. NOTHING else satisfies but Jesus.

Those who seek the Lord will not lack any good thing.
—Psalm 34:10b

I believe many people think reading through the Bible feels daunting, because it's hard to understand and difficult to connect to their everyday life. I pray *revive*DAILY helps to guide readers to understand and apply the daily Bible readings to your life and see the heart of the Lord.

Here's the Deal

Jesus wants you to get to know Him and to receive His great love for you. He desires a personal relationship with you. Studying the Word compels you to sit still and enjoy His presence. Pause the distractions of your life and find a special place to sit each day. Take a deep breath and let go of the worries of the world. Breathe in the promises and the love the Lord has for you.

*Revive*DAILY: *Year One* and *Year Two* is a devotional journey designed to walk with you through the Bible in a span of two years, focusing on seeing the Messiah in each book of the Bible. Following the reviveSCHOOL plan, you will alternate reading sections in the Old Testament and sections in the New Testament, dividing the Bible into ten different segments:

1. *Year One*:
   * Pentateuch
   * The Gospels
   * Historical Books
   * Acts

2. *Year Two*:
   * Poetic Books
   * Paul's Letters
   * Major Prophets
   * Other Letters in the New Testament
   * Minor Prophets
   * Revelation

First, before you even begin, I encourage you to find a cozy spot in your home to make "your place to sit with Jesus". A fun chair in the corner of your bedroom, a cozy nook in a prayer closet or even sitting at a table on your back porch.

As you begin each new day, read the Scripture reading for the day (or listen to the audio version). You will find the daily reading section at the top left of each page. Then read the devotional for a simplified explanation of the Scripture and a personal word of encouragement for your day. But don't stop there! I encourage you to dig a little deeper into the three additional further Scripture verses listed on under each devotional. Rather than write the verses out for you in this devotional,

I want you to take the time to open your Bible and find the Scriptures on your own. Perhaps write them down in the space provided or in your journal. Finding the Scripture on your own will help you get to know your Bible and draw you closer to the Lord. Trust me in this!

When you are done reading each day, write in your journal or in the space below each devotion. An important part of my journey with the Lord is taking time to listen to God's voice. Sit still, ask the Lord questions, and wait to hear His voice: "How does this Scripture apply to my life today? What do you want me to receive from You today? How can I show Your love to others today?"

I am the good shepherd. I know My own sheep, and they know Me.
—John 10:14

If you want to go even deeper, I highly recommend the added study and teaching tools at www.reviveSCHOOL.org. Sign up to receive daily chapter by chapter teachings from the Word.

I am excited to go on this two-year devotional journey through the Word of God with you. I pray it will *revive you*. I bless you with peace and joy in the name of Jesus as you begin, not in your own strength but in the strength of the Lord.

Now to Him who is able to do above and beyond all that we ask or think according to the power that works in us. —Ephesians 3:20

The Lord is with you. The Lord loves you, and you are worthy to receive His great love for you!. The Lord longs for you to love Him with all your heart, soul, mind, and strength. Reading the Bible, His love letter to you, develops this great love. Enjoy the journey with the Lord one day at a time.

In Christ alone and with love,
Laura Kim Martin

Week 1, Day 1: Genesis 1—3
Seed of Jesus and Seed of Satan

Every day is a battle between the two seeds—Satan and Jesus. How does this battle between Satan and Jesus affect your walk with Christ today? The enemy comes to steal, kill, and destroy.

As you walk with Jesus through the everyday battles, remember the victory belongs to the Lord Jesus. He is your God of peace.

The LORD God said, "Since man has become like one of Us, knowing good and evil." —Genesis 3:22

Further Scripture: John 10:10; Ephesians 6:10–11; 1 Corinthians 15:54–57

Week 1, Day 2: Genesis 4—6

What Are My Motives?

The Lord calls believers to check their hearts. Ask yourself, *Am I walking with a seed of Cain, having evil motives, or am I walking with a seed of Abel, having righteous motives?* The Lord longs for you to live with a pure heart. Then you will see Him. May you hold nothing back from the Lord so you may see all God has for you!

The LORD had regard for Abel and his offering, but He did not have regard for Cain and his offering. —Genesis 4:4–5

Further Scripture: Psalm 26:2; Psalm 51:10; Matthew 5:8

Week 1, Day 3: Genesis 7—9
God's Judgment and Redemption: the Flood

Even back in the days when the Lord wiped out the entire earth with a flood, the Lord thought of you and desired to reach you with the Gospel. Therefore He preserved Noah and his family so the seed could continue.

There may be moments when you feel as though your current situation has no purpose, but trust that the Lord had a plan for you, even before the beginning of time: a plan for the seed of Christ to penetrate your life so you could know and receive His love. The Lord even gave us a rainbow to remind us of the promise of His everlasting love between Him and His people.

I am bringing a flood—floodwaters on the earth to destroy every creature under heaven with the breath of life in it. Everything on earth will die. But I will establish My covenant with you, and you will enter the ark with your sons, your wife, and your sons' wives. —Genesis 6:17–18

Further Scripture: Genesis 9:16; Psalm 139:13–14; Jeremiah 29:11

Week 1, Day 4: Genesis 10—12

God's Promises to Abram

The Lord blessed Abram to carry the seed of Christ, even though at the time it didn't make sense because Abram's wife Sarai was barren. The Lord promised to make Abram a great nation, and Abram walked the promise of God out in faith.

You may ask yourself, *How am I going to walk out my calling?* The Word of the Lord says to not fear and that you are called by name. No matter what you pass through, the Lord will be with you. Walk out your calling, knowing with confidence that the Lord is with you!

I will make you into a great nation, I will bless you, I will make your name great, and you will be a blessing. —Genesis 12:2

Further Scripture: Isaiah 41:10; Isaiah 43:1–2; Hebrews 11:8

Week 1, Day 5: Genesis 13—15
The Promise of Offspring

Abram's calling did not make logical sense to him. However, Abram turned to God for clarity, and the Lord gave Abram specifics on his calling. Abram believed God and walked by faith.

The Lord has called you to your own path. To walk by faith is to fear God more than man, to trust God in every circumstance. Today, walk by faith, just as Abram did, while carrying the seed of Christ. Take one step at a time, and the Lord will direct your path.

He took him outside and said, "Look at the sky and count the stars, if you are able to count them." Then He said to him, "Your offspring will be that numerous." Abram believed the Lord, and He credited it to him as righteousness. —Genesis 15:5–6

Further Scripture: Proverbs 3:5–6; 2 Corinthians 5:7; Hebrews 11:1

Week 1, Day 6: Genesis 16—17

God Calls You by Name

God was a personal God to Abram and gave him a new name, Abraham. The Lord *knows* you and calls you by name. When He calls you to something, He will make a way. He will give you all you need, specifically for *you*. How does the Lord reveal to you personally He is with you? May the Lord open your eyes to see what He sees and encourage you to keep walking in faith.

Your name will no longer be Abram, but your name will be Abraham,
for I will make you the father of many nations. I will make you extremely
fruitful and will make nations and kings come from you.
—Genesis 17:5–6

Further Scripture: Deuteronomy 20:4; Psalm 139:1–6;
Hebrews 13:20–21

Week 1, Day 7: Genesis 18
Sarah Laughed at the Impossible

Nothing is too difficult for the Lord. Yet Sarah laughed at God for calling her to have a child in the midst of her barrenness. For Sarah to carry the seed of Jesus, the impossible had to happen, and the Lord had to open her womb. But Sarah laughed.

Do you laugh when God calls you to the impossible? God says to trust in Him. Pour out your heart to the Lord, and trust God to do the impossible.

Is anything impossible for the Lord? —Genesis 18:14

Further Scripture: Psalm 62:8; Jeremiah 32:17; Luke 1:37–38

Week 2, Day 8: Genesis 19

Problems with Being in the World

As the people of Sodom and Gomorrah gave in to their lusts, they acted in the flesh and did not depend on God. The Lord saved Lot but destroyed an entire city. In many ways, this generation, like Sodom and Gomorrah, continues to give in to temptation and live in the flesh, not depending fully on the Lord. Thankfully, Jesus saved everyone because of His grace and mercy through His death, burial, resurrection, and His gift of the Holy Spirit.

Today, give thanks for the grace and mercy of the Lord. Ask yourself, *Am I living in a way that is pleasing to Christ, or am I giving in to temptations and my flesh?* May this be a generation that seeks His face.

So it was, when God destroyed the cities of the plain, He remembered Abraham and brought Lot out of the middle of the upheaval when He demolished the cities where Lot had lived. —Genesis 19:29

Further Scripture: Psalm 24:3–6; Titus 3:3, 5–7

Week 2, Day 9: Genesis 20—21

The Birth of Isaac

This story unfolded out of two mothers' hearts: Sarah for Isaac and Hagar for Ishmael. Sarah sought the Lord and was filled with joy and laughter at the birth of her promised son, Isaac. Hagar despaired because she had to let go of her son and trust the Lord with his future. Yet even in her despair, she sought the Lord for help.

The Lord sees what you are pondering in your heart. May the Lord bless you today as you walk in the hope you have in the Messiah. Delight yourself in the Lord, trust in His time and in His way, and He will give you the desires of your heart.

But God said to Abraham, "Do not be concerned about the boy and your slave. Whatever Sarah says to you, listen to her, because your offspring will be traced through Isaac. But I will also make a nation of the slave's son because he is your offspring." —Genesis 21:12–13

Further Scripture: Psalm 20:4; Psalm 37:3–5; Acts 15:8

Week 2, Day 10: Genesis 22
God's Command to Sacrifice Isaac

The Lord gave Abraham instructions to sacrifice his son Isaac. As difficult as the task was for Abraham, and as much as it did not make sense to kill his seed-bearer, Abraham said, "Here I am, Lord," and obeyed the Lord. However, as Abraham walked out the test, the Lord provided a ram to sacrifice, saving Isaac.

Today, the Lord may be calling you into a season of testing that does not make sense from your perspective. Keep an eternal perspective, one that deepens and strengthens your faith, so that you will lack nothing and reflect more and more of Jesus! Continue to have a heart of surrender saying, "Here I am, Lord." Trust the Lord to provide and fulfill His promises through you.

And all the nations of the earth will be blessed by your offspring because you have obeyed My command. —Genesis 22:18

Further Scripture: Psalm 84:11; Hebrews 11:17; James 1:2–4

Week 2, Day 11: Genesis 23—24

Finding a Wife for Isaac

Abraham's servant sought the Lord after he received orders from Abraham to go and find a wife for Isaac. The servant immediately appealed to the Lord in prayer before beginning this crucial task of finding a seed-bearer.

In the same way, the Lord longs for you to come to Him. He promises He will answer you. He promises when you ask, you will receive. And yet, why do believers so often turn to the Lord as the final step in obedience, walking in their own strength? Today, pause and ask the Lord for help before you go and do the tasks the Lord has for you.

"Lord, God of my master Abraham," he prayed, "give me success today, and show kindness to my master Abraham." —Genesis 24:12

Further Scripture: Psalm 91:15; Jeremiah 33:3; Matthew 7:7

Week 2, Day 12: Genesis 25—26
The Birth of Jacob and Esau

The story of Jacob and Esau was not without sin, and yet the Lord used them and their mother Rebekah when He set the stage for the seed of Christ to continue.

Even when people fall, you can—and you must—*trust* that God is able to work in and through the difficult situation. The key is to stay the course. Keep the faith. As you walk out your faith in Christ, you can hold on to the hope in Christ, knowing His plan prevails. Praise the Lord!

And the Lord said to her: "Two nations are in your womb; two people will come from you and be separated. One people will be stronger than the other, and the older will serve the younger." —Genesis 25:23

Further Scripture: Psalm 130:5–8; Proverbs 19:21; Romans 8:28

Week 2, Day 13: Genesis 27—28

God Promises to Jacob

As you walk with the Lord, remember His promises to Jacob on his journey. The Lord said to Jacob, "Look, I will be with you." Remember the Lord's promises to you because you are on a journey with Him as well. What promises are you holding on to today?

Look, I am with you and will watch over you wherever you go. I will bring you back to this land, for I will not leave you until I have done what I have promised you. —Genesis 28:15

Further Scripture: Exodus 3:12; Psalm 121:5; Romans 8:31

Week 2, Day 14: Genesis 29

The Line of Judah Came through Leah

As you walk with the Lord, may you praise His name. Leah waited to praise the Lord until her fourth son was born. How long will you wait to give praise to the Lord in the midst of your day? The Lord is with you.

And she conceived again, gave birth to a son, and said, "This time I will praise the LORD." Therefore she named him Judah. Then Leah stopped having children." —Genesis 29:35

Further Scripture: Psalm 34:1; Ephesians 5:20; 1 Thessalonians 5:18

Week 3, Day 15: Genesis 30
The Twelve Tribes of Israel

When you read about Jacob's twelve children by four different women, or about how he became prosperous from spotted, striped, and speckled sheep and goats, doesn't it appear messy and complicated? It may seem deceiving, conniving, or even corrupt, but the Lord worked, despite all of this, for the seed of Christ to continue.

Even in the mess, even in the fall of man, the Lord is working and has a plan. As you trust Him and hold on to hope, His plan will prevail—even in the middle of the mess.

Rachel said, "God has vindicated me; yes, He has heard me and given me a son," and she named him Dan. —Genesis 30:6

Further Scripture: Psalm 33:11; Proverbs 19:21; Isaiah 46:10

Week 3, Day 16: Genesis 31
Jacob and Laban Seen by God

God showed up in dreams to both Laban and Jacob, reminding them that He was with them even in the middle of their sinful ways. God sees, and He knows your heart. God sees your sin—even when you deny it or think you can cover it up and escape. He still sees you.

Why do you try to hide? The Lord loves you and will never leave you. Come before Him as you are. Let Him transform you.

If the God of my father, the God of Abraham, the Fear of Isaac, had not been with me, certainly now you would have sent me off empty-handed. But God has seen my affliction and my hard work, and He issued His verdict last night. —Genesis 31:42

Further Scripture: Proverbs 4:25–26; Isaiah 1:18; Matthew 6:22

Week 3, Day 17: Genesis 32—33

Jacob Reconciled with Esau

Jacob was "greatly afraid and distressed" to meet his brother Esau, whom he hadn't seen in years. He prayed and asked the Lord to rescue him, remembering the Lord's promise and calling on his life. The Lord answered Jacob's prayer.

Turn your fears and apprehensions over to the Lord today. If He is leading you to a place of reconciliation, He will provide, and He will answer you. Cry out to the Lord, and watch Him move in your life.

Then Jacob said, "God of my father Abraham and God of my father Isaac … Please rescue me from the hand of my brother Esau, for I am afraid of him; otherwise, he may come and attack me, the mothers, and their children. You have said, 'I will cause you to prosper, and I will make your offspring like the sand of the sea, which cannot be counted.'"
—Genesis 32:9, 11–12

Further Scripture: Genesis 33:10; Psalm 56:3; Isaiah 41:10

Week 3, Day 18: Genesis 34—35

Jacob's Delay in Following God's Instructions

Jacob watched his only daughter be taken advantage of by men who wrongly pursued her. Then he watched his sons retaliate and kill those men. During this time, Jacob turned to God. He remembered God's promise that God would be with Jacob wherever he went.

Even in the midst of your shortcomings or in the middle of hardship, cry out to the Lord! Look back on God's faithfulness in your life and remember the times when the Lord stood with you. God promises you will not be forsaken. He has even more plans ahead for you!

So Jacob said to his family and all who were with him,
"Get rid of the foreign gods that are among you. Purify yourselves and
change your clothes. We must get up and go to Bethel. I will build an altar
there to the God who answered me in my day of distress. He has been with
me everywhere I have gone." —Genesis 35:2–3

Further Scripture: Psalm 120:1; Matthew 28:20; 2 Peter 3:9

Week 3, Day 19: Genesis 36—37
Joseph Sold into Slavery

Reuben and Judah went against the popular opinion of Joseph's brothers. They both spoke up, voiced their concerns about killing Joseph, and offered a different option. In the end, their courage to speak up saved Joseph's life and ultimately saved the lives of the brothers and the seed of Christ as well.

The Lord may put you in a position to speak up. Trust the voice of the Holy Spirit inside you, and take courage. Speaking up in obedience may ultimately save a life ... even if you never know it!

When Reuben heard this, he tried to save him from them. He said, "Let's not take his life." ... Then Judah said to his brothers, "What do we gain if we kill our brother and cover up his blood? Come, let's sell him to the Ishmaelites and not lay a hand on him, for he is our brother, our own flesh," and they agreed. —Genesis 37:21, 26–27

Further Scripture: Esther 4:14; Psalm 31:24; Luke 21:15

Week 3, Day 20: Genesis 38
Unexpected Seed Carrier

As you read the story of Judah and Tamar, you see the Lord use broken people to continue the seed of the Messiah. Despite Judah and Tamar's sin, God still used them. It is interesting how the Lord doesn't use Joseph, Judah's brother, with a seemingly grander life story, to carry the seed of Christ.

If you ever feel as though you don't measure up or you've made too many mistakes, remember God knows what He is doing. He can use anyone's life story for His will and for His glory. He is the perfecter of your faith. God will use you today!

Judah recognized them and said, "She is more in the right than I, since I did not give her to my son Shelah." And he did not know her intimately again. —Genesis 38:26

Further Scripture: Isaiah 43:7; 2 Corinthians 12:9; Hebrews 12:2

Week 3, Day 21: Genesis 39—40

God Blessed Joseph in Everything He Did

The Lord was with Joseph, and whatever he did prospered. Joseph found favor with his boss, Potiphar, who put Joseph in charge of all he owned. Joseph also found favor with the prison warden when he was unjustly imprisoned. Whether at a high place in life or low place in life, the Lord was with Joseph. Joseph remained steadfast in the Lord no matter his circumstances.

The Lord promises to be with you wherever you are. Do not base your feelings today on your circumstances. He delights in you, and He has plans for you.

But the Lord was with Joseph and extended kindness to him.
He granted him favor in the eyes of the prison warden. —Genesis 39:21

Further Scripture: Psalm 139:7–10; Isaiah 26:3–4; Zephaniah 3:17

Week 4, Day 22: Genesis 41—42
Joseph Turned His Attention toward God

During Joseph's rise to success, he turned all the attention toward God. The common theme of Joseph's explanations about wisdom or understanding was God. Joseph feared God. He referenced God above himself, and he did not receive the accolades or the credit.

May you remember that God is in all things, and in Him, all things hold together. Do you pat yourself on the back and receive the praise, or do you remember that everything comes from God? Today, give God all the honor and thanksgiving.

Joseph answered Pharaoh. "It is God who will give Pharaoh a favorable answer." —Genesis 41:16

Further Scripture: Genesis 42:18; Colossians 1:17; James 1:17

Week 4, Day 23: Genesis 43—44

Judah Pleaded to Spare Joseph

Judah pleaded with Joseph to allow him to take the place of their brother, Benjamin, as a slave. Judah longed to spare his brother and explained to Joseph how their father Jacob would die of sorrow if they returned without Benjamin. Judah displayed a selfless, sacrificial love, allowing Joseph to see into this brother's heart.

Judah was the seed-bearer for Christ, who is your ultimate example of selfless and sacrificial love. You are called to love others as Christ loved. Is the Lord asking you to show this selfless and sacrificial love toward someone in your life today?

Now please let your servant remain here as my lord's slave, in place of the boy. Let him go back with his brothers. —Genesis 44:33

Further Scripture: John 15:13; Philippians 2:3–5; 1 John 3:16

Week 4, Day 24: Genesis 45—46

Joseph Revealed His Identity

You only see part of the picture God is writing in your life today. Once again, Joseph gave God credit for redeeming his life so his entire family could be preserved and delivered.

When the Lord provides restoration, it is emotional and powerful because it is all God, just as it was in Joseph's family. Today, hang on to this hope. Do not fear even if those around you are not walking with the Lord. Remember, He is with you. Trust Him.

God sent me ahead of you to establish you as a remnant within the land and to keep you alive by a great deliverance. —Genesis 45:7

Further Scripture: 2 Samuel 22:2–3; Psalm 18:50; Psalm 89:4

Week 4, Day 25: Genesis 47—48

God Is in the Unexpected

God is a God of the unexpected. Israel never expected to see his son again after hearing the news from the brothers that Joseph was dead. And yet the Lord God is able to bring life from death. Not only did Jacob see Joseph again, but he was also able to bless Joseph's sons.

Joseph expected his father to bless the older son with his right hand, but Jacob had other plans for the blessing. Remember, the Lord is faithful, and His ways are higher than your ways. He promises that He is able to do above and beyond anything you can imagine.

Israel said to Joseph, "I never expected to see your face again, but now God has even let me see your offspring." —Genesis 48:11

Further Scripture: Ephesians 3:20; Hebrews 11:6, 21

Week 4, Day 26: Genesis 49—50
Jacob Blessed His Sons

In his final days of life, Jacob, the father of the twelve tribes of Israel, blessed each of his sons by name. He honestly pointed out their character qualities and remembered events in their lives. He also spoke into their future days.

How much more does your Heavenly Father love you? The Heavenly Father sees you. He knows when you fall down. He knows when you give in to temptation. And yet your Heavenly Father loves you and wants to bless you. May you receive His love and walk in it. The Father loves you.

These are the tribes of Israel, 12 in all, and this was what their father said to them. He blessed them, and he blessed each one with a suitable blessing.
—Genesis 49:28

Further Scripture: Romans 8:38–39; Ephesians 1:3–4; 1 John 3:1

Week 4, Day 27: Exodus 1

Fear God: a Deliverer Is Coming

The Lord used the midwives in a mighty way to expand the Hebrew people. The midwives overcame the fear of man and chose to fear God.

When you fear God, you are not dependent on yourself or on things you can control. Instead you live with awe and respect that God is able to handle it all. The Lord longs for you to fear Him and promises to fulfill your desires.

How would you complete this sentence for yourself today? *Since I feared God, God gave me [fill in the blank].*

So God was good to the midwives, and the people multiplied and became very numerous. Since the midwives feared God, He gave them families.
—Exodus 1:20–21

Further Scripture: Exodus 1:17; Psalm 145:19; Luke 1:50

Week 4, Day 28: Exodus 2—3
Cry Out to the Lord

The Israelites cried out to the Lord while in bondage in Egypt. God heard their groaning and remembered His promises. The story of deliverance began as the Lord heard the cries of their hearts.

When you cry out to the Lord, it means you get honest with God. You turn to Him with everything. Be honest with God about the situation you find yourself in today. He will bring you deliverance and set you free from bondage. In Christ there is freedom. Just be honest with the Lord today.

After a long time, the king of Egypt died. The Israelites groaned because of their difficult labor, and they cried out; and their cry for help ascended to God because of the difficult labor. So God heard their groaning, and He remembered His covenant with Abraham, Isaac, and Jacob. God saw the Israelites, and He took notice. —Exodus 2:23–25

Further Scripture: Exodus 3:7–8; Psalm 107:13–14; Galatians 5:1

Week 5, Day 29: Exodus 4—5

Moses Given Powerful Signs

The Lord called upon Moses to help deliver the Israelites. Moses responded with doubts, feelings of inadequacy, and excuses about why he should not be the one. Despite Moses's excuses, the Lord still used him. God explained to Moses in detail how He would help him.

You may have similar excuses as to why you should not be the one the Lord uses in the area He is calling you. Moses didn't think he could speak to people, but the Lord still used him in a mighty way! If the Lord has called you to something, trust that He will equip you with everything you need.

You will speak with him and tell him what to say.
I will help both you and him to speak and will teach you both what to do.
He will speak to the people for you. He will be your spokesman, and you
will serve as God to him. —Exodus 4:15–16

Further Scripture: 2 Corinthians 3:5; Philippians 2:13; Hebrews 13:20–21

Week 5, Day 30: Exodus 6

The Promise of Deliverance

God did not deliver the Israelites the first time around, and Moses voiced his frustration. God responded forthrightly to Moses, explaining who He was and about all His promises. God told Moses He revealed Himself to Abraham, Isaac, and Jacob as "God Almighty," but to Moses, God said, "I Am Yahweh," meaning "I Am Who I Am." This name described His fullness—His eternal existence, sovereignty, unlimited power, and omnipresence. This should have ended Moses's excuses and given him the confidence he needed to press on with the mission God had given him.

What about you? Is it enough to know God Almighty, Yahweh, I Am Lord, is with you and will bless you along the way? Or will you continue to give the Lord excuses as to why you can't follow Him? Remember, He is the great I Am.

Then God spoke to Moses, telling him, "I am Yahweh. I appeared to Abraham, Isaac, and Jacob as God Almighty, but I did not reveal My name Yahweh to them." —Exodus 6:2–3

Further Scripture: Isaiah 46:9–10; John 8:58; Revelation 1:8

Week 5, Day 31: Exodus 7—8

So the Egyptians Would Know

Why did the Lord allow the awful plagues to afflict Egypt? So the Egyptians would know that the Lord was God, and the Israelites would know Him as their Deliverer.

The Lord is your Deliverer too. Because of sin, everyone deserves death, but the Lord delivered the world through His Son Jesus. He will also deliver you from difficult situations in your life, so you will know He is the Lord. Is there anything in your life today the Lord might be allowing in order to prove He is your Deliverer? Turn to Him, with trust, and let Him deliver you.

The Egyptians will know that I am Yahweh when I stretch out My hand against Egypt, and bring out the Israelites from among them.
—Exodus 7:5

Further Scripture: 2 Samuel 22:1–4; Psalm 34:7–8; Galatians 5:1

Week 5, Day 32: Exodus 9—10
Pharaoh's Hardened Heart

Pharaoh's heart was hardened, and he resisted letting the Israelites go. As a result, the Lord continued to multiply signs and wonders in the land of Egypt, specifically through the ten different plagues.

Just as the Lord saw Pharaoh's hardened heart, the Lord sees your heart. He longs for your heart to be surrendered to His ways. Even still, He will show His power and make His name known in all the earth. He is the great I Am.

However, I have let you live for this purpose: to show you My power and to make My name known in all the earth. —Exodus 9:16

Further Scripture: Exodus 7:3; Psalm 67:1–2; Matthew 6:10

Week 5, Day 33: Exodus 11
The Lord's Plan, Power and Purpose

Even after nine plagues afflicted Egypt, Pharaoh's heart remained hardened. He would not let the Israelites go. The Lord gave Moses instructions about the tenth and final plague that would kill all the firstborns in the land of Egypt. The Lord continued to reveal His power and control in the midst of the situation.

In a similar way, the Lord says you will have trials in this life and will suffer. However, He uses these times in your life to restore, confirm, strengthen, and establish you in Christ. May you take heart in the midst of hardship, trusting the Lord has overcome the world. He is working in you, so you will have the strength to endure even more.

The Lord said to Moses, "Pharaoh will not listen to you, so that My wonders may be multiplied in the land of Egypt." —Exodus 11:9

Further Scripture: John 16:33; James 1:2–3; 1 Peter 5:10

Week 5, Day 34: Exodus 12—13
The Lord's Intentional Path

After the tenth plague, Pharaoh finally let the Israelites go. As the Israelites began their journey out of Egypt, the Lord was very intentional. First, God led them on a specific route, not the shortest, but the best one for His people. Then God said He would take care of His people. Finally, God went before the people to lead them.

Remember, God is the same yesterday, today, and forever. Therefore, the same is true for your own journey. The Lord's path is the best one for you, even if it's not the shortest or the easiest. The Lord will care for you. The Lord is going before you and is with you day and night. So keep on walking one step at a time!

When Pharaoh let the people go, God did not lead them along the road to the land of the Philistines, even though it was nearby; for God said, "The people will change their minds and return to Egypt if they face war." So He led the people around toward the Red Sea along the road of the wilderness. —Exodus 13:17–18

Further Scripture: Exodus 13:21; Proverbs 3:5–6; Hebrews 13:8

Week 5, Day 35: Exodus 14—15

Angel of the Lord in the Cloud and Fire

Shortly after the Israelites left Egypt, Pharaoh's heart hardened once again. He pursued the Israelites until they came to a dead end, facing the Red Sea. The Israelites were frightened and cried out to the Lord. In their minds, they had nowhere to turn. And yet, this created another opportunity for God to reveal He is the Lord, the great I Am. In His power, the Lord parted the Red Sea. He saved the Israelites and crushed the Egyptians.

Are you at a place in life that feels like a Red Sea moment? Do you feel as though you have nowhere to turn? Remember, the Lord is with you. The Lord will fight for you. He has a plan. Like the Lord said to the Israelites, "Be quiet," and trust He will bring victory to your situation in a way you never expected!

But Moses said to the people, "Don't be afraid. Stand firm and see the Lord's salvation He will provide for you today; for the Egyptians you see today, you will never see again. The Lord will fight for you; you must be quiet."
—Exodus 14:13–14

Further Scripture: Exodus 14:31; Deuteronomy 20:4; Romans 8:31

Week 6, Day 36: Exodus 16—18
The Lord Will Help You Through

Moses's arms were heavy, literally and figuratively. He could no longer lead the people alone. Aaron helped him to speak. Hur and Aaron supported his hands during the battle with Amalek. Then the Lord sent his father-in-law, Jethro, to advise him in the area of delegation and leadership. Jethro came from the outside and assessed the situation from his perspective.

Moses received assistance with humility. Are you facing a task too heavy for you? Are you overwhelmed? You are not alone. Seek the Lord. He will send the help and insight you need when the task seems too big. Receive it, and God will be with you.

You will certainly wear out both yourself and these people who are with you, because the task is too heavy for you. You can't do it alone. Now listen to me; I will give you some advice, and God be with you. —Exodus 18:18–19

Further Scripture: Exodus 18:24; Psalm 34:17; Matthew 11:28

Week 6, Day 37: Exodus 19—20
God Reminds and God Reveals

Three months after their deliverance from Egypt, the children of Israel set up camp at Mount Sinai. God reminded them of their deliverance with a picture of His tender love for them, saying, "How I carried you on eagles' wings and brought you to Me." Then on the third day, as the consecrated people stood at the foot of the mountain, God revealed Himself in a powerful display. The mountain was in smoke. The Lord descended upon it in fire. The whole mountain quaked violently. The sound of a trumpet grew louder and louder.

Pause for a minute and imagine this: the tender love of a Heavenly Father and the majestic power of an Almighty God. He alone is exalted over all. Remind yourself of His tender love that has carried you. As you seek the Lord today, watch for Him to reveal Himself to you in tender love and powerful splendors.

Mount Sinai was completely enveloped in smoke because the Lord came down on it in fire. Its smoke went up like the smoke of a furnace, and the whole mountain shook violently. As the sound of the trumpet grew louder and louder, Moses spoke and God answered him in the thunder.
—Exodus 19:18–19

Further Scripture: Exodus 19:4; 1 Chronicles 29:11; Isaiah 40:31

Week 6, Day 38: Exodus 21
Framework Regarding Slaves and Personal Injury

After God gave Moses the Ten Commandments on Mount Sinai, He detailed specific ordinances for Moses to share with the people. These ordinances were the framework for judging and resolving civil disputes. The Israelites were fresh out of slavery, and the Lord knew they needed this framework for living in their newfound freedom.

Where do you turn for the framework regarding right and wrong in your life? Do you seek after the world, or do you seek the Word of God for insight? The Word of God is living and effective and sharper than any double-edged sword. Seek God's Word for answers, and He will show you the way.

These are the ordinances that you must set before them. —Exodus 21:1

Further Scripture: Psalm 103:7; Psalm 119:105; Hebrews 4:12

Week 6, Day 39: Exodus 22
Ordinances Reveal God's Heart and Character

The Lord continued to give Moses ordinances for the people of Israel. The Lord knew the nature of His people; He cared for them and explained what consequences would follow their actions. And then, in the middle of explaining the ordinances to Moses, the Lord revealed His character and His heart.

Better than any earthly father, God is your Heavenly Father, and He loves you. If you cry out to the Lord, He will listen to you. He is compassionate. He cares for you, and He understands your needs. He longs for you to call out to Him, and He promises He is there to rescue you.

If you ever take your neighbor's cloak as collateral, return it to him before sunset. For it is his only covering; it is the clothing for his body. What will he sleep in? And if he cries out to Me, I will listen because I am compassionate.
—Exodus 22:26–27

Further Scripture: Psalm 91:15; Psalm 103:8; 2 Corinthians 1:3

Week 6, Day 40: Exodus 23—24
The Consuming Fire

After Moses shared the entirety of the law with the Israelites, they agreed to do all the Lord had spoken and be obedient. Then Moses went up the mountain where the glory of the Lord rested on Mount Sinai, and a cloud covered it. To the eyes of the people, the appearance of the glory of the Lord was like a consuming fire.

Do you ever picture God as a consuming fire, able to consume and utterly destroy? It's an image of God deserving of your reverence and awe. He will conquer your enemies and wipe out evil. Even so, grace is available to all who receive it freely through His Son Jesus. Allow the Consuming Fire to fight for you while you stand in awe of His power.

The appearance of the Lord's glory to the Israelites was like a consuming fire on the mountaintop. —Exodus 24:17

Further Scripture: Deuteronomy 9:3; Psalm 50:3; Hebrews 12:28–29

Week 6, Day 41: Exodus 25
The Presence of God

While on Mount Sinai, the Lord gave Moses specific instructions for construction of the Ark of the Covenant. The Ark served as the place for the presence of God to be with the Israelites at all times. It seems somewhat bizarre for God to place Himself in a tent and inside a box, so He could be near His complaining and grumbling people. But God is humble and merciful. He draws near to sinners.

Thankfully for the new covenant believers, God continues to promise He will always be with us and dwell within us as the power of the Holy Spirit. Today, give thanks for God's presence, which is always with you.

They are to make a sanctuary for Me so that I may dwell among them. You must make it according to all that I show you—the pattern of the tabernacle as well as the pattern of all its furnishings. —Exodus 25:8–9

Further Scripture: Exodus 25:22; Psalm 139:7–10; Matthew 11:29

Week 6, Day 42: Exodus 26
Directions for the Tabernacle

The Lord gave Moses detailed instructions for building the Tabernacle and creating the veil, which would hold the Ark of the Covenant. The Tabernacle served as a church in the wilderness for the Israelites, a place where the Lord's presence stayed among the people. In the construction details, the number fifty was used several times and was often seen when two things are united or joined together.

The number fifty is a definition of the word *Pentecost* and can signify fullness. Fifty is related to the coming of God's Holy Spirit and symbolizes deliverance or freedom from a burden. As you study the Tabernacle and the Lord's presence among His people, pray for the Holy Spirit to bring freedom to your life, releasing you from any burdens you carry. May you find joy in the presence of the Lord.

Make 50 loops on the one curtain and make 50 loops on the edge of the curtain in the second set, so that the loops line up together. Also make 50 gold clasps and join the curtains together with the clasps, so that the tabernacle may be a single unit. —Exodus 26:5–6

Further Scripture: Exodus 26:10–11; Psalm 16:11; Colossians 1:19–20

February 12

Week 7, Day 43: Exodus 27—28

The Priestly Garments: Jesus Your High Priest

God gave Moses detailed instructions for building the courtyard of the Tabernacle. The Tabernacle was a place for the people to present themselves before the Lord. Only the priests could approach the altar, and they had to wear very specific priestly clothing.

As a believer in Christ, you are a priest with Christ in you, set aside from others. You are clothed in garments of salvation and robes of righteousness. It's nothing you have to earn or even put on yourself. It's a gift from Him. Live freely, clothed in the righteousness of Christ and in His presence all day long! He loves you. He has called you as a priest to reflect His love and give Him glory!

These are the garments that they must make: a breastpiece, an ephod, a robe, a specially woven tunic, a turban, and a sash. They are to make holy garments for your brother Aaron and his sons so that they may serve Me as priests. . . . These must be worn by Aaron and his sons whenever they enter the tent of meeting or approach the altar to minister in the sanctuary area, so that they do not incur guilt and die. This is to be a permanent statute for Aaron and for his future descendants. —Exodus 28:4, 43

Further Scripture: Psalm 100:4; Isaiah 61:10; Galatians 3:27

Week 7, Day 44: Exodus 29

The Cleansing and Anointing of the Holy Priests

The Lord described to Moses exactly how Aaron and his sons should prepare to become priests. They would go through a time of consecration and offer sacrifices for the people. After these specific instructions, God made it clear that He would dwell among the people, so they would know He was the Lord their God.

In the New Testament, consecration is for every believer as he or she presents and surrenders his or her life as a living sacrifice to the Lord. It's saying, "Lord, I am living for You. I am no longer living for myself, the world, or anything else. Use me for Your glory." In your sacrifice to Him, as His chosen priest, remember the Lord dwells within you, He is the Lord your God!

I will consecrate the tent of meeting and the altar; I will also consecrate Aaron and his sons to serve Me as priests. I will dwell among the Israelites and be their God. And they will know that I am Yahweh their God, who brought them out of the land of Egypt, so that I might dwell among them. I am Yahweh their God. —Exodus 29:44–46

Further Scripture: Romans 12:1; 2 Timothy 2:21; 1 Peter 2:9

Week 7, Day 45: Exodus 30—31

Skilled Workers Provided

In order for the building instructions God gave Moses to be completed, the Lord specifically chose the craftsmen for service. God filled them with His Spirit and with wisdom, understanding, and ability for their calling as craftsmen.

May you find comfort trusting that when God has a plan for His people and calls you to something, He will provide everything you need and will empower you through His Spirit. When you work as unto the Lord, His power will fill you and equip you. Remember, He goes before everything He has commanded you to do!

Look, I have appointed by name Bezalel son of Uri, son of Hur, of the tribe of Judah. I have filled him with God's Spirit, with wisdom, understanding, and ability in every craft to design artistic works in gold, silver, and bronze, to cut gemstones for mounting, and to carve wood for work in every craft. I have also selected Oholiab son of Ahisamach, of the tribe of Dan, to be with him. I have placed wisdom within every skilled craftsman in order to make all that I have commanded you. —Exodus 31:2–6

Further Scripture: Joshua 1:9; 1 Corinthians 12:4–8; Colossians 3:23

February 15

Week 7, Day 46: Exodus 32—33
Moses Interceded for the People

After God's anger rose up against the Israelites because they chose to make and worship a calf-god, Moses and God had an honest, face-to-face talk, like friends. Despite His great frustration, God showed an even greater and more intimate love for Moses and His people by continuing to lead and deliver them.

The Lord loves you deeply, no matter your shortcomings. Even when it seems He would want to walk away from you, He will draw near to you as you draw near to Him. The Lord longs for you to know Him in a personal, honest, face-to-face way. Do you talk to the Lord as though He were a friend? As you follow the Lord and spend time speaking with Him, the closer you will be to Him, like friends.

The Lord spoke with Moses face to face,
just as a man speaks with his friend. —Exodus 33:11

Further Scripture: John 15:12–15; James 2:23; James 4:8

Week 7, Day 47: Exodus 34—35

Forty Days and Forty Nights with God

Moses spent another forty days and forty nights with God on Mount Sinai. This time he fasted and did not eat or drink. Moses spent time talking with and listening to God. As he came down from the mountain, Moses's face radiated brightly because he had spent time in God's presence.

When you spend time in the presence of God, in His Word, praying, and listening to Him, you will be transformed. The key is taking time away from the distractions of the world to spend time with God. God is a God of transformation! It may be a process, but the more time you abide with Christ, the more you are being made into His image and will reflect His love and His glory!

As Moses descended from Mount Sinai—with the two tablets of the testimony in his hands as he descended the mountain—he did not realize that the skin of his face shone as a result of his speaking with the Lord.
—Exodus 34:29

Further Scripture: Acts 4:13; Romans 12:2; 2 Corinthians 3:18

Week 7, Day 48: Exodus 36
Provision for Building the Tabernacle

Moses summoned every skilled person the Lord had given wisdom and understanding for building the sanctuary. Their hearts stirred to work and do the tasks at hand. Morning after morning, the sons of Israel brought contributions and offerings to use for construction. Not only did they bring what was sufficient, the people brought more than enough. They listened to their hearts and responded in obedience as the Lord led them.

When the Lord gives a plan for something and calls His people to it, He will make a way. He will equip you with all wisdom and knowledge so you may bear fruit in every good work. Listen to the stirrings of your heart. Respond to the Lord. And remember, in Christ, you will have more than enough.

So Moses summoned Bezalel, Oholiab, and every skilled person in whose heart the Lord had placed wisdom, everyone whose heart moved him, to come to the work and do it. They took from Moses' presence all the contributions that the Israelites had brought for the task of making the sanctuary. Meanwhile, the people continued to bring freewill offerings morning after morning. . . . The materials were sufficient for them to do all the work. There was more than enough. —Exodus 36:2–3, 7

Further Scripture: 2 Corinthians 9:8; Colossians 1:9–10; Hebrews 13:20–21

Week 8, Day 49: Exodus 37—38
Repeat Details

Once again, Moses, the author of Exodus, inspired by God, recounted the exact details of the Tabernacle construction process. Have you ever wondered why Moses wrote the features out in such full detail—not once but twice? As you compare the two, see how similar and exact the two accounts were. In a similar way, the writers of the New Testament often repeated truths they wanted the early church to understand. Paul said he repeated truths for believers' protection.

Pay attention to the things that repeat or even happen three or four times in your life. God may be trying to get your attention, keep you safe, or make sure you understand something. God is an intentional God. Don't overlook some of the obvious ways He is trying to speak to you.

Bezalel made the ark of acacia wood, 45 inches long, 27 inches wide, and 27 inches high. —Exodus 37:1

Further Scripture: Philippians 3:1; 2 Peter 1:12; Jude 1:5

Week 8, Day 50: Exodus 39
As the Lord Commands

As you read the detailed instructions for making the ephod, breast-plate, and priestly garments, ten different times you see the phrase, "as the Lord commanded Moses." When you read a phrase repeated this many times in one chapter, take notice. The skillful Israelites obeyed everything the Lord commanded. Not one detail was left undone.

In the New Testament, Jesus said the greatest command is to love the Lord with all your heart, soul, and mind and to love others as yourself. Are you obedient to this commandment? Obedience to the Lord is love. As you receive grace from Jesus, you are able to walk out His commands in faith.

The Israelites had done all the work according to everything the Lord had commanded Moses. Moses inspected all the work they had accomplished. They had done just as the Lord commanded. Then Moses blessed them.
—Exodus 39:42–43

Further Scripture: Matthew 22:35–39; Romans 1:5; 2 John 1:6

Week 8, Day 51: Exodus 40

Physical Signs of God's Presence

When Moses finished work on the Tabernacle, God filled it with His glory in the form of a cloud. God placed a cloud over it by day and a fire inside the cloud by night as a sign to the people that He was with them along their journey. These physical signs served as a visible reminder of God's presence. He was with them, and His glory was all around.

Remember, God is with you on your journey. Open your eyes to see God in your midst. And if you don't sense Him, ask Him to reveal Himself to you! The Lord is your Deliverer.

For the cloud of the Lord was over the tabernacle by day, and there was a fire inside the cloud by night, visible to the entire house of Israel throughout all the stages of their journey. —Exodus 40:38

Further Scripture: Judges 18:6; Psalm 25:4–5; Psalm 121:8

Week 8, Day 52: Leviticus 1—3
The Burnt Offering, Grain Offering, and Fellowship Offering

While Exodus is like a design manual for the Tabernacle, Leviticus is a user manual. It's a codebook for the Law. It begins by describing the burnt offerings, grain offerings, and peace or fellowship offerings. The people sacrificed their most costly possessions or livelihood at the altar as an offering to the Lord. The sacrifices were a soothing aroma to God and allowed the people to be found acceptable by Him. This alone was reason enough to make the sacrifice at the altar.

Disciples who give up everything to follow Christ also make this sacrifice. It too is pleasing to God. As you worship God, you are called to present yourself as a living sacrifice. You are to hold nothing back. Is there anything you are holding back today that needs to be presented to God as a sacrifice in worship to Him? As you lay it down before Him, remember, it will please the Lord.

Then the Lord summoned Moses and spoke to him from the tent of meeting:
"Speak to the Israelites and tell them: When any of you brings an offering
to the Lord from the livestock, you may bring your offering from the herd or
the flock. . . . He must bring it to the entrance to the tent of meeting so that
he may be accepted by the Lord." —Leviticus 1:1–2, 3

Further Scripture: Mark 8:34; John 12:3; Romans 12:1

Week 8, Day 53: Leviticus 4—5
Atonement for Sin

In today's reading, this message is repeated: If a person sins, a priest will make atonement on his behalf for his sin, and he will be forgiven. It is important to understand what this means. Atonement means reconciliation. God provides a way for humankind to come back into a loving, peaceful relationship with Him despite sin. Because God loves you, He seeks to reconcile Himself to you.

In the Old Testament, the high priests' sacrifices accomplished atonement for themselves and for the people because of sin. In the New Testament, Jesus Christ gave His life as a ransom for you. If you believe in Jesus Christ as your Savior, your sins are forgiven. Today, rest in that promise. Your sins are forgiven as a child of God. Thank the Lord for this free gift of reconciliation to God.

He must prepare the second bird as a burnt offering according to the regulation. In this way the priest will make atonement on his behalf for the sin he has committed, and he will be forgiven. —Leviticus 5:10

Further Scripture: Mark 10:45; Romans 5:11; Hebrews 7:27

Week 8, Day 54: Leviticus 6
No More Guilt

You know the feeling of guilt you experience after sinning? You try to ignore it or wish it away, but the guilt lingers and even gets heavier. The Lord spoke to Moses, giving him instructions for "when a person sins." Notice, God didn't say *if* someone sins but *when*. The Lord knew His people would sin. Therefore, He instructed Moses on the guilt offering, so the people's sins would be forgiven, and they would no longer incur guilt.

In a similar way, Jesus came to make atonement for your sin. Instead of carrying the burden of guilt and shame, He longs for you to know you are forgiven and can walk in freedom! Turn to Him, confess your sins, and you will be forgiven. He loves you and wants you to let go of the guilt you have been carrying. Be honest with Him today. Let His love wash over you.

In this way the priest will make atonement on his behalf before the Lord, and he will be forgiven for anything he may have done to incur guilt.
—Leviticus 6:7

Further Scripture: 2 Corinthians 3:17; 2 Corinthians 7:9–10; 1 John 1:9

Week 8, Day 55: Leviticus 7

The Peace Offering

The people of Israel received instructions on peace offerings, sometimes referred to as fellowship offerings. The peace offering focused on wholeness or completeness. The Israelites would sense completeness with God as they brought sacrifices. Completeness with God can feel like joy and peace of mind, which comes from knowing God is at peace with you. Likewise, Paul instructed believers to present their requests to God with thanksgiving and supplication, and then, the peace of God will cover them completely.

Jesus is your peace and brings completeness to your life. His peace will come upon you when you stop trying to control every situation and instead give every moment over to the Lord. What are you still trying to control that you may need to surrender as a sacrifice to the Lord? Make today a day of surrender, a peace offering to God!

The Lord spoke to Moses: "Tell the Israelites: The one who presents a fellowship sacrifice to the Lord must bring an offering to the Lord from his sacrifice." —Leviticus 7:28–29

Further Scripture: Psalm 29:11; Ephesians 2:17–18; Philippians 4:6–7

Week 8, Day 56: Leviticus 8–9

The Israelites Experience God's Glory in the Tabernacle

Moses, Aaron, and Aaron's sons did just as the Lord commanded them to do so that the glory of the Lord would appear. The seven-day process of ordination was detailed and involved, but even so, they obeyed every detail. On the eighth day, the Lord honored His word, and the glory of the Lord came as a fire, causing all the people to fall facedown and shout. They worshipped the Lord with humility and joy.

God demonstrated His glory for you through the death, burial, and resurrection of Jesus Christ. May you never cease bowing down in worship to the Lord with humility and joy! As you worship the Lord, you will experience His transforming glory!

When they came out, they blessed the people, and the glory of the Lord appeared to all the people. Fire came from the Lord and consumed the burnt offering and the fat portions on the altar. And when all the people saw it, they shouted and fell facedown on the ground. —Leviticus 9:23–24

Further Scripture: Leviticus 9:6; Matthew 17:5–6; Romans 6:4

Week 9, Day 57: Leviticus 10
God Wants Obedience Not Sacrifice

Even in the midst of the marvelous presentation of God's glory, Aaron's two sons, who were priests, went against the commands of the Lord and presented unauthorized fire before Him. The Lord gave them immediate judgment and burned them to death.

As a royal priesthood of Christ, even in the middle of doing the work of the Lord, you may be tempted to put "unauthorized fire" before God. You may be tempted to live selfishly in the area of addiction, pride, or the worship of other gods. Remember, as Christ's chosen priests, you are called out of darkness, out of sin, and into His marvelous light, filled with grace and power from the Lord. Resist the temptation to do your own thing. Today, may you draw strength from the Lord to stand strong.

Aaron's sons Nadab and Abihu each took his own firepan, put fire in it, placed incense on it, and presented unauthorized fire before the Lord, which He had not commanded them to do. Then fire came from the Lord and burned them to death before the Lord. —Leviticus 10:1–2

Further Scripture: Romans 6:22–23; James 1:13–15; 1 Peter 2:9–10

Week 9, Day 58: Leviticus 11—12
Set Apart for God's Glory

God wanted the Israelites to be holy because He is holy. For the Israelites, it meant eating specific food. God wanted His people to be set apart, and eating this specific way was an outward act of obedience and holiness.

As followers of Christ, you are chosen, and you are holy. You are called not only to be set apart from sin and the world but also to be set apart for God's purposes. Rather than focusing on what you eat or don't eat, choose to put on compassion, kindness, humility, gentleness, and patience. Today, whatever you do, do everything for God's glory.

For I am Yahweh your God, so you must consecrate yourselves and be holy because I am holy. You must not defile yourselves by any swarming creature that crawls on the ground. For I am Yahweh, who brought you up from the land of Egypt to be your God, so you must be holy because I am holy.
—Leviticus 11:44–45

Further Scripture: Deuteronomy 7:6; 1 Corinthians 10:31; Colossians 3:12

Week 9, Day 59: Leviticus 13
Jesus Accepts You as You Are

Skin infections and rashes are no fun! If you've ever had even a pimple on your face, you know how awkward and self-aware it makes you. It's hard to imagine the Israelites having to go to a priest for every rash, boil, or skin infection. Can you feel their humiliation from being forced to live outside the community until they were completely healed?

Because of Jesus' love and grace, you belong and are accepted into the body of Christ. Open your eyes to see people on the outside who feel as though they don't belong because of their physical differences. Or maybe you are the one who feels as though you don't belong. Remember, you are forever a part of God's family, and nothing will separate you from His love. May His love shine upon you today.

He will remain unclean as long as he has the infection; he is unclean.
He must live alone in a place outside the camp. —Leviticus 13:46

Further Scripture: Psalm 139:14; Matthew 5:44–45; Romans 8:38–39

Week 9, Day 60: Leviticus 14

Faith in Christ Makes You Pure

God made a way for people to come to Him despite their inadequacies and differences. Israelites used the hyssop plant to treat skin diseases or homes with mold to become clean again and to no longer be a target of judgment. Hyssop was a sign of purity and spiritual cleansing.

God's love is the atonement for your sins. He is the way, the truth, and the life. He makes a way for you when you cannot see it. No matter what you have done or the scars you may bear, you are covered by the grace and love of Jesus Christ. He considers you pure and white as snow. Receive His love for you today.

What is left of the oil in the priest's palm he is to put on the head of the one to be cleansed. In this way the priest will make atonement for him before the Lord. The priest must sacrifice the sin offering and make atonement for the one to be cleansed from his uncleanness. —Leviticus 14:18–19

Further Scripture: Psalm 51:7; John 14:6; John 19:28–30

Week 9, Day 61: Leviticus 15

The Lord's Love Covers the Seen and Unseen

The Lord clearly sees all things, and nothing is hidden from His eyes. Even in the middle of bodily discharge, the Lord knows, He sees, and He makes a way for His people to come back into His holy presence.

In the same way the priests made atonement for the Israelites, Jesus made atonement for you. He sees the sin you think is hidden from Him. He says, "I am here to forgive you and reconcile you to Myself." He longs for you to have clean hands and a pure heart. Turn to Him, and He will receive you as you are, purifying you with His grace-filled love.

The priest is to sacrifice one as a sin offering and the other as a burnt offering. In this way the priest will make atonement for her before the Lord because of her unclean discharge. You must keep the Israelites from their uncleanness, so that they do not die by defiling My tabernacle that is among them. —Leviticus 15:30–31

Further Scripture: Psalm 24:3–4; Hebrews 4:13; 1 Peter 1:22–23

Week 9, Day 62: Leviticus 16
Day of Atonement—Jesus Is Your Substitution

The Day of Atonement was a significant annual event for the Israelites. Just in case their sins hadn't been covered by any of the various offerings, this day purified them and allowed them to be clean before the Lord. The Israelites went through many ceremonial steps. They placed their wrongdoings on a goat and sent it into the wilderness in an effort to get rid of their sin.

In the New Covenant, Jesus is the Lamb of God who takes away your sin. As believers in Christ the Messiah, you no longer have to go through the ceremonies and rituals to find freedom and forgiveness. You are freed from your sin and can live in righteousness because of Christ's own sacrifice. Now that's something to celebrate and give thanks for!

Atonement will be made for you on this day to cleanse you, and you will be clean from all your sins before the Lord. —Leviticus 16:30

Further Scripture: Leviticus 16:22; John 1:29; 2 Corinthians 5:21

Week 9, Day 63: Leviticus 17

Life Is in the Blood

The Lord instructed His people once again. This time He specifically outlined how they were to make sacrifices before Him. The word *blood* is mentioned thirteen times in this chapter. The power of blood brings forgiveness in both the Old and New Testaments.

Blood serves as the atonement in your life. God sent His Son Jesus and purchased your forgiveness with His blood. In Christ alone, and in no other, you have abundant life. Seek Him, and you will find life abundantly because the blood of Christ covers you.

For the life of a creature is in the blood, and I have appointed it to you to make atonement on the altar for your lives, since it is the lifeblood that makes atonement. —Leviticus 17:11

Further Scripture: John 10:10; Ephesians 1:7; 1 John 2:2

Week 10, Day 64: Leviticus 18
Don't Follow Your Old Ways

Through Moses, the Lord told the Israelites to follow Yahweh's commands. Essentially, the Lord said, "Don't follow the practices of your old ways, and don't follow the practices of the land you are going to inhabit in the future. Instead, follow the commands of your current living situation."

Often times you may be tempted to go back to your old ways, or you may want to look ahead to what is on the horizon. In Christ, you are a new creation—the old is gone, and the new has come. You have the power of the Holy Spirit inside you, and you are to live in that power, not in the flesh. Today, don't live the way you used to live. You have a heavenly calling. The Holy Spirit living inside you will give strength for today to walk the ways of the Lord.

Do not follow the practices of the land of Egypt, where you used to live, or follow the practices of the land of Canaan, where I am bringing you. You must not follow their customs. . . . Keep My statutes and ordinances; a person will live if he does them. I am Yahweh." —Leviticus 18:3, 5

Further Scripture: 2 Corinthians 5:17; Philippians 3:18–20; Philippians 4:12–13

Week 10, Day 65: Leviticus 19
Yahweh Is Holy

God instructed Moses to speak directly to the entire Israelite community. He restated the Ten Commandments. After each commandment, the phrase, "I am Yahweh," is repeated. When you read something over and over in a chapter, pay attention. "I am Yahweh," can be translated, "I Am Who I Am," and highlights God as the author of these holiness laws. The Lord also commanded the Israelites to be holy because He is holy.

You are called to be an imitator of Christ. Because God is holy, and God is who He says He is, you are to love others and live your life as a sweet aroma of Christ.

The Lord spoke to Moses: "Speak to the entire Israelite community and tell them: Be holy because I, Yahweh your God, am holy." —Leviticus 19:1–2

Further Scripture: Leviticus 19:18; Matthew 5:48; Ephesians 5:1–2

Week 10, Day 66: Leviticus 20
Punishment for Molech Worship and Sexual Offenses

The Lord gave straight forward and very clear statutes to the people so they would be set apart. He longed for His people to be holy as He is holy. For example, if a man committed adultery with a married woman, both the woman and the man were to be put to death. Oh, how far away from these commands culture has drifted. It should be emphasized that this was the Old Testament Law.

Yes, in Christ, you are forgiven and covered by the blood of Jesus. Yes, His grace washes over you. But even as a New Testament believer, you are to resist temptation, flee from evil, and do what is right in the eyes of the Lord. Please don't give the enemy a foothold. If you are married, please love, respect, and honor your spouse. Fill yourself up with the Spirit daily so you will not give into the flesh.

If a man commits adultery with a married woman—if he commits adultery with his neighbor's wife—both the adulterer and the adulteress must be put to death. —Leviticus 20:10

Further Scripture: Ephesians 5:18, 25; James 4:7

Week 10, Day 67: Leviticus 21
Jesus' Blood Covers All

If any of Aaron's descendants throughout the generations had a physical defect, they could not come near to present food offerings to God. They couldn't go near the curtain or approach the altar.

Give thanks today for the blood of Jesus the Messiah, the ultimate High Priest, who without defect or blemish cleansed you from your sin so you could spend forever with the eternal God. Jesus came to love, to serve, and to heal those with physical defects. May you love others the way Jesus loves others, even those who look differently from the way you look. Jesus paid the price for everyone!

The Lord spoke to Moses: "Tell Aaron: None of your descendants throughout your generations who has a physical defect is to come near to present the food of his God. No man who has any defect is to come near: no man who is blind, lame, facially disfigured, or deformed." —Leviticus 21:16–18

Further Scripture: Matthew 4:24; Hebrews 9:14; 1 Peter 1:18–19

Week 10, Day 68: Leviticus 22
Hope in Jesus—The Only Holy Priest

Following the regulations from the Lord was a serious matter. The phrase, "That person will be cut off from My presence; I am Yahweh," may be hard for some to fathom, as it is spoken from a kind, loving, gracious, Father God. And yet that's how seriously the Israelites were to take the regulations.

Can you imagine being cut off from the Lord's presence? A life of complete darkness: no hope, no glimpse of the light. Today, give thanks for the Lord's presence. Give thanks for the Holy Spirit's presence in your life every day, all day, wherever you go! In His presence you will find rest, peace, and hope from an all-knowing, all-powerful Lord and Savior. And thanks to Jesus' atonement, nothing will ever separate us from His presence.

Say to them: If any man from any of your descendants throughout your generations is in a state of uncleanness yet approaches the holy offerings that the Israelites consecrate to the Lord, that person will be cut off from My presence; I am Yahweh. —Leviticus 22:3

Further Scripture: Psalm 16:11; Psalm 139:7–10; Romans 8:38–39

Week 10, Day 69: Leviticus 23—24
The Sabbath and the Feasts

The phrase "sacred assembly" occurs eleven times in just one chapter. These assemblies served as a time for people to set aside their routine work and activities and focus on worshipping the Lord. The Lord described each of the eight different days designated as sacred assemblies, such as Passover, the Festival of Unleavened Bread, and the Day of Atonement. You too were created to worship the Lord. It may be through fasting, sacrifices and offerings, rejoicing in His goodness, or resting in His promises.

As a New Testament believer, you are no longer instructed to celebrate these specific sacred assemblies. However, Paul instructed believers to rejoice always and in everything give thanks. Today, give thanks, and remember the Lord's faithfulness in your life. Give thanks for the trials that have strengthened your faith and the joys in life that display God's goodness and kindness. The Lord is worthy of your praise and thanksgiving!

The Lord spoke to Moses: "Speak to the Israelites and tell them:
These are My appointed times, the times of the Lord that you will proclaim
as sacred assemblies." —Leviticus 23:1

Further Scripture: Lamentation 3:22–23; 1 Corinthians 10:31;
1 Thessalonians 5:16–18

Week 10, Day 70: Leviticus 25
Sabbath Years and Jubilee

The Lord gave Moses clear instructions for the Israelites to observe a Sabbath rest for the land every seventh year. The Lord explained in detail how this would work. The Israelites would have a sufficient crop every sixth year to provide enough to carry them through the Sabbath year and even the year following the Sabbath. God promised the Israelites would live securely in the land if they kept His statutes and ordinances and carefully observed them. Can you imagine physically not working for an entire year, trusting the Lord to provide everything you need? And yet, what was their alternative? They could have taken matters into their own hands, doing what they wanted and what they thought best.

In the same way, the Lord instructs you to rest in Him, trusting He will provide as you follow His ways. So why is it so hard to let go of control, rest with unwavering faith in God's promises, and do things His way? Today, seek the Lord for rest, and trust in His ways and His plans for your day. Let go of control and walk by faith.

But there will be a Sabbath of complete rest for the land in the seventh year, a Sabbath to the Lord: you are not to sow your field or prune your vineyard. You are not to reap what grows by itself from your crop, or harvest the grapes of your untended vines. It must be a year of complete rest for the land. . . . You are not to cheat one another, but fear your God, for I am Yahweh your God. You are to keep My statutes and ordinances and carefully observe them, so that you may live securely in the land.
—Leviticus 25:4–5, 17–18

Further Scripture: Psalm 147:7–9; Matthew 6:24; Matthew 11:28–29

Week 11, Day 71: Leviticus 26
Covenant Blessings and Discipline

If the Israelites followed God's statutes and faithfully observed His commands, the Lord promised to bless them abundantly. Not only would He bless the work of their hands, but His presence would also be with them, bringing them ultimate peace and freedom. They had a choice to follow God or go their own way. God even gave them a second chance through confessing their sins, offering blood sacrifices, and turning back to Him. God desires strongly for His people to follow Him and trust Him.

The same is true today. The Lord, through the blood of Jesus, longs for you to follow Him and His ways each day. In Him, there is freedom, love, and peace. You will find blessings as you maintain the discipline to follow Jesus and resist temptation. As a believer, the Holy Spirit takes residence in you, and He is with you always. Rest in that promise today, and make a choice to seek the Lord your God with all your heart, soul, mind, and strength.

I will place My residence among you, and I will not reject you. I will walk among you and be your God, and you will be My people. I am Yahweh your God, who brought you out of the land of Egypt, so that you would no longer be their slaves. I broke the bars of your yoke and enabled you to live in freedom. —Leviticus 26:11–13

Further Scripture: Isaiah 57:15; 1 Corinthians 3:16; 1 John 4:12

Week 11, Day 72: Leviticus 27

The Cost to Following

As Leviticus comes to an end, God gave Moses final commands for the Israelites. Specifically, they discussed making vows to the Lord and how the vows could be redeemed (essentially breaking the vows through a determined sum of money).

As believers, there is a cost to following Christ. Jesus said if you want to be His disciple, you must bear your own cross and follow Him. Jesus said believers who do not count the cost and hold loosely to all earthy things cannot be His disciples. However, in all this, the beautiful truth is that Christ gave His life for you. Through His precious blood, Jesus came as the atonement for sinners. And life with Christ is free and full when you surrender all and follow Him. He is your forever hope.

If the vow involves one of the animals that may be brought as an offering to the Lord, any of these he gives to the Lord will be holy. —Leviticus 27:9

Further Scripture: Luke 14:27, 33; 1 Peter 1:18–19

Week 11, Day 73: Numbers 1—2

The Census of Israel

The Lord commanded Moses and Aaron to take a census of the entire Israelite community, counting their names one by one. The Lord was bringing order to the Israelites and beginning to build Israel's army. Pay attention as you read the names and numbers in each ancestral house. Can you imagine counting all those people one at a time—no computers, no paper or pens? Still, the Lord commanded that each name be counted one by one. The task was worth the time and effort to the Lord.

In the same way, the Lord knows your name. He has an ultimate plan for you. No matter what community you belong to, you have a role and are important to the entire body of Christ. He's counting on you to bring Him glory!

Take a census of the entire Israelite community by their clans and their ancestral houses, counting the names of every male one by one.
—Numbers 1:2

Further Scripture: Isaiah 43:1; John 10:14; Ephesians 4:11–12

March 15

Week 11, Day 74: Numbers 3

The Serving and Caring Levites

After the Lord gave commands and job assignments to all the Israelites, He focused on the 22,000 Levites. The Levites' job was to assist Aaron and his sons by attending to the service of the Tabernacle. They were specifically instructed to take care of all the furnishings. What a role!

Many times, jobs that deal with the "caring of things" go unnoticed in life until something is dirty, out of place, or falling apart. Then you realize how important it is to have a group serving and caring behind the scenes. The world may not view these roles as important or highly esteemed, but as followers of Christ, you are called to serve just as Jesus came to serve. If you are following the Lord and His plans for your life, there's no better place to be, even if it involves scrubbing toilets!

The Lord spoke to Moses: "Bring the tribe of Levi near and present them to Aaron the priest to assist him. They are to perform duties for him and the entire community before the tent of meeting by attending to the service of the tabernacle." —Numbers 3:5–7

Further Scripture: John 12:26; Romans 12:4–7; Galatians 5:13

Week 11, Day 75: Numbers 4

Duties of the Kohathites, Gershonites, and Merarites

The Lord assigned the Kohathites, the Gershonites, and the Merarites to transportation duties. They were given specific tasks to complete in the process of transporting the Tent of Meeting. As the Lord outlined specific transportation assignments, it was a reminder that He was in the details of life. Previously God said He would go ahead of Moses and the Israelites in a pillar of cloud and a pillar of fire, so the Israelites knew they would be moving. Then He gave them detailed instructions on how to build the Tent of Meeting. If God commanded the Israelites to build it and said they would be moving, then it only made sense that God had transportation details taken care of!

Remember, if the Lord has called you to something, He is going to have a plan for all the delicate details. The Lord promises He will counsel you and show you the way to go. Doesn't that give you great relief? God has a plan!

Their registered men numbered 8,580. At the Lord's command they were registered under the direction of Moses, each one according to his work and transportation duty, and his assignment was as the Lord commanded Moses.
—Numbers 4:48–49

Further Scripture: Exodus 13:21; Exodus 35:10–11; Psalm 32:8

Week 11, Day 76: Numbers 5—6
The Aaronic Blessing

After giving instructions regarding purity laws and vows, it was almost as though the Lord paused and took a deep breath. Again, God spoke to Moses with instructions for Aaron and his sons on how to bless the Israelite people. This Aaronic blessing brings protection, favor, deliverance, hope, and more.

God continues to be the example to follow about how to deal with people. Even in the midst of details and structure, remember to pause and see the people around you as human beings with emotions and feelings. Sometimes life's details keep you so busy that you may forget to bless people. No matter where you are today, pause for just a minute, and bless someone with the love of Jesus.

The Lord spoke to Moses: "Tell Aaron and his sons how you are to bless the Israelites. Say to them: May Yahweh bless you and protect you; may Yahweh make His face shine on you and be gracious to you; may Yahweh look with favor on you and give you peace. In this way they will pronounce My name over the Israelites, and I will bless them." —Numbers 6:22–27

Further Scripture: John 1:16; 2 Corinthians 9:11; Philippians 2:4

Week 11, Day 77: Numbers 7

Accepting Offerings

When Moses finished setting up the Tabernacle, he anointed and consecrated it, along with all the furnishings, the altar, and its utensils. Afterwards, the leaders of Israel presented an offering in front of the Tabernacle. The Lord commanded Moses to accept this offering. Then the Lord told Moses to use the offering for specific purposes. Finally, Moses gave the offering to specific people.

The Lord presented a model for receiving offerings. It is a great example to keep in mind as you receive gifts from God. If the Lord allows something to be given to you, then accept it. Open your eyes to why the Lord gave it to you, so you know how to use it. And, if there is anyone you need to pass the gift along to, do so. Remember, all good and perfect gifts are from the Lord. Give thanks for God's goodness today!

The Lord said to Moses, "Accept these from them to be used in the work of the tent of meeting, and give this offering to the Levites, to each division according to their service." —Numbers 7:4–5

Further Scripture: Psalm 84:11; 2 Corinthians 9:8; James 1:17

Week 12, Day 78: Numbers 8—9

Wait and Ask the Lord

The Israelites prepared to celebrate the second Passover a year after they first observed Passover in Egypt. Some men came to Moses with questions after hearing the commands on how to observe this sacred assembly. When they asked Moses for clarification, Moses responded, "Wait until I find out what the Lord commands concerning you." Moses could have just answered on his own or told the men how he thought the Lord would answer. Instead, Moses paused and told the men to wait. Then Moses confidently asked the Lord, believing the Lord would have an answer for the men.

How often do you rush into making decisions or giving answers to people in your life without seeking the Lord's counsel? In this situation, Moses provided a great example of not rushing into an answer or giving advice without seeking the Lord first and foremost. As believers, you have the Holy Spirit dwelling inside you ready to counsel you moment by moment. Walk this out in your own life today, and watch the Lord guide you in all ways.

These men came before Moses and Aaron the same day and said to him, "We are unclean because of a human corpse. Why should we be excluded from presenting the Lord's offering at its appointed time with the other Israelites?" Moses replied to them, "Wait here until I hear what the Lord commands for you." Then the Lord spoke to Moses: "Tell the Israelites . . ."
—Numbers 9:6–10

Further Scripture: Psalm 32:8; John 14:26; James 1:5

Week 12, Day 79: Numbers 10—11
The Lord Hears Your Complaints

The Israelites complained about hardship, and the Lord's anger literally burned among them, consuming parts of the camp. Then some became dissatisfied with the manna the Lord had provided. They wanted something different—they wanted meat. In response, the Lord gave them quail, and the people who complained for a different type of food died while eating it. Have you noticed a pattern yet? The people become dissatisfied, God answers, and the people are still dissatisfied. How exhausting!

The Lord longs for you to find your satisfaction in Him alone. You are to crave God's presence in your life more than anything else. The lies of the enemy will tell you otherwise. Today, examine your heart, and ask the Lord if you are craving things of this world for satisfaction rather than Him. Remember, in the Lord's presence there is fullness of joy.

The Lord answered Moses, "Is the Lord's power limited? You will see whether or not what I have promised will happen to you."
—Numbers 11:23

Further Scripture: Psalm 16:11; Jeremiah 15:16; Philippians 2:13–15

Week 12, Day 80: Numbers 12—13
Scouting Out Canaan

God commanded Moses to send twelve men to scout out the land of Canaan. After forty days, they returned to the Israelites with two different reports. The majority of the scouts came back fearful, intimidated, and with negative attitudes about going into the land. But Caleb spoke up, full of faith, believing they could certainly conquer the land.

Whenever the Lord leads you into new situations, you can choose to respond with a negative or positive attitude. You can choose to fear or have faith. You can choose to believe you are defeated before it even begins, or you can choose to believe you are a conqueror in all situations. With God by your side and the power of the Holy Spirit within you, you have all you need for seemingly impossible situations. Remember, with God, all things are possible. God has not given you a spirit of fear but of power, love, and sound judgment. Walk in these promises today as the Lord leads you to new adventures!

Then Caleb quieted the people in the presence of Moses and said, "We must go up and take possession of the land because we can certainly conquer it!" But the men who had gone up with him responded, "We can't go up against the people because they are stronger than we are!" —Numbers 13:30–31

Further Scripture: Luke 1:37; Romans 8:37; 2 Timothy 1:7

Week 12, Day 81: Numbers 14
Caleb's Different Spirit

Out of the twelve men who scouted the land for forty days, only Caleb and Joshua remained alive. The Lord saw that Caleb had a different spirit and had followed Him completely. Caleb walked in faith and humility. He mourned alongside Moses, Aaron, and Joshua for the sins of the Israelites. He had faith God would be with him and the others in this new land.

Can you imagine if the Lord said those words about you? "[Fill in your name] has followed Me completely." When God leads you to something, do you fully trust Him and His faithfulness, or do you waiver and doubt? Today, make the choice to trust that God will be with you always, and with humility, follow Him completely. The Lord is rich in faithful love, a love that will never fail you.

But since My servant Caleb has a different spirit and has followed me completely, I will bring him into the land where he has gone, and his descendants will inherit it. —Numbers 14:24

Further Scripture: Numbers 14:18; Psalm 119:133; James 4:6

Week 12, Day 82: Numbers 15—16

Aaron and Moses Intercede to Save the People

The Israelite community continued to act in rebellion toward God. Korah, a Levite, along with 250 prominent Israelite men and leaders of the community, questioned Moses and Aaron's ordained positions as leader and priest. Three different times Moses's and Aaron's reactions to the rebellion were to fall facedown before the Lord. They sought the Lord in complete humility and surrender on behalf of the Israelite people. Even when the people criticized Moses and Aaron, they continued to seek the Lord's mercy to save the people and not penalize the entire nation of Israel.

What do you do when you are desperate for the Lord to move? Do you fall on your face before Him in complete surrender? Moses and Aaron knew the power of the Lord, and they came before Him with all they had. Whatever you are facing today, fall on your face before the Lord in worship and complete surrender, expecting Him to move powerfully in your situation!

But Moses and Aaron fell facedown and said, "God, God of the spirits of all flesh, when one man sins, will You vent Your wrath on the whole community?" —Numbers 16:22

Further Scripture: Galatians 2:20; Hebrews 11:6; James 4:10

Week 12, Day 83: Numbers 17—18

Chosen Appointed Royal Priest

From among twelve staffs, one belonging to the head of each ancestral house, the Lord chose Aaron's. Overnight it was Aaron's staff that miraculously went from being a lifeless piece of wood to sprouting, forming buds, blossoming, and producing almonds! Then the Lord commanded that Aaron's staff be placed in front of the Testimony as a sign to the rebels in the community, putting an end to their complaining about whom the Lord had appointed for priestly service.

As believers, the Lord has called you by name. Through Christ, you go from death to life. Just as the white blossoms on the staff symbolized purity and holiness to the Aaronic priests, you too, as a chosen member of the royal priesthood of Christ, are to be holy and live pure in Christ. As you remain in Christ, you will produce much fruit. Today, when you walk out your calling, remember that the Lord's presence, the Holy Spirit, resides in you at all times. You are not alone. His rod and staff will comfort you.

The next day Moses entered the tent of the testimony and saw that Aaron's staff, representing the house of Levi, had sprouted, formed buds, blossomed, and produced almonds! —Numbers 17:8

Further Scripture: Psalm 23:4; Romans 8:11; 1 Peter 2:9

Week 12, Day 84: Numbers 19—20
Years of Wandering

Once again, the Israelites complained and grumbled to Moses and Aaron about a lack of water. Once again, Moses and Aaron fell on their faces and sought help from the Lord. And once again, the Lord responded with a plan to display His miraculous provision. The Lord instructed Moses to speak to a rock while the Israelites watched, and the rock would yield water. However, Moses raised his hand and struck the rock twice with his staff. Moses clearly did not follow the exact commands of the Lord. Yet God displayed mercy, and the rock still produced water for the people. Moses acted in anger and impatience. This act of disobedience caused God to prevent Moses from entering the Promised Land.

Although God is a forgiving God, there are consequences for behavior. Your actions demonstrate your trust in God's faithfulness. As you walk in the Spirit, you are filled with the fruit of the Spirit: love, joy, peace, patience, kindness, goodness, faithfulness, gentleness, and self-control. If your life lacks one or more of these, take a minute today to come before the Lord. Spend time in His presence, read through His Word, worship Him with thanksgiving, confess anything that comes to mind, and allow Him to fill you up. When you are refreshed with the Spirit, you will be strengthened for the journey ahead.

Then Moses raised his hand and struck the rock twice with his staff, so that a great amount of water gushed out, and the community and their livestock drank. But the Lord said to Moses and Aaron, "Because you did not trust Me to show My holiness in the sight of the Israelites, you will not bring this assembly into the land I have given them." —Numbers 20:11–12

Further Scripture: 2 Corinthians 12:9–10; Galatians 5:22–23a; Ephesians 5:18

Week 13, Day 85: Numbers 21—22

The Bronze Snake—Jesus Lifted Up

The Israelite people grew impatient because of the journey, and they spoke against God. So the Lord sent poisonous snakes among the people, and their bites caused many Israelites to die. Once again, the people pleaded for help, and Moses interceded with the Lord on their behalf. And once again, the Lord showed mercy and grace to the Israelites by creating a way to rescue them from the snakes. The Lord instructed Moses to make a bronze serpent and set it up on a pole. When those bitten by snakes looked at the pole, they recovered, and their bites were healed.

Think about how this parallels with the saving grace of Jesus. When life gets to be too much and the journey feels beyond what you can bear, you may complain to God and forget His faithful promises. But God has an ultimate plan. He sent Jesus to be lifted up on the Cross. Everyone on the journey who looks up to Him is saved from death, healed of sins, and freed from bondage. In looking up to Christ and believing in Him, you will have eternal life. Turn to Christ and look up to Him, giving thanks for His many promises in your life.

Then the Lord said to Moses, "Make a snake image and mount it on a pole. When anyone who is bitten looks at it, he will recover." —Numbers 21:8

Further Scripture: Isaiah 45:22; John 3:14–15; Acts 4:12

Week 13, Day 86: Numbers 23—24

From the Mouth of a Donkey

The Lord got Balaam's attention when He opened the mouth of a donkey and allowed the donkey to speak to Balaam. From the time Balaam met with the Angel of the Lord in the middle of a road, he spoke only the messages God put in his mouth, even when it was not the message King Balak expected to hear. The Lord used Balaam to point Balak and Israel to the coming Star, the King, Christ the Messiah.

If the Lord can speak the message of truth through a donkey and a hired servant, then remember, He can speak through anyone. If the Lord lays a message on your heart as you meet with Him, be obedient and bold, and share it with others. God can use anyone to be His mouthpiece. Your adequacy comes from God, not yourself.

Balaam said to Balak, "Stay here by your burnt offering while I seek the Lord over there." The Lord met with Balaam and put a message in his mouth. Then He said, "Return to Balak and say what I tell you."
So he returned to Balak, who was standing there by his burnt offering with the officials of Moab. Balak asked him, "What did the Lord say?"
—Numbers 23:15–17

Further Scripture: Numbers 24:17; 2 Corinthians 3:5; 2 Corinthians 11:5–6

Week 13, Day 87: Numbers 25—26
Israel Worships Baal—Phinehas Intervenes

The Israelites were in the mountains of Moab near the Jordan River Valley. In the middle of the camp, the Israelites gave in to temptation, and in this case, their sexual desires. In response, God's anger burned against the Israelites. He wanted to kill all the men who had aligned themselves with the god Ba'al of Peor. However, one man, Phinehas, noticed what was happening and stood up for what was right. In his zealousness, he killed a man and woman having sexual relations near the entrance of the Tabernacle, a place reserved for the sacred presentation of offerings to God. Because of Phinehas's bold and courageous act against this sin, the Lord ended the plague, and no one else was killed. A line was drawn in the sand, and there was a shift in the rebellion of Israel.

Who are you in this harsh reality? Are you the one giving in to temptation and living in sin? Or are you the one zealous enough to follow the Lord and stand up for what is right? The world and Satan want to lure you into sinful ways: an emotional or sexual affair, sex before marriage, or the temptation of pornography. You know it is not from the Lord, but you have grown numb to sin and enjoy the temporary pleasures it brings. As followers of Christ, draw a line in the sand today. Turn away from the darkness of sin and walk into the light of Christ. The Lord will welcome you with open arms of forgiveness. If you see a brother or sister stumbling in this area, be zealous and say something. Don't stand by and watch them live in sin. Be a light for Jesus today!

The Lord spoke to Moses, "Phinehas son of Eleazar, son of Aaron the priest, has turned back My wrath from the Israelites because he was zealous among them with My zeal, so that I did not destroy the Israelites in My zeal."
—Numbers 25:10–11

Further Scripture: Psalm 106:30–31; 1 Corinthians 10:13; Galatians 6:1

Week 13, Day 88: Numbers 27—28
Laws of Inheritance

The daughters of Zelophehad stood before Moses and boldly asked for their father's property. The women came from a father whom the Lord had killed in the wilderness because of his sin. Despite their family's sin, the Lord answered the women's bold request by giving them their inherited property.

The Lord knows everything about your past and your present, and He still loves and cares for you. In Christ, you are no longer called an orphan; you are called God's child. When you put your hope in Christ, you receive an inheritance in Him that is imperishable, uncorrupted, and unfading. It will be yours forever as you walk with Jesus. So walk boldly, like these women, in the promise of your inheritance as a son or daughter of the King of kings and Lord of lords.

"Why should the name of our father be taken away from his clan? Since he had no son, give us property among our father's brothers." Moses brought their case before the Lord, and the Lord answered him, "What Zelophehad's daughters say is correct. You are to give them hereditary property among their father's brothers and transfer their father's inheritance to them."
—Numbers 27:4–7

Further Scripture: John 14:18; Ephesians 1:11–12; 1 Peter 1:4

Week 13, Day 89: Numbers 29—30

Calendar of Public Sacrifices: Jesus the Sacrifice and High Priest

Once again Moses instructed the Israelites on everything the Lord commanded regarding sacrifices and offerings. Every year during the many festivals, the Israelites gave up their resources in the form of sacrifices and offerings to make atonement for their sins. This was all the Israelites knew in the way of atonement.

However, in the New Testament, Christ came and offered a sacrifice for sin forever. With His life, He paid the price of sin once and for all. Through this one offering, Jesus has perfected forever those who are sanctified in Him. You are forgiven forever; therefore, sacrifices and offerings are no longer necessary. Praise the Lord for this sacrificial act of love.

"You must offer these to the Lord at your appointed times in addition to your vow and freewill offerings, whether burnt, grain, drink, or fellowship offerings." So Moses told the Israelites everything the Lord had commanded him. —Numbers 29:39–40

Further Scripture: Ephesians 5:2; Hebrews 10:10–12, 17–18

Week 13, Day 90: Numbers 31
War with Midian: Physical War and Spiritual War

The Lord instructed Moses about how the Israelites were to execute vengeance upon the Midianites, who had allowed sexual sin to creep into the Israelite camp. This battle destroyed all the impure people. After the Israelites succeeded in this battle, they went through a purification process for themselves and the goods they obtained before they were allowed back into the community.

God desires purity from His people. You are called into a battle every day. When you go through the daily battle, a purification process naturally occurs in your life. Anything in you that is not of the Lord will not last during the battle. These difficult times help to get rid of pride, lust, selfishness, control, and other fleshly desires that may have crept into your life. What will the Lord purify in your life? The Lord allows you to go through the fire so that you may reflect more of Him. Today let your heart take courage, for the battle belongs to the Lord.

The Lord spoke to Moses, "Execute vengeance for the Israelites against the Midianites. After that, you will be gathered to your people." . . . "Also purify everything: garments, leather goods, things made of goat hair, and every article of wood." . . . "After that, you may enter the camp."
—Numbers 31:1, 20, 24

Further Scripture: 1 Samuel 17:47; Malachi 3:2–3; Ephesians 6:10–13

Week 13, Day 91: Numbers 32

Pressing Forward into the Promises of God

The Reubenites and the Gadites came up with their own plan for their families and livestock, and it didn't include crossing the Jordan River with the rest of the Israelites. They liked the land they were on and decided it was best for them. As a result, they didn't think they needed to go into battle or into the Promised Land with the other tribes. Moses was upset with their lack of trust and loyalty to God's original plan.

As followers of Christ, Jesus calls you to keep your hands to the plow and follow Him by faith. However, temporary things may tempt you to stop walking by faith. You are called to walk by faith and to trust in the Lord with all your heart, not depending on your strength. Today, you may be in a place where you are tempted to rely on your own strength. Be encouraged to press on in faith, trusting that the Lord's plan will be the best for your life! He loves you, and His plan is incredible!

They said, "If we have found favor in your sight, let this land be given to your servants as a possession. Don't make us cross the Jordan."
But Moses asked the Gadites and Reubenites, "Should your brothers go to war while you stay here?" —Numbers 32:5–6

Further Scripture: Proverbs 3:5–6; Luke 9:62; 2 Corinthians 5:7

Week 14, Day 92: Numbers 33
From Egypt to Jordan—Start Fresh

The Israelites needed to start fresh in the land the Lord was giving them. The Lord knew if they left any of the previous inhabitants in the land, those inhabitants would become stressful to His people, like thorns in their eyes and sides.

Sometimes in life, when you start a new job, move to a new home, or begin at a new school, you may try to merge the previous people, places, or things with the new ones. You want to make both sides happy and avoid causing pain or heartache to anyone. However, in reality, it may lead to unhappiness on both sides, creating a stressful situation. The Lord was commanding the Israelites to eliminate all of the old ways and just start fresh. Maybe you need to hear this today. Make the hard decision and start fresh. Be strong and courageous as you take steps forward. The Lord will work it out for good!

But if you don't drive out the inhabitants of the land before you, those you allow to remain will become thorns in your eyes and in your sides; they will harass you in the land where you will live. And what I had planned to do to them, I will do to you. —Numbers 33:55–56

Further Scripture: Numbers 33:52–53; Proverbs 16:1–4; Romans 8:28

Week 14, Day 93: Numbers 34
Details of the Promised Inheritance

The Lord gave Moses specific instructions on how to communicate the inheritance of the land to the Israelites. Even though they were walking into the Promised Land and knew they had an inheritance coming, Moses still needed to communicate the inheritance to the people, detailing the borders and assigning a leader from each tribe to distribute the land.

As a believer, you have an inheritance from the Lord—eternal life. Like Moses, you need to communicate to others about this inheritance. Don't keep this knowledge to yourself or assume others already know the details of your inheritance in Christ. This is one inheritance that is available for everyone to receive! Some people may never know about the inheritance of Jesus Christ unless you share it!

The Lord spoke to Moses, "Command the Israelites and say to them: When you enter the land of Canaan, it will be allotted to you as an inheritance with these borders." —Numbers 34:1–2

Further Scripture: Numbers 34:13; Ephesians 1:18–19; Hebrews 9:15

Week 14, Day 94: Numbers 35–36

Lead with Humility and Seek God's Wisdom

At the end of the Book of Numbers, leaders from the clan of Manasseh returned to Moses and questioned the decision made regarding the inheritance of Zelophehad's daughters. Moses answered the command of the Lord and affirmed the leaders were right. Then Moses relayed a new command from the Lord concerning Zelophehad's daughters, their inheritance, and whom they should marry. Moses responded in humility, and he sought the Lord for wisdom before answering.

Have you ever been questioned by someone who wanted a different answer from the one you originally gave? It takes great humility to say someone else is right because that implies you were wrong. No one likes to be wrong. However, when the Lord is your rock and your strong foundation, being right or wrong will not faze you. As you make Christ your solid foundation, humbly acknowledging Him and all His ways, you will not be shaken. Today, allow the Lord to be your rock, and your ways will not be shaken.

So Moses commanded the Israelites at the word of the Lord,
"What the tribe of Joseph's descendants says is right. This is what the Lord
has commanded concerning Zelophehad's daughters."
—Numbers 36:5–6

Further Scripture: Psalm 16:8; Psalm 62:6–8; 1 Corinthians 10:3–4

Week 14, Day 95: Deuteronomy 1—3
Please Let Me

In the opening chapters of the Book of Deuteronomy, Moses readied the people for what was ahead. As he prepared the new generation of Israelites for the Promised Land, Moses reminded them of all that had taken place up to this point. In doing so, Moses recalled how he pleaded with the Lord to "please" reconsider the decision to not allow him into the Promised Land. But the Lord said no once again. Even so, God softened His answer and allowed Moses to see the land with his own eyes by going to the top of Pisgah, overlooking the land.

Have you ever asked the Lord to reconsider His decision for your life? "Can I please move back to my old home?" "Will you please make my child well again?" "Can I please have my job back?" It's hard to not have what you want or what you think is best for your life, but God promises He has a plan and will work all things together for good. It may not always make sense at the time, but choose to rest in the Lord, trusting that He has plans not to harm you but to give you a future and a hope.

At that time I begged the Lord . . . Please let me cross over and see the beautiful land on the other side of the Jordan, that good hill country and Lebanon. —Deuteronomy 3:23, 25

Further Scripture: Isaiah 55:8; Jeremiah 29:11; Romans 8:28

Week 14, Day 96: Deuteronomy 4—6
Instructions for the Promised Land—The Shemah

Moses gave the Israelites the most important commandment to remember before they entered into the Promised Land. They were to love the Lord with all their heart, soul, and strength. These verses are known as the *Shemah* and are the greatest commandments. The words from the Lord were to be in their hearts. Yes, teach them to your children. Yes, talk about them when you come and go. Yes, bind them to your hand and forehead. Yes, write them on the doorposts of your house and gate. But first, put them in your heart.

As brothers and sisters in Christ, the Lord is interested in your heart relationship with Him, not about the Law or the outward appearance. First, examine your heart and your love for the Lord. Living Christ's love on the outside will happen naturally when your heart is filled up with a love for Christ.

Listen, Israel. The Lord our God, the Lord is One. Love the Lord your God with all your heart, with all your soul, and with all your strength. These words that I am giving you today are to be in your heart. Repeat them to your children. Talk about them when you sit in your house and when you walk along the road, when you lie down and when you get up. Bind them as a sign on your hand and let them be a symbol on your forehead. Write them on the doorposts of your house and on your gate.
—Deuteronomy 6:4–9

Further Scripture: Proverbs 4:23; Proverbs 21:2; Luke 6:45

Week 14, Day 97: Deuteronomy 7—9

Remember What You Have Been Through

As the Israelites approached the Promised Land, Moses reminded them of God's faithfulness to them over the years: deliverance out of bondage in Egypt and His provision and power through their wandering in the wilderness.

Whenever you prepare to enter a new season, take time to reflect and remember God's faithfulness in your life. Take note of the specific wonders of His power and tender care along the way. And as you look ahead to the future with its unknowns, do not be afraid. Remember, God is the same yesterday, today, and tomorrow. He will be with you all the days ahead in faithful, powerful ways!

Do not be afraid of them. Be sure to remember what the Lord your God did to Pharaoh and all Egypt: the great trials that you saw, the signs and wonders, the strong hand and outstretched arm, by which the Lord your God brought you out. The Lord your God will do the same to all the peoples you fear. —Deuteronomy 7:18–19

Further Scripture: Psalm 77:11–12; Psalm 98:3; Hebrews 13:8

Week 14, Day 98: Deuteronomy 10—12

Blessed and Chosen

Out of all the peoples of the Earth, the Israelites were blessed and chosen by God to be His. From the highest heavens above to everything on the earth below, it all belongs to the Lord.

As a follower of Christ, the Lord chose you—yes, you—to love and bless and call His own. You are chosen. You are set apart. You are known. You are loved beyond what you can imagine. The Lord called you out of darkness and into His marvelous light. Breathe in these grace-filled truths, and let all the lies of the enemy fall to the side. Today, proclaim the praises of the Lord God Almighty!

The heavens, indeed the highest heavens, belong to the Lord your God, as does the earth and everything in it. Yet the Lord was devoted to your fathers and loved them. He chose their descendants after them—He chose you out of all the peoples, as it is today. —Deuteronomy 10:14–15

Further Scripture: Deuteronomy 14:2; Jeremiah 1:5; 1 Peter 2:9

Week 15, Day 99: Deuteronomy 13—14

Listen to and Follow God

Moses continued to give instructions to the Israelites regarding the days ahead in the Promised Land. Over and over, Moses reminded them to love the Lord their God with all their hearts and warned them not to follow false prophets or have other gods. Moses commanded the Israelites to follow God and fear Him. As the Israelites kept His commands and listened to His voice, they displayed their love for their Lord.

The same is true for believers today. As you draw closer to Jesus, you will become more attune to hearing His voice and keeping His commands because you love Him and desire to obey Him. Just as a sheep hears the voice of its shepherd and walks toward that voice, you are to follow your Shepherd's voice. What is He saying to you today?

You must follow the Lord your God and fear Him.
You must keep His commands and listen to His voice; you must worship
Him and remain faithful to Him. —Deuteronomy 13:4

Further Scripture: John 10:27; John 14:5; Revelation 3:20

Week 15, Day 100: Deuteronomy 15—16

No Stingy Hearts

Moses continued to instruct the Israelites on how to live in the Promised Land. He commanded the Israelites to be generous to others and not have stingy hearts. The Lord is generous, giving good gifts to His children. How much more can His children be generous in return by not holding on to things?

Ask the Lord today for a generous heart. Ask Him to reveal areas in your life that need greater generosity. You can give your time, your resources, your possessions, even your entire life as an offering to the Lord. The more you walk in a spirit of generosity, the more the Lord will bless you through it all. The Lord loves a cheerful giver!

Give to him, and don't have a stingy heart when you give,
and because of this the Lord your God will bless you in all your work and in
everything you do. —Deuteronomy 15:10

Further Scripture: Luke 11:13; 2 Corinthians 9:7; 1 Timothy 6:18–19

April 11

Week 15, Day 101: Deuteronomy 17—18
The Promised Prophet

Moses made a bold statement in the middle of talking about pagan prophets with the Israelites. Confidently, Moses said God would raise up a prophet like himself, and all must listen to the prophet that is to come. Fast forward to the New Testament where John, Peter and Stephen all refer to Moses as a prophet. They go on to confirm Jesus, not only as a prophet, but as the promised Messiah. Moses came as a faithful servant in God's household to write about the Law. And while Jesus' life parallels Moses' life in many ways, Jesus came so all may have eternal life.

As believers, you receive freedom, grace, and eternal life in Jesus Christ, the Promised Prophet. God raised up this Prophet, the Messiah, for you to listen to! What is Jesus saying to you today?

The Lord your God will raise up for you a prophet like me from among your own brothers. You must listen to him.
—Deuteronomy 18:15

Further Scripture: John 1:45; Acts 7:37; Hebrews 3:5–6

Week 15, Day 102: Deuteronomy 19—20

Battle Preparations

As the Israelites prepared to enter the Promised Land, the Lord prepped them for the battles ahead. Moses commanded the people to listen and to not be cowardly, afraid, alarmed, or terrified. It's almost as though Moses gave them a war manual.

You may never be called to fight on the front lines of a physical war. However, every day as a believer in Christ, you are in a spiritual battle against the world, your own flesh, and Satan. You are to stand firm and equip yourself with the armor of God. The Lord has victory over all, and He promises to go with you to fight your enemies! Today is your day to stand and not be afraid. The Lord will help you through whatever you face. It's going to be a great day of victory for you in Christ Jesus!

He is to say to them: "Listen, Israel: Today you are about to engage in battle with your enemies. Do not be cowardly. Do not be afraid, alarmed, or terrified because of them. For the Lord your God is the One who goes with you to fight for you against your enemies to give you victory."
—Deuteronomy 20:3–4

Further Scripture: Psalm 20:7; Isaiah 41:10; Ephesians 6:12–13

Week 15, Day 103: Deuteronomy 21—22
Stubborn and Rebellious Children

Moses's instructions to the Israelites included the law and penalty regarding stubborn and rebellious children. In the event of children who would not listen to their parents or were drunkards and gluttons, the parents were to bring their children to the elders of the city. A *drunkard* is a person affected by alcohol to the extent of losing control of one's behavior. A *glutton* is a person with a remarkably great desire or capacity for something, whether it's work or food or drink or material items. Both a drunkard and a glutton excessively seek something other than the Lord for their satisfaction.

New Testament believers can also be stubborn and rebellious. Satan may tempt you into justifying overeating, overworking, overdrinking, or overspending to the point you no longer listen to the voice of the Lord, just like rebellious children who don't listen to the voice of their parents. The Lord says to seek Him every day, and you will find Him when you seek Him with all your heart. The Lord's arms are always open to welcome His sons and daughters back into His unconditional love. Today, listen to the voice of the Lord, and turn back to Jesus for your satisfaction.

They will say to the elders of his city, "This son of ours is stubborn and rebellious; he doesn't obey us. He's a glutton and a drunkard." Then all the men of his city will stone him to death. You must purge the evil from you, and all Israel will hear and be afraid. —Deuteronomy 21:20–21

Further Scripture: Psalm 81:11–13; Matthew 5:6; Luke 15:20

Week 15, Day 104: Deuteronomy 23—24

Care for the Foreigners, Widows, and Orphans

The Lord had a plan for the Israelites to care for needs in the community. When they harvested grain from the fields, fruit off the olive trees, or grapes in the vineyard, if they forgot to gather some of the crop, they were told to leave it. These "leftovers" would go to foreigners, orphans, and widows. The Lord specifically highlighted these less fortunate groups in the community, prioritizing their care.

Open your eyes to see the foreigners, orphans, and widows around you. Who has the Lord placed in your circle for you to care for and help look after? The Lord calls you to love others as Christ has loved you. Today, ask the Lord for a plan for you to love and care for the foreigners, widows, and orphans around you.

When you reap the harvest in your field, and you forget a sheaf in the field, do not go back to get it. It is to be left for the foreigner, the fatherless, and the widow, so that the Lord your God may bless you in all the work of your hands. —Deuteronomy 24:19

Further Scripture: Psalm 82:3; John 13:34; James 1:27

Week 15, Day 105: Deuteronomy 25—26
Check Your Heart

Moses reiterated the commands, statues, and ordinances to this second generation of Israelites. They looked back and remembered God's faithfulness and redemption. They reviewed all the details of the Law. And then Moses confirmed once again to the Israelite people that they must follow the Lord their God with all their hearts and with all their souls.

You may not be part of the Israelite community, but the same truth applies to your relationship with Jesus. Pause and check your heart. If your heart doesn't love the Lord fully, then following Him will begin to feel hard and burdensome. So check your heart today. Get honest with yourself and ask, "Do I love the Lord with all my heart?" Pause and listen. The heart drives your actions. When you have your heart aligned with the Lord, everything else in life will flow freely.

The Lord your God is commanding you this day to follow these statutes and ordinances. You must be careful to follow them with all your heart and all your soul. —Deuteronomy 26:16

Further Scripture: Proverbs 4:23; Jeremiah 31:33; Matthew 22:37–38

Week 16, Day 106: Deuteronomy 27
Write It Down

Moses instructed the Israelites to write the words of the law on stones covered with plaster after they crossed into the land God had promised them. Moses did not want the people to forget the commands of the Lord. In today's world, you don't have to write the Word of the Lord on stones covered with plaster, yet the practice of writing out Bible verses is still a wise discipline.

Do you have a favorite journal, decorative notecards, a chalkboard in your home, or a whiteboard at work? All these tools can be used to write down the Word of the Lord and point you to God's truth as you go through your day. Write a Bible verse on a notecard and put it by your computer, close to the steering wheel in the car, or on your bathroom mirror. Take time to write down a Bible verse that holds meaning to you. Then as you read the verse throughout the day, give thanks to the Lord for His truth in your life.

Write all the words of this law on the stones after you cross to enter the land the Lord your God is giving you, a land flowing with milk and honey, as Yahweh, the God of your fathers, has promised you. —Deuteronomy 27:3

Further Scripture: Deuteronomy 6:9; Psalm 119:105; Habakkuk 2:2

Week 16, Day 107: Deuteronomy 28
Stay on Track

The Lord told the Israelites that if they listened to His commands and followed them carefully, He would move them upward and never downward. He said they would always be the head and never the tail. However, for this to happen, the Israelites were instructed to never turn to the right or the left nor worship other gods.

Do things in life on your right or left ever sidetrack you? The Lord longs for you to keep seeking Him. He longs for you to keep walking in relationship with Him. He doesn't want you to live with Jesus plus a few side gods—He wants you to live solely in Jesus and His grace. A relationship with Jesus is enough. He promises to meet all your needs and bless you abundantly along the way.

The Lord will make you the head and not the tail; you will only move upward and never downward if you listen to the Lord your God's commands I am giving you today and are careful to follow them. Do not turn aside to the right or the left from all the things I am commanding you today, and do not go after other gods to worship them.
—Deuteronomy 28:13–14

Further Scripture: Joshua 1:7; Psalm 24:5–6; Proverbs 4:25–27

Week 16, Day 108: Deuteronomy 29–30
Choose Life

Moses addressed the Israelites at a final community talk before his death and before they crossed over into the Promised Land. He told the people they had a choice and commanded them to love the Lord their God, to walk in His ways, and to keep His commands. Moses even told them this decision was not difficult or beyond their reach—it was near to them in their mouths and in their hearts. Moses understood he couldn't force the Israelites to make the decision to love the Lord, yet he made one final plea with them to choose life in the Lord God. Like a loving father with his children, Moses desperately longed for the Israelites to walk with God and not turn away to other gods.

As a believer, you made the decision for life in Christ Jesus when you received Him as your Savior. However, you will be tempted to turn and look away from Christ. Today, fix your eyes on Jesus. Remain steadfast and hold on to your faith in Christ without wavering, for the Lord has promised to be faithful.

This command that I give you today is certainly not too difficult or beyond your reach. . . . But the message is very near you, in your mouth and in your heart, so that you may follow it. —Deuteronomy 30:11, 14

Further Scripture: 1 Corinthians 15:58; Hebrews 10:23; Hebrews 12:2

Week 16, Day 109: Deuteronomy 31
Walk with Courage

As Moses began the change of command and commissioning of Joshua as the next leader, he repeated these powerful words of encouragement three times: "Be strong and courageous; don't be terrified or afraid of them. For it is the Lord your God who goes with you; He will not leave you or forsake you."

Moses and Joshua anticipated the change in their lives as they looked ahead. You too will have times of change in your life when you will face an uncertain future, and you will have a choice. You can walk with fear and trembling or you can be strong and courageous, trusting the Lord is with you and will not leave you. Whatever you face today, may you feel strengthened by the Lord who is with you, empowering you to walk with courage. The Lord is with you and will help you face whatever the future holds. You can do this!

Be strong and courageous; don't be terrified or afraid of them. For it is the Lord your God who goes with you; He will not leave you or forsake you.
—Deuteronomy 31:6

Further Scripture: Isaiah 43:2; Jeremiah 29:11; Psalm 32:8

Week 16, Day 110: Deuteronomy 32—34
How Will You Choose to Walk?

Before Moses died in the land of Moab at the age of 120, he sang a final song and stated a final blessing over the Israelites. His words were full of memories and truth about the good times, the hard times, and the days ahead Moses knew were coming for the people. The Israelites were a chosen group, saved and protected by the Lord, to bear witness of the Lord's mighty power. Moses was a man of God, a prophet like no other, who saw God face-to-face and was God's chosen leader of His people. Even though Moses foretold how the Israelites would respond to God in the days ahead, there was still a sense of "now what?" in his words. How would the Israelites really walk with God after Moses died? They had every reason to follow the Lord with all their hearts, souls, and minds. But what would they decide?

As believers, the same is true for you. How will you choose to spend today? Will you follow the Lord with all your heart? Will you walk in His ways? Will you remember His faithfulness from yesterday? Or will you make the choice to turn away and seek your own interest? Today, choose to believe the Lord loves you unconditionally and longs for you to love Him with all your heart. As you receive the truth of His love, you will have strength to walk firmly in His ways and love others.

How happy you are, Israel! Who is like you, a people saved by the Lord?
He is the shield that protects you, the sword you boast in.
Your enemies will cringe before you, and you will tread on their backs.
—Deuteronomy 33:29

Further Scripture: Psalm 28:7; Psalm 143:8; Romans 16:25–27

Week 16, Day 111: Matthew 1
Meaning of Names

As part of God's plan for the world, Joseph and Mary had a virgin-born son. When you hear the news that someone has had a baby, many times the first question you ask is, "What did the parents name the baby?" After an angel of the Lord appeared to Joseph in a dream, he obediently named their son, Jesus, the Greek form of the Hebrew name Joshua, which means "Yahweh saves." Joseph and Mary may not have realized the magnitude of Jesus' name at the time of His birth, that their newborn son was born to be the Savior of the world. He was, as the prophets foretold, Immanuel—God with us.

Think about the meaning of your own name, and pray through what it means. Ask the Lord to reveal to you how He wants to use you to impact the kingdom of God. Give thanks for Jesus, Yeshua, the great I Am, who was born to save and deliver you from your sins.

---

*She will give birth to a son, and you are to name Him Jesus,
because He will save His people from their sins.* —Matthew 1:21

Further Scripture: Genesis 32:28; Luke 2:11; 1 John 4:10

Week 16, Day 112: Matthew 2
Dreams Can Direct Steps

Joseph, Mary, and Jesus moved from Jesus' birthplace in Bethlehem to Egypt before settling in Nazareth, where Jesus eventually grew up. Each time they moved or altered their travel plans, it was because Joseph had a dream. After each dream, Joseph immediately obeyed and moved his family to where he was told to go—even if it meant leaving in the middle of the night.

As a believer in relationship with Jesus, He will speak to you, and He may even do so in a dream. Dreams may come and go in your life, and sometimes you may think nothing about them. However, next time you have a dream, pause, write it down, and ask the Lord what He's telling you through that dream. If He reveals something to you, then act on it in faith and obedience. Joseph moved in faith. He acted immediately, and in doing so, he saved his son. The wise men were warned in a dream not to go back to Herod; they immediately took a different route and were saved. Praise the Lord for guiding and directing your steps, even speaking to you through dreams.

After they were gone, an angel of the Lord suddenly appeared to Joseph in a dream, saying, "Get up! Take the child and His mother, flee to Egypt, and stay there until I tell you. For Herod is about to search for the child to destroy Him." So he got up, took the child and His mother during the night, and escaped to Egypt. —Matthew 2:13–14

Further Scripture: Psalm 119:60; Joel 2:28; Matthew 2:12

Week 17, Day 113: Matthew 3
Baptism by the Holy Spirit and Fire

John the Baptist, a forerunner for Christ, preached a message focused on repentance and the coming kingdom of heaven. He foretold of the One who was to come, Jesus, who would baptize His followers with the Holy Spirit and fire. Repentance often leads to an outward change in people's lives, but Jesus brings true inner transformation.

When you become a follower of Christ and repent, you receive fire and the gift of the Holy Spirit. Fire burns up the chaff. The chaff represents areas in your life that do not reflect Christ, such as selfishness, pride, worshipping other gods and idols, or anger. The Holy Spirit works within you, refining you, essentially burning these areas out of your life with a continual fire, so you reflect more of the light of Christ. Just as God the Father delights in His beloved Son Jesus, so also Jesus delights in you and loves you. He loves when you seek Him and walk closer with Him. Allow the Holy Spirit to work in your life today. May His power work through you, so you may be a bright, shining light and a forerunner for Christ's ultimate return!

I baptize you with water for repentance, but the One who is coming after me is more powerful than I. I am not worthy to remove His sandals. He Himself will baptize you with the Holy Spirit and fire. His winnowing shovel is in His hand, and He will clear His threshing floor and gather His wheat into the barn. But the chaff He will burn up with fire that never goes out. —Matthew 3:11–12

Further Scripture: Ezekiel 36:26; Matthew 3:17; Acts 1:5

Week 17, Day 114: Matthew 4

Immediate Obedience

When Jesus called the first disciples to follow Him, all four men—Simon, Andrew, James, and John—*immediately* left their nets, their boats, and their fathers to follow Jesus. *Immediately* means right away, without delay, instantly. The disciples responded *immediately*, and right away they witnessed Jesus preaching the good news of the kingdom and healing people with diseases and sicknesses.

Today's culture is fast-paced, and many things in life are immediately at your fingertips. People don't like to wait for anything, and technology continues to allow for this instant-gratification lifestyle. However, when it comes to following Jesus and living in obedience, do you act *immediately*? You may doubt you truly hear from the Lord and don't take the next step of obedience. Today, walk in *immediate* obedience and watch the Lord's faithful hand in your life! Leave a job, turn away from a distraction, repent from sin, ask for forgiveness, go on a mission trip, or give a gift the Lord has put on your heart. Maybe you have never said yes to Jesus and received His love for you in faith. Stop overanalyzing it and follow Christ! Today is the day for an *immediate* yes to Jesus!

Immediately they left their nets and followed Him. —Matthew 4:20

Further Scripture: Matthew 21:2–3; 2 John 1:6; Revelation 14:12

Week 17, Day 115: Matthew 5
Love the People Hard to Love

Jesus sat down on a mountain with His disciples gathered around Him and poured out wisdom for everyday living as a disciple and follower of Christ. This sermon became known as the Sermon on the Mount, and in it, Jesus addressed issues of the heart. The disciples knew they were to love the Lord, but Jesus went further, teaching them to love their enemies, even pray for their enemies.

This may seem impossible. However, with Christ's unconditional love covering you, He equips you to love others, even your greatest, meanest, most selfish enemy. Today, ask the Lord to give you a heart of compassion and love for those unloving people in your life. Maybe someone has said an unkind word to you or to your kids. Begin by praying for them. Then ask the Lord to bless their socks off and overwhelm their life with Jesus' precious love! In praying for them, believe the Lord has a plan for their lives and will turn this difficult relationship around for good. As people observe you loving your enemy, you become a light on a hill and salt on the earth for Jesus. People will see something different in you—the love of Jesus. And maybe, just maybe, your love will draw someone to Jesus.

But I tell you, love your enemies and pray for those who persecute you, so that you may be sons of Your Father in heaven. —Matthew 5:44–45

Further Scripture: Proverbs 25:21; Romans 12:9–10; 1 John 4:7

Week 17, Day 116: Matthew 6
Don't Worry About Today

The disciples continued listening to Jesus' teachings from the Sermon on the Mount. Jesus taught practical lessons about how to walk with God in giving, praying, fasting, and handling material items. And then Jesus said to these men, "Do not worry about your life." These disciples had just left their livelihoods and their families to follow Jesus. Can you imagine the thoughts going on in their minds about how they would eat, drink, or even have clothing? Yet Jesus continued to tell them that rather than worry, they were to seek first the kingdom of God and those things would be provided.

As a follower of Christ, you are to seek the Lord and pursue a life with Him above all other concerns in life. Jesus promises that when you seek Him first, all the things you truly need will be provided. Therefore stop worrying and remember—God's got it! He knows what you will eat or wear even before it happens. When you catch yourself worrying today, stop and say a prayer of thanksgiving for God's faithfulness and His promise to provide for you as you seek Him first.

But seek first the kingdom of God and His righteousness, and all these things will be provided for you. Therefore don't worry about tomorrow, because tomorrow will worry about itself. —Matthew 6:33–34

Further Scripture: Proverbs 3:5–6; Philippians 4:6–7; Colossians 3:1–2

Week 17, Day 117: Matthew 7

Love without Judgment

In the middle of the Sermon on the Mount, Jesus told His disciples to not judge others. You can't love and judge at the same time. Think about that for a minute. When you judge someone, you have no idea what has happened to them during their day, in their past, or even throughout their upbringing.

Think about your own life, and remember the Lord loves you *and* the person you are judging equally. Jesus models how you are to love others with compassion. It's with this same love and compassion you are loved today. Jesus loves you unconditionally, and He asks you to love others with that same love. Today, every time you have a judgmental thought toward someone, ask the Lord to give you eyes to see what He sees and a heart to love them as He loves them.

Do not judge, so that you won't be judged. For with the judgment you use, you will be judged, and with the measure you use, it will be measured to you. —Matthew 7:1–2

Further Scripture: Mark 12:31; Romans 14:10; James 4:11

Week 17, Day 118: Matthew 8

The Greatest Faith

A centurion came to Jesus and asked Him to heal his servant who was lying at home paralyzed and in terrible agony. This Gentile commander in the Roman army amazed Jesus. He showed an unnecessary love toward his servant and displayed humility in the presence of Jesus, ignoring his own earthly position and ranking. And he displayed faith, believing Jesus could heal miraculously just by saying a word.

As a follower of Christ, empowered by the Holy Spirit, you have the strength to walk in love, humility, and faith, causing Jesus to be "amazed" by you today. No matter what you may be walking through, approach the situation with love, humility, and faith like the centurion. Maybe you too will be amazed at how the Lord will move through the situation!

Hearing this, Jesus was amazed and said to those following Him,
"I assure you: I have not found anyone in Israel with so great a faith!"
—Matthew 8:10

Further Scripture: Matthew 8:13; John 20:29; Colossians 1:10–11

Week 17, Day 119: Matthew 9
See, Feel, and Love Like Jesus

Jesus continued to go throughout the towns and villages, preaching the good news and healing people with diseases and sicknesses. As Jesus went out, He *saw* the crowds of people, and He *felt* compassion for them.

As a believer of Christ, you are to be Jesus' love to those around you. Do you *see* people and their needs around you, or do you quickly pass them by, busily making your way to your next event? Open your eyes to really *see* people like Jesus does, asking the Holy Spirit to guide your way. And when the Lord brings someone to your attention, what do you *feel?* Jesus *felt* compassion for the weary and worn out. Do you *feel* anything, or do you just pass them by, believing they can care for themselves or hoping someone else will take care of them? People are messy, but as a follower of Christ, you are to *see, feel, and love* those around you. Jesus told the disciples to pray to the Lord of the harvest to send more workers because the harvest is abundant. Today, you can be an answer to Jesus' prayer. Open your eyes to *see* someone hurting, *feel* compassion toward them and put Jesus' *love* into action.

When He saw the crowds, He felt compassion for them, because they were weary and worn out, like sheep without a shepherd. —Matthew 9:36

Further Scripture: Zachariah 7:9–10; Matthew 9:37–38; Colossians 3:12

Week 18, Day 120: Matthew 10

Jesus' Instructions for His Apostles: Don't Be Afraid.

As Jesus commissioned the disciples with authority, He said to them three times, "Don't be afraid."

Today, as you go about your own day, as you live your life for Christ, guess what remains the same? Don't be afraid. Jesus will give you words to speak when you think you have nothing to say. Jesus will share everything with you and nothing will be hidden. Jesus is more powerful than anything or anyone. Jesus knows every hair on your head, and you are worth more than a sparrow, who Jesus also cared for. He loves you, child of God! So today, *don't be afraid*. You have all authority from Jesus because it has been given to you. Walk on and do not fear.

But even the hairs of your head have all been counted.
So, don't be afraid therefore; you are worth more than many sparrows.
—Matthew 10:30–31

Further Scripture: Isaiah 41:10; Psalm 56:3; 2 Timothy 1:7

Week 18, Day 121: Matthew 11
Truth Revealed to the Humble

In Jesus' prayer to His Father, the Lord of heaven and earth, He shared that truths are revealed to infants, not the wise and the learned. The Greek word for *infants* is literally, *babies*. Using the word for *babies*, Jesus meant humble and sincere. Therefore, Jesus was saying humble and sincere seekers would know and find the truth.

You see, you don't need to be at the top of your class intellectually or even proud of how much knowledge you have. Rather, Jesus longs for you to come to Him willing to receive all He has for you. He reveals Himself to the person with the heart of a child, walking in humility and sincerely hungry for truth. As you approach Jesus in humility, He says the kingdom of heaven will be yours. Let go of feeling as though you need to have it all together, and instead, come as you are.

At that time Jesus said, "I praise You, Father, Lord of heaven and earth, because You have hidden these things from the wise and learned and revealed them to infants." —Matthew 11:25

Further Scripture: Matthew 5:3; Matthew 18:4; Mark 10:15

Week 18, Day 122: Matthew 12

Heart Overflow

As Jesus referenced the Pharisees' evil words, He gave the illustration of a tree being known by its fruit. He explained that a bad tree produces bad fruit, just as a good tree produces good fruit. The Pharisees spoke evil words about Jesus, which revealed the nature of their hearts.

It is important to remember the Lord is interested in your heart above all else because what comes out of your mouth is an overflow of your heart. If the words of your mouth hurt others or are displeasing to the Lord, it may be time to do a heart check. What are you filling your heart with? When you fill your heart with things from the Lord, like truth from His Word, it will transform you. Set your heart daily on the Lord, and watch transformation take place in the words that come out of your mouth.

For the mouth speaks from the overflow of the heart. —Matthew 12:34

Further Scripture: Luke 6:45; Romans 12:2; Ephesians 3:16–17a

Week 18, Day 123: Matthew 13

The Mystery of the Kingdom of Heaven

Jesus shared seven parables referring to the mystery of the kingdom of heaven. For believers, the kingdom of heaven is a treasure. Even if you sell everything you have and all that remains is this one treasure, the kingdom of heaven, it is enough. Christ's saving grace, redeeming power, righteousness, peace, joy, and eternity with Him are worth letting go of everything else.

Are you still hanging on to something that is preventing you from experiencing all of the kingdom of heaven? Ask the Lord to purge your heart today, so you can freely enjoy all the kingdom of heaven has to offer. Let go of anything hindering you. *Just let go.* When you seek Jesus with all your heart, He will be found.

The kingdom of heaven is like treasure, buried in a field, that a man found and reburied. Then in his joy he goes and sells everything he has and buys that field. —Matthew 13:44

Further Scripture: Jeremiah 29:13–14; Matthew 6:33; Romans 14:17–19

Week 18, Day 124: Matthew 14
Walking on Water

The story of Jesus walking on water in the middle of a storm and calling out to Peter to join Him powerfully illustrates Jesus as King. Jesus had control and authority, even over the wind and the waves. As the storms began, Jesus was praying alone on the mountain. However, just when the disciples needed help, Jesus appeared to them walking on the water, telling them to take courage and not be afraid. Jesus reached out his hand to Peter and said to him, "You of little faith, why did you doubt?"

Just like the disciples, you will find yourself in the middle of a storm in life. Maybe even today, the winds of your storm are swirling around you. Jesus promises He is interceding for you. He will reach out His hand to help you. Today, take courage. Have the faith to walk out of the boat, trusting the Lord will be with you and will help you. Do not walk in doubt. Grab hold of the hand of Jesus and confidently walk in faith that He is with you!

Immediately, Jesus reached out His hand, caught hold of him, and said to him, "You of little faith, why did you doubt?" When they got into the boat, the wind ceased. —Matthew 14:31–32

Further Scripture: Isaiah 43:2; 2 Corinthians 1:8; 1 Timothy 6:15

Week 18, Day 125: Matthew 15
Humbly Ask for Help

As Jesus withdrew to the area of Tyre and Sidon, a Canaanite woman cried out, asking Jesus to heal her demon-possessed daughter. This mother was in great distress and had been walking through a terrible trial, and yet she found hope in Jesus. Jesus responded slowly in His answer to this unlikely candidate for healing. She was a Gentile and a pagan enemy of Israel. Even so, she humbly knelt before Jesus with strong faith that He could heal her daughter and pleaded with Him to help. Jesus saw her faith, saw her belief in Him, and restored her daughter.

As you face trials in life and find yourself in distress, humbly come before Jesus. Don't assume you aren't a likely candidate or good enough for Jesus to help. He loves all people. Jesus may have a different timeframe from the one you want, but sit before Him, talk with Him, and share your heart with Jesus the Messiah. The process of waiting and humbling yourself brings glory to the Lord. The Lord sees you and knows you. No matter what you face today, keep your faith in Jesus. He is your helper.

But she came, knelt before Him, and said, "Lord, Help me!"
—Matthew 15:25

Further Scripture: Matthew 25:23; Hebrews 11:6; 1 Peter 1:7

Week 18, Day 126: Matthew 16
You Are the Christ!

Jesus asked His disciples who people said He was. Since the disciples were out doing ministry as they had been commissioned to do, they had answers to give to Jesus. Then Jesus looked at His disciples and asked them directly, "But . . . who do you say that I am?" The disciples had left everything and followed Jesus. They witnessed His miracles of healing, restoring, and providing for people. They walked with Him. Peter answered, "You are the Messiah, the Son of the living God."

Today, ask yourself that same question. As you receive Jesus in your own life and walk with Him, who do you say Jesus is? Your answer may change from day to day, depending on your experiences in life. Jesus may be your Savior, your Friend, your Strength, your Help, your Burden-Bearer, your Joy, or your Hope. Today, be ready to bear witness to others. You may be the only witness they have in life. Let your light shine before all men.

"But you," He asked them, "Who do you say that I am?"
—Matthew 16:15

Further Scripture: John 15:27; Acts 22:15; 1 Peter 3:15

Week 19, Day 127: Matthew 17
His Transformation Before Men

Jesus took Peter, James, and John up on a high mountain where they witnessed Jesus physically transform in front of them. And if that wasn't enough of an experience, Moses and Elijah appeared and talked with Jesus. Suddenly, God the Father spoke from heaven and proclaimed three revealing points: Jesus is the Son of God, the Father loves Jesus, and all must listen and obey Jesus. After God the Father spoke, the disciples fell facedown and were terrified. Not only was Jesus transformed, but Peter, James, and John's lives were also transformed as they went away with Jesus.

As a follower of Christ, God gives you the gift of the Holy Spirit and transforms your life as you spend time in His presence. You may be thinking, *Wait. I believe in Jesus, but I'm not feeling transformed.* As an example for you, Jesus intentionally went away to a mountain to spend time with the Father. Today, get away from the busy, the routine and the chaos. Spend time alone with the Lord, earnestly asking the Lord to transform you more and more into His image. As you make spending time with the Lord a regular routine, He promises His Spirit will transform your heart.

He was transformed in front of them, and His face shone like the sun.
—Matthew 17:2

Further Scripture: Psalm 139:23–24; Romans 12:2; Ephesians 4:22–23

147

Week 19, Day 128: Matthew 18

Forgive Seventy Times Seven

Jesus instructed the disciples to live differently from the way the world lives. He told them to forgive not just seven times but seventy times seven. In other words, to forgive as many times as necessary. Jesus told a parable that illustrated to the disciples that if those who don't forgive will be forever tortured for not forgiving a fellow brother or sister.

Forgiveness. Some of you may run from that word. However, forgiveness is the key to your belief in Jesus. When you confess your sins to Jesus, He is faithful and forgives you fully from all unrighteousness. His death on the Cross covered your sins. You are forgiven forever. You are loved unconditionally. In addition, Jesus says you are to love others, just as He loves you. And yet when it comes to forgiving one another, you make excuses, you run from it, and you avoid it. But it never goes away; bitterness may even set in. Today, ask the Lord to help you to forgive.

Forgiveness doesn't come from your own strength but from the unconditional love and grace you receive from the Father. So walk it out by trusting and obeying all He is asking you to do in faith. Jesus promises His peace will be with you.

Then Peter came to Him and said, "Lord, how many times could my brother sin against me and I forgive him? As many as seven times?" "I will tell you, not as many as seven," Jesus said to him, "but 70 times seven. . . . So My heavenly Father will also do to you if each of you does not forgive his brother from his heart." —Matthew 18:21–22, 35

Further Scripture: Ephesians 1:7–8; Colossians 3:13; 1 John 1:9

Week 19, Day 129: Matthew 19

All Things Are Possible with a Heart Set on Christ

Jesus continued teaching the disciples about the kingdom of heaven and explained it is easier for a camel to go through the eye of a needle than for a rich person to enter heaven. Why is it so hard for a rich man to enter the kingdom of heaven? From an earthly, outside perspective, the rich man is able to do life on his own and in his own strength. But God is full of grace and love, and Jesus promised the disciples that with God all things are possible.

God looks at the heart and knows when a person trusts and believes in Jesus as Lord and Savior. Therefore, even if you have all the riches you want, but your heart is set on Christ, it is possible for you to enter His kingdom. Jesus wants your heart to trust fully in Him. Today, is there anything you are trusting in more than God? He desires for you to keep your heart surrendered to Jesus the King, ensuring that He is the God of all your life. If you are to boast in anything, boast in Jesus!

"Again, I tell you, it is easier for a camel to go through the eye of a needle than for a rich person to enter the kingdom of God." . . .
But Jesus looked at them and said, "With men this is impossible,
but with God all things are possible." —Matthew 19:24, 26

Further Scripture: Psalm 20:7; Ephesians 2:8–9; Colossians 3:2

Week 19, Day 130: Matthew 20

Mercy and Compassion

Jesus was leaving Jericho when two blind men cried out, asking Him for mercy and to open their eyes. Even as Jesus was on the way to the next place of ministry, He took the time to stop and ask what they wanted. He showed compassion and touched their eyes so they could see.

In the same way, Jesus has stopped and showed you compassion because of His great love for you. If your eyes have been opened by His love and mercy in your own life, then you can show that same compassion to someone along your way. Today, take the time to show someone the same mercy and compassion Jesus showed the blind men.

There were two blind men sitting by the road. When they heard that Jesus was passing by, they cried out, "Lord, have mercy on us, Son of David!" The crowd told them to keep quiet, but they cried out all the more, "Lord, have mercy on us, Son of David!" —Matthew 20:30–31

Further Scripture: 2 Corinthians 1:3; Titus 3:5; 1 Peter 2:10

Week 19, Day 131: Matthew 21
Listen and Obey

As Jesus and the disciples approached Jerusalem and came to Bethphage on the Mount of Olives, Jesus spoke directly to the disciples, giving them specific actions to go and do. The disciples trusted His voice. They listened even though they were receiving seemingly random instructions to go get a donkey and a colt belonging to someone else. They gave everything up, even the robes off their backs, and proclaimed the name of Jesus, saying, "Hosanna in the highest heaven!" And because of their obedience, the city was shaken as King Jesus rode in on a colt.

This act of obedience was the disciples' role in preparing the way for Jesus. You too have a role in preparing the way for King Jesus. Today, ask the Lord what your role is as Jesus makes His return. *Listen to His voice, and go in obedience.* Just as the disciples had an impact for the glory of the coming King, so will you as you walk it out, trusting and obeying the voice of the Lord.

The disciples went and did just as Jesus directed them.
They brought the donkey and the colt; then they laid their robes on them,
and He sat on them. —Matthew 21:6–7

Further Scripture: Matthew 21:10; Luke 9:23; John 10:27

Week 19, Day 132: Matthew 22

All Are Invited; Few Will Accept

A king gave a wedding banquet for his son. However, those who were invited didn't want to come. Even after being summoned a second time, those who were invited paid no attention, going away to mind to their farms and businesses. Finally the king extended the invitation to everyone, both good and evil people in the kingdom. The banquet filled with guests. One man came dressed in clothes that were disrespectable for the king's wedding banquet, and he was cast out.

In a similar way, the Lord your God is welcoming you into the kingdom of heaven through faith in His Son Jesus. Your response to the invitation reveals your heart. Do you have a need for Jesus the King in your life? Are you too consumed or overly interested in building your own kingdom through your career? Have you said yes to the invitation from Jesus but in your heart mocked the concept of Jesus as your Lord and Savior? Jesus says, "Love the Lord your God with all your heart, with all your soul, and with all your mind." *All are welcome into the kingdom of heaven.* Will you say yes in your heart?

For many are invited, but few are chosen. —Matthew 22:14

Further Scripture: Matthew 22:29; Romans 1:5–6; Revelation 17:14

Week 19, Day 133: Matthew 23
Humble Yourself

Jesus spoke to the crowds and His disciples about the Pharisees and the scribes. He described their outward appearance and how they liked to *look* religious. They liked to have the *proper place* at the banquets. They liked having a *status greeting* as Rabbi, thinking they deserved honor. Jesus pointed out that these things were not what was important.

Similar to the Pharisees and the scribes, your designer, well-put-together outfits are not important. Your official title is not important. Your corner office with expensive furniture is not important. *Jesus wants your heart.* He wants your heart surrendered to Him because Jesus said the humbled will be exalted. Blessed are the poor in spirit, for theirs is the kingdom of heaven. Stop trying so hard. Sit and purify your heart. Stay in a place of humility, and as the Lord sees your heart, you will be exalted into the kingdom of God!

The greatest among you will be your servant. Whoever exalts himself will be humbled, and whoever humbles himself will be exalted.
—Matthew 23:11–12

Further Scripture: Matthew 5:3; Matthew 23:37b; James 4:10

Week 20, Day 134: Matthew 24

Signs of the End Times

The disciples asked Jesus, "What will be the sign of Your coming and of the end of the age?" And Jesus responded: persecution, lawlessness, false messiahs, false prophets, wars and rumors of wars, famines, earthquakes, nation will rise up against nation and kingdom against kingdom, and many will betray one another and hate one another. These events are the beginning of birth pains, just like a mom contracting and laboring before delivering a newborn baby.

The world will go through a similar labor before Jesus' return. So don't be alarmed when these events happen around you but rather recognize Jesus' return is near! Don't live in fear. Take notice of the birth pains occurring, and live with the hope you have in Christ.

Today, take the opportunity to proclaim God's love to the world as you prepare for the return of Christ.

See that you are not alarmed, because these things must take place, but the end is not yet. . . . All these events are the beginning of birth pains.
—Matthew 24:6, 8

Further Scripture: Matthew 24:14; Mark 13:32; 2 Peter 3:10

Week 20, Day 135: Matthew 25

Don't Delay!

Jesus instructed the disciples to be alert and ready for the day He would return. He clearly advised them to live faithfully with what they had been given, not comparing or complaining about the gifts, talents, and treasures entrusted to them. Jesus simply wanted those gifts used for His glory.

How would you live if you knew Jesus were returning next week? Would you hide under a rock and sleep away the days? No way! The joy of the Lord is your strength! As He instructed the disciples, Jesus instructs you to live life intentionally because of the eternal hope found in Him. It may mean studying your Bible to learn more about Jesus' love for you as you prepare to live with Him forever. It may mean sharing your hope and faith in Jesus with those you love, regardless of feeling nervous or fearful. Living intentionally may look like using your gifts of hospitality, teaching, or serving unashamedly in faith. No more hiding your gifts or living in fear. When you live life fully with all the Lord has given you, Jesus says, "Well done, good and faithful servant! I will now put you in charge of more!" Today, don't delay. Ask the Holy Spirit to guide you to live life to the fullest and prepare you to be ready for the return of Jesus the King!

Therefore be alert, because you don't know either the day or the hour.
—Matthew 25:13

Further Scripture: Galatians 5:25; Ephesians 3:20; 1 Peter 4:10

Week 20, Day 136: Matthew 26
Giving Everything to Jesus

While Jesus reclined at a table in Simon's house, a woman came to Him with an alabaster jar of very expensive, fragrant oil. She poured the oil over His head. Jesus received this sacrificial offering as a way of preparing Him for burial, something the disciples did not fully understand at the time. The disciples witnessed this scene from a logical viewpoint, upset to see the woman "waste" an expensive amount of perfume. But Jesus understood the woman's heart. He honored her for breaking the jar and pouring the oil over Him. It was an act of love and devotion to Jesus the King and fulfilled the Scriptures.

As you offer your heart to Jesus, are you holding anything back? Release the things you feel like you need control over: your future, your children, your finances, your health, or your schedule for the day. Today, pour out your broken heart before the Lord and say, "Jesus, have it all!" Even if it doesn't make sense, offer the Lord all you are and all you have in faith. The Lord will bless you as you worship Jesus the King with a broken heart.

I assure you: Wherever this Gospel is proclaimed in the whole world, what this woman has done will also be told in memory of her. —Matthew 26:13

Further Scripture: 2 Kings 9:6; Psalm 51:16–17; Psalm 62:8

Week 20, Day 137: Matthew 27
Pain

Jesus unjustly died on the cross. Although the crowd hailed, "This is Jesus, the King of the Jews," putting Jesus to death did not make sense according to the laws of the time. However, Jesus' death was the will of the Father, who gave up His only Son so that whoever believes in Jesus would have eternal life. Jesus went through physical pain. He was mocked. He was pierced for your transgressions and bruised for your iniquities. He suffered both physically and emotionally. In those final moments, the prophecies were fulfilled as Jesus died. He suffered much so that you could be set free and have eternal life.

Today, reflect and give thanks for the pain Jesus suffered on the Cross. It's hard to linger in the rawness of the pain Jesus endured for sin. It'd be easier to move on to the fact that yes, Jesus was resurrected! But don't miss the pain He suffered. It was real. You may like to skip over your own pain and move on to happier times. But the truth is, everyone suffers. Everyone endures pain. Jesus, the King of kings, is your Savior. He understands and can sympathize with your pain. He was willing to endure the suffering and death for you, beloved child of God. *As you press into the pain Jesus suffered and the pain in your own life, the Lord promises He is with you.* He will help you endure the pain. And from that pain, you are promised a resurrected life. Your hope is found in Christ alone!

When the centurion and those with him, who were guarding Jesus, saw the earthquake and the things that had happened, they were terrified and said, "This man really was God's son!" —Matthew 27:54

Further Scripture: Isaiah 53:5; John 3:16; Hebrews 4:15–16

Week 20, Day 138: Matthew 28
Go and Tell of the Risen Lord!

"Come and see . . . Jesus has been resurrected, just as He said He would be!" the angels proclaimed. They instructed Mary Magdalene and the other Mary to go and tell what they have seen and heard. As the women went on their way, they met Jesus along the path. After worshipping Jesus at His feet, He too told them to go and tell. Then the disciples saw Jesus resurrected just as He foretold to them. And although they worshipped Him, some still doubted what they saw. Had Jesus truly been resurrected?

Just like the disciples, Jesus is alive in you! He has told you to *go and tell* others about His great love. Will you worship Him and go, or will you continue to doubt the Jesus you have seen alive in your life? Today move from doubt to faith, and live for Christ just as He commanded His disciples! Jesus promises He will be with you always, even to the end of the age.

When they saw Him, they worshiped, but some doubted. . . .
"Go, therefore, and make disciples of all nations, baptizing them in the name of the Father and of the Son and of the Holy Spirit, teaching them to observe everything I have commanded you. And remember, I am with you always, to the end of the age." —Matthew 28:17, 19–20

Further Scripture: Psalm 96:3; Galatians 2:20–21; Revelation 14:6–7

Week 20, Day 139: Mark 1
Let's Go!

Jesus knew His mission: to preach the good news of God, which is that truth is fulfilled, the kingdom of God has come near, and all must repent and believe in the good news. He went out teaching in full authority. At one point in the midst of teaching, healing, and driving out demons, He went away alone early in the morning to pray. His disciples soon found Him, saying, "Everyone's looking for You!" Jesus responded, "Let's go. This is why I have come!"

Jesus is God in human form. It's important to remember He is fully human. He knew His mission and calling, and He has delegated this same mission and calling to your life. Just like Jesus, you will have busy seasons. You will have demanding times where everyone is looking for you. Therefore, Jesus models the importance of getting away from all the activity to pray. He also models a positive, "Let's go!" attitude when it's time get back to the mission. Today, take time to pray and seek the Lord. And when it's time to get back to work, practice saying, "Let's go! This is what God has called me to." Work not in your own strength but from the strength and power of the Holy Spirit, equipping you for each step on your mission.

And He said to them, "Let's go on to the neighboring villages so that I may preach there too. This is why I have come." —Mark 1:38

Further Scripture: Philippians 2:13; Colossians 1:28–29; 2 Timothy 1:9

Week 20, Day 140: Mark 2
Jesus Sought the Lost

Levi hosted a dinner at his home for Jesus and the disciples. The dinner party also included tax collectors and sinners—in other words, people who specifically violated God's Law. As the scribes and Pharisees questioned Jesus about His decision to associate with this part of the community, Jesus reminded them of His purpose. Jesus came to seek the lost. Jesus came to save people from their sins, not to look down on them. Jesus came to dwell among the sinners.

As a believer in Christ, you are called to be Jesus' love to sinners. As a child of God, you are called to *go out*. You are called to live among sinners and reflect Jesus' love. He promises to empower you, to give you strength, and to give you the words to say when you go out as His witness. Today, ask the Lord to give you eyes to see the "sinners and tax collectors" in your community. Then go sit with someone you normally wouldn't. Invite a family over to your home who doesn't go to your church. Go out of your way to love someone like Jesus does. You are a light in the world.

When Jesus heard this, He told them, "Those who are well don't need a doctor, but the sick do need one. I didn't come to call the righteous, but sinners." —Mark 2:17

Further Scripture: Matthew 1:21; John 1:14; Acts 13:47

Week 21, Day 141: Mark 3

Facing Opposition in Ministry

After seeing Jesus preach, heal, and cast out demons, the crowds continued to follow Him. He went up to a mountain and appointed twelve apostles to partner with Him to preach and to have authority to drive out demons. Then, He returned home, and still the crowds followed Him. Jesus' ministry was busy, and He was in high demand. He even had a team around Him to walk out His mission. However, when Jesus went home, His own family tried to restrain Him, calling Him "out of His mind." Jesus' family didn't welcome Him and say, "Welcome home and put Your feet up. You are doing amazing work of Your Heavenly Father, and we support You." No, even Jesus, the servant of God, received opposition and accusations about His ministry from His own family.

Can you relate? As you study God's word and live your life for Christ, have you found those closest to you giving you a hard time? You are promised as you walk with Jesus that you will face opposition. So today, be strong. Remember who you are in Christ and what He has called you to. Greater is He who is in you than he who is in the world.

When His family heard this, they set out to restrain Him, because they said, "He's out of His mind." —Mark 3:21

Further Scripture: Romans 8:31–32; Ephesians 6:12; Philippians 1:27–29

Week 21, Day 142: Mark 4
Walk in Faith and Not Fear

Jesus and the disciples left the crowd and went into a boat on the Sea of Galilee. Suddenly, a fierce windstorm came upon them, and their boat filled with water. The disciples reacted to the storm in fear and accused Jesus of not caring for them. Jesus simply stood up, rebuked the wind, and said to the sea, "Silence! Be still!" Immediately, the storm ceased.

At some point in life, you will find yourself in an unexpected "storm on the sea." It may be a sudden car accident, a financial crisis, a sickness of a child or loved one, or a depression that won't go away. Will you respond in fear like the disciples or in faith? Fear is a lack of confidence in God, whereas faith is a trust in God. Jesus asked the disciples, "Why are you fearful? Do you still have no faith?" Even in the middle of the crisis, Jesus can *calm the storm* and bring peace to you. He can make the hard things more doable. He can bring joy to your sadness. He will always provide. And He can bring a peace that passes all understanding. Turn to Him in the middle of your storm with faith that He is with you and will bring you peace.

He got up, rebuked the wind, and said to the sea, "Silence! Be still!"
The wind ceased, and there was a great calm. Then He said to them,
"Why are you fearful? Do you still have no faith?" —Mark 4:39–40

Further Scripture: Psalm 46:1–2; Psalm 107:28–30;
2 Thessalonians 3:3

Week 21, Day 143: Mark 5

The Touch of a Servant

A woman who suffered from bleeding for twelve years had faith and believed if she could just touch Jesus, she would be made well. Just as she believed in faith, as soon as she touched Him, her body was cured. Even though a crowd surrounded Jesus, He sensed power had gone out from Him. When He realized the woman had touched Him, He said to her, "Daughter, your faith has made you well. Go in peace and be free from your affliction."

Do you understand this woman's pain and struggle? She had been untouchable for years because of her affliction. And now because of her faith and the touch of Jesus, she was healed. Do you need a touch from the Lord today? What does it look like for you to reach out in faith and touch Jesus? Quiet yourself and pray. Humbly repent and ask the Lord to take away your pain and set you free. Share your affliction and burden with a trusted person. No matter the depth of sin or the span of years you have carried this burden, release it today. *Reach out and touch Jesus.* His power is greater than all your fear and doubt. Have faith and praise the Lord for His love for you and for the hope you have in Him.

Then the woman, knowing what had happened to her, came with fear and trembling, fell down before Him, and told Him the whole truth. "Daughter," He said to her, "your faith has made you well. Go in peace and be free from your affliction." —Mark 5:33–34

Further Scripture: Jeremiah 17:14; Philippians 4:7; James 5:15–16

Week 21, Day 144: Mark 6
God of Miracles for Today!

Jesus and the disciples went away again to rest and get refreshed. But once again, the crowds came. Even so, Jesus had compassion on them and began to teach them many things. They were spiritually hungry for His teachings. However, as evening came, they were also physically hungry. Rather than send them away to the nearby villages, Jesus took what He had—five loaves of bread and two fish—and blessed the food. Miraculously, all five thousand ate and were filled, with leftovers filling twelve baskets.

There may be times in your life when you look around and wonder, *How am I going to make it?* Look to Jesus. Ask Him to provide all of your needs for today. He cares for you, and He says to not worry about tomorrow because tomorrow has enough worries of its own. As you seek first His kingdom and His righteousness, He will provide for you both spiritually and physically. He is the God of miracles!

Everyone ate and was filled. Then, they picked up 12 baskets full of pieces of bread and fish. —Mark 6:42–43

Further Scripture: Psalm 81:10; Matthew 6:34; Philippians 4:19

Week 21, Day 145: Mark 7
The Touch of Jesus

Jesus exemplifies servanthood. He lived out His compassion for people with action. When a deaf man who also had speech difficulty was brought to Him, Jesus didn't shy away. Rather Jesus modeled to His disciples how to do ministry. First He depended upon the Lord. Then, He loved and had compassion for the man. Jesus took action by touching him, and He ministered with authority from the Lord. Through the ministry and power of Jesus, the deaf man was healed, his ears were opened, and he also began to speak clearly.

Friend, as you see the needs of others, remember you do not carry their burdens and ailments on your own. Seek the Lord for His power, His authority, and His compassion. You are able to do all things through His strength at work within you. You will get weary if you try to do ministry by your own strength and in your own flesh. If ministry and people's needs are weighing you down right now, take a deep breath, and look to heaven. Ask the Lord for help. Then put your compassion into action and watch God's grace become sufficient.

So He took him away from the crowd privately. After putting His fingers in the man's ears and spitting, He touched his tongue. Then, looking up to heaven, He sighed deeply and said to him, "Ephphatha!" (that is, "Be opened!"). —Mark 7:33–34

Further Scripture: Isaiah 49:10; Matthew 11:28; 2 Corinthians 12:9

Week 21, Day 146: Mark 8
Get Behind Me, Satan!

Peter took Jesus aside and attempted to convince Jesus to stop speaking about His upcoming death to the disciples. Jesus rebuked Peter and firmly said, "Get behind Me, Satan." And it was over. The enemy's intention to persuade Jesus to not suffer and die was easily diffused by the truth.

You may find yourself in a situation you know is not from the Lord. You may feel temptation creeping in to overtake you. The thoughts and lies in your head may feel so overwhelming that you don't want to get out of bed in the morning. In these moments, stand firm and know the Lord your God is with you. Remember, you have authority in the name of Jesus to say out loud, "Get behind me, Satan!" As you submit to the Lord, the enemy will flee. Remember to focus on God's promises and the truth in His Word. Jesus had to walk His authority out, and so will you. Walk in confidence—Jesus is at work within you!

But turning around and looking at His disciples, He rebuked Peter and said, "Get behind Me, Satan, because you're not thinking about God's concerns, but man's!" —Mark 8:33

Further Scripture: Luke 10:19; James 4:7; 1 John 2:14

Week 21, Day 147: Mark 9
A Servant of All

As the disciples walked along their way, they argued. Although Jesus wasn't with them, He asked them what they had been arguing about. They remained silent and didn't answer, but Jesus knew. He knew their thoughts before they even had them. The disciples argued about who was the greatest. Jesus sat them down like a parent talking to children and spoke clearly. If you want to be the greatest, then serve one another. Don't seek to be the first; seek to be the last.

As a follower of Christ, you are called to walk in humility, thinking of others more highly than yourself. When you serve others, you point people to Jesus, not to yourself. And that's the whole point: *to glorify Jesus and His power and strength at work within you.* Next time you have the option to go first, pause for a second, and let someone else go ahead of you. In doing this, the Lord will honor you. He sees your heart and knows your thoughts.

Sitting down, He called the Twelve and said to them,
"If anyone wants to be first, he must be last of all and servant of all."
—Mark 9:35

Further Scripture: Psalm 139:1–3; John 3:30; James 4:10

Week 22, Day 148: Mark 10
True Servanthood

James and John asked Jesus to seat them at His right and left in His glory. In response to this request, Jesus taught the disciples a lesson on power and the struggle of desiring a place of honor. He pointed out that people in high positions like to exercise power over others. In contrast, a follower of Jesus is great by becoming a servant. Rather than being served like royalty, it means serving others, even giving your life for the sake of others. This was the purpose of Jesus' life—He came to serve and give His life so others could live forever.

In a similar way, you too are not called to fame, riches, power, and position, but you are called to serve. If you are asking yourself how to love a family member, how to deal with a spouse, or how to bless your coworkers, start by asking the Lord how to serve them. Begin by humbling yourself like Jesus, and serve the people God has put in your life regardless of what you think you deserve. By doing so, you will honor the Lord.

On the contrary, whoever wants to become great among you must be your servant, and whoever wants to be first among you must be a slave to all. For even the Son of Man did not come to be served, but to serve and to give His life—a ransom for many. —Mark 10:43–45

Further Scripture: Romans 5:6–8; 1 Peter 5:3–6; 1 John 2:6

Week 22, Day 149: Mark 11
Producing Fruit

Jesus spotted a fig tree with leaves in the distance, but when He got closer, He saw it had no fruit. It just looked good on the outside. In a similar way, Jesus became upset when He entered the temple complex and found this place of worship had become more like a market than a sanctuary. Both the temple complex and the fig tree looked good on the outside, but upon closer inspection, there was no evidence of fruit in either.

Jesus said to the disciples, "Have faith in God." That's the bottom line . . . have faith. When you have faith in God, you are connected to Jesus. The more you abide in Jesus, the more fruit you will bear. Be careful of only looking like a Christian on the outside while on the inside, you're not connected to Jesus. Maybe you go to church on Sundays, but the rest of the week, you don't even think about living life with Christ. Jesus wants you to walk in faith daily *with Him*. In doing so, you will be able to move mountains.

The next day when they came out from Bethany, He was hungry. After seeing in the distance a fig tree with leaves, He went to find out if there was anything on it. When He came to it, He found nothing but leaves, because it was not the season for figs. —Mark 11:12–13

Further Scripture: Matthew 21:43; John 15:5; Galatians 5:22–23

Week 22, Day 150: Mark 12

The Widow's Coins

Jesus and the disciples were at the Temple treasury. Jesus watched as individuals dropped their money into thirteen trumpet-shaped chests used for the worshippers to place their freewill offerings. Jesus saw the rich people offering large sums of money, and He also saw a widow offering a small amount of two tiny coins. But Jesus saw more than people putting money into the treasury, He saw their hearts as they gave. Even though the amount the widow gave was physically worth very little, spiritually, the gift of her heart was greater than all the others.

Jesus had previously shared with the disciples that the greatest commandment was to love the Lord their God with all their heart, soul, mind, and strength. The widow put this love of the Lord her God into action. As you give your money, time, or talent to the Lord, give from a place of loving Jesus with all you have. He doesn't call you to give just because it's a duty or a law. No, He wants you to give because of your love for Him. And because you love Jesus, you love others. Therefore, it is a *joy* to give with all you are and with all you have. Today, check your heart. Are you giving from a heart that loves Jesus or because you feel it's your Christian duty?

And a poor widow came and dropped in two tiny coins worth very little.
Summoning His disciples, He said to them, "I assure you: This poor widow
has put in more than all those giving to the temple treasury."
—Mark 12:42–43

Further Scripture: Matthew 6:21; 2 Corinthians 8:1–3;
2 Corinthians 9:7

Week 22, Day 151: Mark 13
Watch! Be Alert!

Jesus prepared His disciples for the end times. In this chapter, He encouraged them seven times with the same message: watch out, don't be alarmed, be on watch, be alert. He wanted the disciples to be aware and watch for signs of the end, but He didn't want them to be afraid. Jesus prepared them, telling them everything they needed to know in advance.

Just as the disciples were to have this attitude in preparation for the end times, so are you as a follower of Christ. As you go about your day, are you watchful for signs of the end and living life with this eternal, hopeful perspective? No matter what may happen, be it earthquakes, wars, persecution, or false prophets, you are to be on guard while not alarmed. Remember, you have the hope of salvation. Walk in confidence, asking the Lord for wisdom to discern your days. Today, trust Jesus regardless of the circumstances or events happening around the world. Jesus prepared you about what would happen, so don't be afraid. The Lord is with you!

And you must watch! I have told you everything in advance.
—Mark 13:23

Further Scripture: Luke 12:35–36; 1 Corinthians 16:13–14; Revelation 16:15

Week 22, Day 152: Mark 14

Stay Awake and Pray!

Jesus prayed to His Father in the Garden of Gethsemane. He told His disciples to sit nearby and pray. Three times Jesus found the disciples asleep. And three times Jesus asked them, "Couldn't you stay awake?"

As you await the return of Christ, devote yourselves to prayer and stay alert. Jesus warned that the Spirit is willing, but the flesh may be weak. Therefore you must continue to pray. It sounds simple, but the disciples fell asleep and couldn't stay awake for even an hour. As a follower of Christ waiting for His return, how is your prayer life? Spend time in prayer, and watch how it gives you strength for the day.

Stay awake and pray so that you won't enter into temptation.
The spirit is willing, but the flesh is weak. —Mark 14:38

Further Scripture: Romans 13:11; Colossians 4:2; 1 Thessalonians 5:17

Week 22, Day 153: Mark 15
Jesus Endured Pain and Crucifixion

Jesus not only faced physical pain before His crucifixion, He endured emotional pain as well. People passed by and yelled insults, the chief priests with the scribes mocked Jesus, and even a criminal crucified alongside Jesus taunted Him. Jesus endured it all until His death on the Cross.

As followers of Christ, persecution for your faith will come. As you live boldly for Jesus in this culture, be prepared for insults, mocking, and taunting. Jesus endured the emotional and physical pain by keeping His eyes on His mission from the Father. Sometimes emotional suffering hurts more than physical pain. May you live your life in such a way that people will know the Jesus inside you, even if it means enduring hardship, suffering, and persecution. Even then, be courageous—Jesus has conquered the world!

In the same way, the chief priests with the scribes were mocking Him to one another and saying, "He saved others; He cannot save Himself! Let the Messiah, the King of Israel, come down now from the cross, so that we may see and believe." Even those who were crucified with Him were taunting Him. —Mark 15:31–32

Further Scripture: John 15:18; John 16:33; 2 Timothy 3:12

Week 22, Day 154: Mark 16

Jesus Is Alive!

The women arrived at Jesus' tomb early in the morning with spices to anoint His body. Instead of finding His body in the tomb, an angel met the women and shared the news that Jesus had been resurrected and gone ahead of them to Galilee. Just as Jesus had promised, He would see the women again! As the women went away from the angel, they were so bewildered with the news that Jesus was alive that they didn't say anything as they went on their way.

Have you ever seen God move in such a big way that it took a while for the miracle to sink in? Maybe your body was healed, the Lord provided finances for something that seemingly impossible, you passed a test you felt certain to fail, or your difficult marriage turned around in a moment. Just like the women who witnessed the miracle of Jesus' resurrection, sometimes it takes a while to articulate the power and amazement of Jesus in your life. But just as the women eventually shared the amazing news of Jesus' resurrection, the Lord will give you words and opportunities to go into all the world and share about His miraculous power in your life!

So they went out and started running from the tomb, because trembling and astonishment overwhelmed them. And they said nothing to anyone, since they were afraid. —Mark 16:8

Further Scripture: Matthew 7:28; Acts 3:11–12; Romans 15:18–19

Week 23, Day 155: Luke 1

The Angel Announces the Birth of Two Sons

God sent the angel Gabriel to a young virgin named Mary. He shared with her the news, "Do not be afraid, Mary, for you have found favor with God. Now listen: You will conceive and give birth to a son, and you will call His name Jesus. Therefore, the Holy One to be born will be called the Son of God." Then the angel reminded her of this truth: "Nothing will be impossible with God." Mary responded in humility and surrender, saying, "I am the Lord's slave. May it be done according to your word."

No matter what you face today, no matter the magnitude of your responsibility, your calling, or your trial, believe these truths for your own life: do not be afraid, God sees you, His favor is upon you, you have a purpose, and nothing will be impossible with God. Today, walk with the Lord, having the same faith and humility as Mary. The Lord has a plan for you, and He makes the impossible *possible*!

For nothing will be impossible with God. —Luke 1:37

Further Scripture: Isaiah 41:10; Jeremiah 32:17–18; Matthew 17:20

Week 23, Day 156: Luke 2

Understanding Jesus' Humanity

Jesus wasn't just born with all wisdom and favor as an infant. Over the years, He sat and listened to scholars and teachers of the Mosaic Law. He asked them questions, and He was obedient to His parents. With time, Jesus increased in wisdom, stature, and in favor with God and people.

Like Jesus, you will continue to grow in wisdom as you spend time in the Word of God, discussing Scripture with other believers, and living obediently to the Lord. The Lord doesn't expect you to have it all together the moment you say yes to Him. You don't have to have it all together because His grace is sufficient in your weakness. Continue to place yourself in positions where you will grow in Christ. Walk with perseverance and endurance, pressing on to know Him more.

And Jesus increased in wisdom and stature, and in favor with God and with people. —Luke 2:52

Further Scripture: Hebrews 5:12–14; James 1:2–4; 1 Peter 2:2–3

Week 23, Day 157: Luke 3

One Is Coming

John the Baptist, the miraculous son of Zechariah and Elizabeth, traveled around the River Jordan, preaching a baptism of repentance for the forgiveness of sins. Three different people groups asked, "What then should we do?" They wondered if perhaps John was the Messiah who had been foretold. But John corrected them, saying One was coming who was more powerful and would baptize people with the Holy Spirit and fire.

There was a hunger and humility in the question, "What then should we do?" The people knew they needed repentance. They knew they needed to take action and make a heart change. John knew they would find ultimate fulfillment through the Savior of the world. Jesus would come to save them from their sins, and then His fire would begin to transform their hearts.

Today, ask the Lord in humility, "What then should I do?" Is there something in your life you need to repent of in order to create a pure heart and make a real life change? Or maybe the Lord has you going through a trial to purify your heart. Ask the Lord, listen to His voice, and He will reveal to you what to do. Remember, He loves you His grace is enough.

Tax collectors also came to be baptized, and they asked him, "Teacher, what should we do?" . . . John answered them all, "I baptize you with water, but One is coming who is more powerful than I. I am not worthy to untie the strap of His sandals. He will baptize you with the Holy Spirit and fire."
—Luke 3:12, 16

Further Scripture: Psalm 51:10; Malachi 3:3; 1 Peter 1:7

Week 23, Day 158: Luke 4
The Temptation of Christ

Jesus spent forty days fasting in the wilderness. The devil seized this time to tempt Jesus in three specific ways. Each time, Jesus resisted the temptation by quoting Scripture, and the devil departed from Him for a time.

Every day, you will face temptation. The enemy's purpose is to steal, kill, and destroy. The devil prowls around like a lion seeking to devour anyone along the way. *How will you stay strong and not give in?* The Word of God says to resist the devil, and he will flee from you. Combat each temptation with the truth found in God's Word. Identify the lies from the enemy and replace the lie with the truth. If the devil says you are not good enough, say out loud, "I am perfectly and wonderfully made." If the enemy says you are all alone, say out loud, "I am not alone, the Lord my God is with me wherever I go." Spend time with Jesus, and read His Word, so you will have the truth on your heart. The Holy Spirit promises to guide you in all your ways as you walk with Him.

And Jesus answered him, "It is said: Do not test the Lord your God."
After the Devil had finished every temptation, he departed from
Him for a time. —Luke 4:12–13

Further Scripture: John 10:10; 1 Peter 5:8; James 4:7

Week 23, Day 159: Luke 5
Jesus Calls His First Disciples

As Jesus ministered and performed miracles, people were drawn to follow Him and give Him praise. From the fishermen to the man with a serious skin disease, from the paralyzed man to the tax collector, at some point Luke described each of them in a *lowly position—a place of humility.* But as they each witnessed Jesus' power, *they got up.* They were impacted by Jesus in such a way it caused them to get up and follow Him or get up and testify to others about His power.

As believers of Jesus, this is a model for you to follow as you enter Jesus' presence, seeking His power and healing touch in your own life. Today, enter into a place of humble worship and adoration with Jesus. As you experience His power and strength in your life, get up and proclaim it to others. The power of Jesus is not for you to contain; it's for you to get up and share with others!

After this, Jesus went out and saw a tax collector named Levi sitting at the tax office, and He said to him, "Follow Me!" So, leaving everything behind, he got up and began to follow Him. —Luke 5:27–28

Further Scripture: Luke 5:25; James 4:10; 1 Peter 5:6

Week 23, Day 160: Luke 6

Finding Rest in the Lord of the Sabbath

The Pharisees began to question Jesus about properly honoring the Sabbath. Jesus incorporated rest in the midst of an ongoing ministry schedule and demanding crowds. It may not have fallen on a specific day or hour, but Jesus still took time to rest and spend time with His Father. This is the heart behind the Sabbath. And yet Jesus' actions were judged from the outside as being unlawful.

As believers, you are no longer tied to the law of the Sabbath. *The Lord wants you to rest in Him and abide in Him.* If you are busy judging others or even yourself, wondering if you are resting "enough" or doing "enough," you will miss the whole meaning of Sabbath. Be at rest with Jesus as your rock and your salvation. Trust in Him. Take time to rest in Him away from others so you will be filled with His love and grace to jump right back into life and ministry as the Lord leads. When you serve from a place of rest and through the power of the Holy Spirit, it gives the Lord glory. Try it. Take a deep breath and rest today.

Then He told them, "The Son of Man is the Lord of the Sabbath."
—Luke 6:5

Further Scripture: Psalm 37:7; Psalm 62:5–8; Luke 6:12

Week 23, Day 161: Luke 7

Showing Compassion—One Person at a Time

Jesus traveled to a town called Nain with His disciples and a large crowd. As they were walking, Jesus noticed a coffin being carried out. Inside the coffin was a dead man, the only son of a widow. In the midst of large crowds coming and going, Jesus saw the widow and had compassion for her. Jesus went to the coffin and told the dead man to get up. The man got up, and Jesus gave him back to his mother.

Jesus saw a widow crying even though He was in the middle of a large crowd of people, and He had compassion for her. But He didn't stop there; He discerned the situation and took action by responding to a need. As a believer, you are called to do the same. As you go on your way today, open your eyes to *see* the needs of others and to *love* them like Jesus. *Ask* the Holy Spirit to lead you in how to respond with *action*. When every person takes time to love people like Jesus, it could change the world!

When the Lord saw her, He had compassion on her and said, "Don't cry."
—Luke 7:13

Further Scripture: Psalm 103:13; 2 Corinthians 1:3–4; 1 John 3:17

Week 24, Day 162: Luke 8

Peace in the Storm

The disciples literally cried out to Jesus, "We're going to die!" They had been sailing along on the lake, and they suddenly found themselves in a fierce windstorm. The water was swamping their boat, and they were in danger. They called out to the Lord. Jesus rebuked the wind and waves, and the storm stopped. Peace came.

Do you ever feel as though you are going along your normal life when, suddenly, you find yourself in a windstorm? You think to yourself, "There is no way out, this is so hard, so bad, that surely I will die in this storm?" Here's the key to remember in the midst of your storm: *Cry out to Jesus.* Remember His power is within you. Jesus rebuked the wind and the waves. You can rebuke anything in the name of Jesus. Stand firm and know He is God. He will bring His peace when you call upon His name.

They came and woke Him up, saying, "Master, Master, we're going to die!" Then He got up and rebuked the wind and the raging waves. So they ceased, and there was a calm. He said to them, "Where is your faith?"
—Luke 8:24–25

Further Reading: Psalm 34:4; Psalm 138:3; Colossians 3:15

Week 24, Day 163: Luke 9
Deny Yourself Daily

The disciples helped Jesus pass out baskets of bread and fish the Lord had miraculously provided for five thousand men (plus women and children) from five loaves and two fish. Jesus continued to teach and instruct the disciples. He said to them, "If you want to come with Me, you have to deny yourself, take up your cross daily, and follow Me." Essentially He was saying that to be a true disciple of His, you have to deny yourself. Yes, it will be painful because carrying a cross was a painful and humiliating execution.

Daily means *every day*. Every day, Jesus asks you to deny yourself, even through the pain and suffering, and follow Him. What does denying yourself look like for you today? Jesus promises by following Him and giving up your own pleasures and desires, you will find your true self. You will find joy. You will find peace. You will find freedom. Regardless of what the world may say, press on daily, and trust Him. He is faithful.

Then He said to them all, "If anyone wants to come with Me, he must deny himself, take up his cross daily, and follow Me." —Luke 9:23

Further Reading: Daniel 1:8; Romans 8:12–13; 1 Peter 2:11

Week 24, Day 164: Luke 10
The Right Choice

While Jesus was traveling, he came to Bethany, and Lazarus's sisters, Mary and Martha, welcomed Him inside their home. As Jesus sat in their home and talked, Martha was distracted by many things while Mary sat at His feet and listened to what He said. Martha was bothered by Mary's act of sitting and listening to Jesus as His disciple. Martha wanted Mary to give her a hand. However, Jesus confirmed Mary's choice to sit and listen by telling Martha that Mary had made the right choice.

You live in a busy world. Like Martha, there are many, many tasks at hand. Your day could be filled for twenty-four hours doing tasks and staying busy. And if it's not your tasks you need to do, it's friends and family and coworkers in need of your help. And yet the right choice in all the busyness is sitting at the feet of Jesus and listening to what He says. No matter what your day holds, take time to sit and listen to Jesus. This may look like opening the Bible and reading Scripture. This may mean sitting still and praying and pausing long enough for the busyness of the world to calm down around you. So today, *stop doing so much.* Even if your checklist is not checked off. Sit even before you begin the checklist. Listen to Jesus and all He has to speak to your heart. He says, "That is the right choice." Make the right choice today.

The Lord answered her, "Martha, Martha, you are worried and upset about many things, but one thing is necessary. Mary has made the right choice, and it will not be taken away from her." —Luke 10:41–42

Further Reading: Luke 10:39; John 15:4; James 4:8a

Week 24, Day 165: Luke 11
How to Pray Like Jesus

After the disciples saw Jesus get away for a time to pray, they asked Him to teach them to pray. And Jesus said to them, "Whenever you pray, say: Father, Your name be honored as holy. Your kingdom come. Give us each day our daily bread. And forgive us our sins, for we ourselves also forgive everyone in debt to us. And do not bring us into temptation."

Jesus later explained to His disciples to keep asking, keep searching, and keep knocking on the door, because Jesus said that the one who asks receives, the one who searches finds, and the one who knocks will find an open door. *Start your day praying the prayer Jesus told His disciples to pray.* And if you have a day when you feel hopeless and alone, remember Jesus is with you. Seek Him, and you will find Him. Keep asking—He promises He'll answer. His faithfulness stretches to the heavens. He is the God of the impossible, and He loves you today.

He said to them, "Whenever you pray, say: Father, Your name be honored as holy. Your kingdom come. Give us each day our daily bread."
—Luke 11:2–3

Further Reading: Psalm 36:5; Psalm 86:15; Jeremiah 29:13

Week 24, Day 166: Luke 12
Keep Watch; Be Ready

Jesus told His disciples to be ready over and over. Have your lamps lit. Be alert because the Son of Man is coming. How about you? Are you living ready for Christ's return?

If you knew a guest was coming for dinner tonight, you'd get ready and prepare food. If you knew your car would be broken into tomorrow, you would remove precious items or even open the windows so they wouldn't be damaged. But if you knew Christ was returning tomorrow, what would you do today? If you haven't surrendered your life to Christ and trusted Him as your Lord and Savior, then that is the best place to start. And if you are already a believer, ask the Holy Spirit to speak to your heart today about what it means for you to live ready for His return. Walk in faith and in obedience to what He's asking you to do. The Holy Spirit will give you the words and power to walk it out. Trust the Lord to empower you to remain ready for His return.

You also be ready, because the Son of Man is coming at an hour that you do not expect. —Luke 12:40

Further Scripture: Matthew 5:14–15; Romans 13:12; 1 John 2:5

Week 24, Day 167: Luke 13

Everyday Compassion

Jesus had compassion for people and the power to heal the sick. Much to the dismay of the synagogue leaders, Jesus showed compassion to the sick seven days a week. While He taught on the Sabbath, He healed a woman disabled by a spirit. She went on to glorify the Lord because of her healing. The synagogue leaders were upset that Jesus healed on the Sabbath. However, Jesus had such a heart for the lost and sick, He healed them—no matter what day it was.

As you go throughout your day, open your eyes and see people around you. Ask the Lord to give you compassion for others every day of the week. Allow the Holy Spirit to work within you for the kingdom of God, giving glory to His name. Rest in the Lord and draw strength from Him.

Then He laid His hands on her, and instantly she was restored and began to glorify God. —Luke 13:13

Further Scripture: Psalm 30:2; Psalm 34:3–4; Psalm 62:5–8

Week 24, Day 168: Luke 14

Banquet Lessons

Jesus told a parable about guests arriving at a wedding banquet. Some guests walked in and chose the most favorable positions. Then the host told them to move and sit at the lowest place, bringing humiliation to those guests. However, the guests who chose the lowest place at the table were invited to move up higher.

As a follower of Christ, you are called to walk in humility and think of others before yourself. If there is an open parking spot and another car pulls up at the same time, humility lets that person go ahead of you and take the spot. If you are waiting for a favorite cupcake with friends and there is only one favorite flavor left, humility lets your friend have the last favorite cupcake while you try something new. Today, think of others before you think of yourself. When you live in such a way, you walk out the love of Christ. The Lord will honor your heart as you walk in humility. Open your eyes to see the way He blesses you for your unselfish and humble attitude.

For everyone who exalts himself will be humbled, and the one who humbles himself will be exalted. —Luke 14:11

Further Scripture: Proverbs 11:2; Philippians 2:3–4; 1 Peter 5:6

Week 25, Day 169: Luke 15
Jesus Seeks the Lost

Jesus told a parable about a man with one hundred sheep who lost one of them. This man left the ninety-nine and went after the one sheep, searching until he found it. After the one sheep was found, the man went to all his friends and family and asked them to rejoice with him in finding the one lost sheep.

In this story, Jesus illustrated His great love for you. Do you realize Jesus loves each person so deeply that He will go after even one person who has not come to Him and repented? He doesn't miss the one. He seeks the one.

You are called to love like Jesus. But before you can love like Jesus, you need to *receive His great love for you.* Start every day believing you are a child of God, holding on to the truth that He loves you just as you are. His love is long and wide and deep and high. Today, receive His great love for you so that out of His love for you, you are able to love others and seek after the one in your own life.

I tell you, in the same way, there will be more joy in heaven over one sinner who repents than over 99 righteous people who don't need repentance.
—Luke 15:7

Further Scripture: Psalm 103:11; Ephesians 3:17–18; 1 John 4:19

Week 25, Day 170: Luke 16
Heaven—and Hell—Are Real

Luke shared the story of a rich man and a poor man. When the rich man, who had lived a life of luxury and lavishly feasted every day of his life, died, he was tormented in hell. In contrast, when the poor man, who had been covered with sores during his life, died, angels carried him away to heaven. While the rich man suffered in hell, he requested to cool his tongue for relief from the heat. He begged Abraham to go to his five brothers and warn them about hell, so they wouldn't endure the same suffering.

Heaven and hell are real. Sometimes people like to think maybe hell isn't that bad. But yes, as described in this passage, hell is truly an awful place. Jesus came so that you may have eternal life in heaven forever. If you receive His gift of salvation and follow Him, you do not have to suffer in hell for eternity. The choice is yours. Will you believe in Jesus during your days on earth? Or will you be your own god? The Lord longs for you to receive His love. He wants to spend eternity with you forever. And for those choosing to believe in Jesus, don't hold back sharing with others. You could help save them from eternity in hell. Today, go and share Jesus, and help save a life!

Besides all this, a great chasm has been fixed between us and you, so that those who want to pass over from here to you cannot; neither can those from there cross over to us. —Luke 16:26

Further Scripture: Matthew 16:26; Colossians 3:2–4; 1 John 5:11–12

Week 25, Day 171: Luke 17
The Lord Sees

While Jesus was traveling, ten men with serious skin diseases met him. They stood at a distance and asked Jesus to have mercy on them. Jesus sent them on their way, telling them to go and show themselves to the priests. While they were going, the ten men were healed. Just one of the ten returned to thank Jesus. To this one man who did something different, Jesus said, "Go on your way. Your faith has made you well." This one man was not only a leper and an outcast from society, but he was also also a Samaritan, a foreigner. Even still, the Lord healed him physically and spiritually. The Lord saw his faith.

The Lord sees you, and He loves you. You may feel different. You may stand apart from the crowd as you make choices to follow Christ. Jesus is with you and sees you as you follow Him rather than the crowd. Today, follow the voice of the Lord. Humble yourself and give thanks to the Lord, even if you stand out as the different one. Remember, the Lord created you; you are perfectly and wonderfully made. Walk in faith, believing His love is with you.

But one of them, seeing that he was healed, returned and, with a loud voice, gave glory to God. He fell facedown at His feet, thanking Him. And he was a Samaritan. . . . And He told him, "Get up and go on your way. Your faith has made you well." —Luke 17:15–16, 19

Further Scripture: Psalm 139:13–14; Colossians 3:17; Revelation 19:5

Week 25, Day 172: Luke 18

Be Persistent in Prayer

When Jesus was with His disciples, He shared a story about a persistent widow who went before a judge seeking justice against her adversary. The widow was so persistent and refused to give up to the point the judge called it pestering. The judge eventually gave her the justice she asked for because he was tired of her persistence. He just gave her what she wanted!

Jesus told this parable because He knew the disciples would need "to pray always and not become discouraged." Raise your hand if this is you! Have you sought the Lord for days, weeks, or even years for the same loved ones to receive Jesus as their Savior? Or for the prodigal son or daughter to come home? Or for your marriage to turn around for good? Or for wisdom and clarity on a decision? *The Lord knows.* He knows the tendency to become discouraged in the midst of waiting. Jesus says to pray always and don't be discouraged. Today, once again, come before Jesus with your requests. He hears you, and He will answer you. The answer may be no, it may be yes, or it may be to wait a bit longer. But He has promised—He will answer you when you seek Him with all your heart.

He then told them a parable on the need for them to pray always and not become discouraged. —Luke 18:1

Further Scripture: Isaiah 40:31; Matthew 7:7; 1 Thessalonians 5:16–18

Week 25, Day 173: Luke 19
Seek and Save Mission

While Jesus was traveling through Jericho, the crowds followed Him. A rich tax collector named Zacchaeus climbed up a tree so he could see Jesus. As Jesus passed by, He saw Zacchaeus and told him to come down because Jesus must stay at his house. Zacchaeus hurried down and joyfully welcomed Jesus into his home. Zacchaeus's life was transformed as he made Jesus Lord of his life. Jesus, the Son of Man, came to seek and save the lost. Jesus saw Zacchaeus in a tree and wanted to spend time with him. In doing so, one life was changed forever as Zacchaeus received the love of Jesus.

Today, open your eyes to see the people who are watching you live your life for the Lord. And then do the next thing. Invite them into your home for a meal or be willing to go into their home. Show them the love of Jesus by spending time with them. It may require you to get outside your comfort zone, but that's how Jesus lived His life. He was criticized for going to a tax collector's home, and yet He went and loved anyway. His mission is now your mission—to seek and save the lost. As you go on your way, open your eyes to see someone to love like Jesus!

"Today salvation has come to this house," Jesus told him, "because he too is a son of Abraham. For the Son of Man has come to seek and to save the lost."
—Luke 19:9–10

Further Scripture: Romans 1:16; Romans 10:1; 1 Corinthians 9:22–23

Week 25, Day 174: Luke 20
Meeting the Sadducees's Challenge

The scribes and the chief priests wanted to get rid of Jesus so they looked for a way to get their hands on Him. They asked Jesus many questions, trying to trap Him. Jesus discerned their craftiness in questioning Him and was slow to speak, using wisdom when answering them. He answered so well, they no longer dared to ask Him anything.

As you walk with Jesus, those around you may question you in an attempt to make you stumble in your faith. Remember, craftiness is a tool of the enemy. Just as the serpent was crafty with Eve in the garden, the enemy will send crafty people your way to try and shake your faith in Christ. But like Jesus, through the power of the Holy Spirit, you are filled with discernment and wisdom for all situations. When you respond, slow down as you speak, and don't take offense from others. Walk in the authority you have in Christ, and speak truth in love. Love never fails.

Some of the scribes answered, "Teacher, You have spoken well." And they no longer dared to ask Him anything. —Luke 20:39–40

Further Scripture: Genesis 3:1; Luke 12:12; Ephesians 4:14–15

Week 25, Day 175: Luke 21
The Coming of the Son of Man

Jesus the Messiah is returning. Therefore, Jesus repeatedly told His disciples to be ready, to be on guard, to look for the signs, and to not be surprised! He wanted their minds to be ready and not dulled from drunkenness and the worries of life. If their minds were dulled, the day would catch them off guard.

Notice how Jesus said to be on guard so your mind is not dulled from drunkenness *and* the worries of life. But *how* are you to be on guard? Jesus says by prayer, thanksgiving, and setting your mind on the hope in Him. Prayer will give you the strength to stand firm and not be ashamed of the Gospel. As you embrace the anxieties of life, resist the temptation to worry or to seek out temporary pleasures. Rather, press into Jesus and remain steadfast. In doing so, you will be ready for Christ's return.

Be on your guard, so that your minds are not dulled from carousing, drunkenness, and worries of life, or that day will come on you unexpectedly like a trap. —Luke 21:34–35

Further Scripture: Luke 21:36; Colossians 4:2; 1 Peter 1:13

Week 26, Day 176: Luke 22

The Lord's Supper

While Jesus ate His final meal with the disciples, He shared with them His desire to eat this Passover meal with them before He suffered death on the Cross. He knew this time was near. Jesus served as a sin offering, dying for all the sins of the world so you could be saved. Years after Jesus' final meal with His disciples, believers in Jesus still participate in the re-creation of this meal. Communion, or the Lord's Supper, is a form of worship and remembrance of Jesus' sacrificial life for those who follow Him.

You may walk into church on any given Sunday and be given the opportunity to partake in communion. It may even be at your home with family and friends or at a wedding ceremony. As you partake in the Lord's Supper, you are asked to *remember* what Christ did for you on the Cross. You are asked to *participate* in how Christ lived His life. And finally, you are asked to *proclaim* His death until He returns again. Today, give thanks for Jesus and His life sacrificed to save the world.

And He took bread, gave thanks, broke it, gave it to them, and said, "This is My body, which is given for you. Do this in remembrance of Me." In the same way He also took the cup after supper and said, "This cup is the new covenant established by My blood; it is shed for you."
—Luke 22:19–20

Further Reading: 1 Corinthians 11:24, 26; Hebrews 10:10, 14

Week 26, Day 177: Luke 23
The Son of Man Reality

Jesus, the Son of Man, was fully God and fully human. The whole assembly wanted Jesus charged as a criminal, but Pilate found no grounds for charging him. Since Jesus was considered a Galilean, Pilate brought in Herod Antipas, the ruler of Galilee, to help make the decision. Still, Herod agreed with Pilate and found no reason to charge Jesus with death. However, they agreed to whip Him, mock Him, and insult Him. Eventually Pilate gave into the cries of the assembly and agreed to crucify Jesus, even if there was no substantial reasoning. Therefore, Jesus endured humiliation and physical pain until He died on the Cross.

Your Savior, Jesus, the Son of Man, understands and can sympathize with you and your pain. The Word says you will suffer. You will face trials. You will be persecuted. Similarly, Jesus endured suffering, trials, and persecution. However, Jesus does not leave you alone. Even today, whatever you face, turn to the Lord. He understands the pain and suffering, and He promises to give you the strength you need to endure. Jesus promises He is at work in the middle of your pain and will restore, establish, strengthen, and support you. Ask Him for help. Turn to Him in your moment of weakness, and He will strengthen you. Remember today, you are not alone in your agony.

But they kept up the pressure, demanding with loud voices that He be crucified. And their voices won out. So Pilate decided to grant their demand and released the one they were asking for, who had been thrown into prison for rebellion and murder. But he handed Jesus over to their will.
—Luke 23:23–24

Further Scripture: Hebrews 4:15; James 1:2–3; 1 Peter 5:10

Week 26, Day 178: Luke 24
How to Engage with the Risen Lord

The disciples were startled and frightened when they first saw Jesus resurrected and physically with them again after His death on the Cross. However, Jesus spent time with them. They invited Him to stay with them for the evening. They shared bread together. Then He took the time to explain the Scriptures concerning His role as the Messiah and how the prophecies were fulfilled. He walked with them and blessed them to send them out as His witnesses. And then Jesus left them again and ascended to heaven. Because the disciples spent this time with Jesus, it helped ease their worries and fears. They sought truth and answers with Jesus. Then after Jesus ascended into heaven, they had great joy and continually praised God.

In a similar way, you will find joy when you spend time in Jesus' presence, seeking Him for answers to your questions. It is important for you to take time to spend with Jesus. Yes, life is busy, and there are many places to turn to with answers to your questions or solutions for your fears. But follow the example of the disciples. Today, take time to sit in Jesus' presence, study His word, and seek Him in prayer. As you seek Him, He will guide you along your path of life. You will be filled with joy and strength for the day.

After worshiping Him, they returned to Jerusalem with great joy.
And they were continually in the temple complex praising God.
—Luke 24:52–53

Further Scripture: Psalm 16:11; Psalm 28:7; Jeremiah 15:16

Week 26, Day 179: John 1
The Word Became Flesh

John began his Gospel with the message that Jesus is life and this life is the light of men. Jesus as the light shines into the darkness. What if you said throughout your day these phrases of truth: "Jesus is my life. Jesus is my light?"

What are some things getting in the way of Jesus as your life? Is work your life? Is shopping your life? Are your loved ones your life? Today, *make Jesus your life*. Give Him all your affections and receive the abundant life found in Him alone. Jesus is also the light. The light shines in the darkness. There is absolutely no darkness in Jesus. If the light of Christ has grown dim in your life and darkness is growing around you, spend time with Jesus. Walk with Him and practice His truth. His light will grow within you and set you free.

Life was in Him, and that life was the light of men. The light shines in the darkness, yet the darkness did not overcome it. —John 1:4–5

Further Scripture: John 14:6; Romans 8:2; 1 John 1:5–7

Week 26, Day 180: John 2

The First Sign

Jesus, His mother, and His disciples were guests at a wedding in Cana of Galilee. His mother turned to Jesus and told Him the hosts had run out of wine. Understanding her son's power, Jesus' mother turned to the servants and said to them, "Do whatever Jesus says to do." Jesus performed His first miracle, turning water to wine. Jesus told the servants what to do, and they did it. They didn't question Him. They didn't argue. They just did it. Because of their immediate obedience, the water turned into good wine. Jesus publically displayed His glory, and His disciples believed Him.

What would happen if you listened to Jesus like the servants? Whatever He told you to do, you just did it. Whatever you read in the Word of God about His promises and truth, you believed immediately. You don't question it. You don't ask someone else what they think. Rather, you listen and obey immediately. In walking in immediate obedience, you begin to experience Jesus working in miraculous ways, like the servants seeing the water turn to wine. If they had waited, argued, rationalized, or asked someone else to do it, they would have missed the miracle. Today, listen to the voice of the Lord, and just do it.

"Do whatever He tells you," His mother said to the servants. . . .
"Fill the jars with water," Jesus told them. So they filled them to the brim.
Then He said to them, "Now draw some out and take it to the chief
servant." And they did. —John 2:5, 7–8

Further Reading: Genesis 17:23; Isaiah 30:20b–21; John 2:11

Week 26, Day 181: John 3

The One from Heaven

God loved the world so much He sent His only Son Jesus to earth. Jesus' purpose was to come to earth so that everyone who believed in Him would have eternal life. Jesus came not to judge the world but to save the world.

God gave up His Son out of a *great love*. Have you ever had to give something up? Maybe you sent a child overseas to work with orphans, and you gave up the dream of living near your grown child. Yet because you gave your child and dream up, hundreds of orphans' lives have been impacted. Maybe the Lord led you to give up a vehicle so the ministry family would have a working car. Because you gave up your car, this family impacted an entire city for the Gospel. It's worth the sacrifice, right? God gave up His only Son, and now the entire world can be saved and have eternal life. But just like the family would have to receive the vehicle as a gift, you must receive the gift of God's Son as a gift, a free gift of salvation. As you receive this gift, you will be saved from death and your sins through Jesus' life. Today, receive the gift of salvation if you haven't made this decision. And if you have, ask the Lord if there is anything He wants you to give up so that His love, grace, and power can spread to others.

For God so loved the world in this way: He gave His one and only Son, so that everyone who believes in Him will not perish but have eternal life. For God did not send His Son into the world that he might condemn the world, but that the world might be saved through Him. —John 3:16–17

Further Reading: Romans 10:9–10; 1 John 4:8; Revelation 22:17

Week 26, Day 182: John 4
Son of God

Jesus traveled through Samaria on His way to Galilee. But Jesus chose the path less traveled by other Jews and stopped at Jacob's well for a drink. He was worn out from His journey. He was without His disciples and alone, which was rare for Him. And then a Samaritan woman came near Him to draw water. Although tired and thirsty Himself, Jesus set His needs aside and took the time to love, listen, discern, and respond to this woman at the well. That day, as Jesus took time to show love to this woman, her life was changed forever as she believed in Jesus as the Son of God. Even the town was impacted, and many Samaritans began to believe in Jesus.

Are you worn out from the journey? Do you feel as though you need time to sit and be served a drink of water? Jesus felt the same way. And yet, in the middle of that worn-out moment, someone came along for Jesus to love. As you rest and sit by a pool or read a book at a coffee shop, remember to keep your eyes open to whoever the Lord brings your way to love like Jesus. You may even be in your home and you just want to put your feet up and chill, but your child comes by and needs you. In those moments of weariness, call upon the Lord for strength to love and show grace. In these moments of weakness, *Jesus' love shines through in a mighty way*. Continue to rely on His love in and through you to impact the lives of others at unexpected and inconvenient times. You never know what an impact Jesus' love can make in one person's life.

Jacob's well was there; so Jesus, wearied as he was from his journey, was sitting beside the well. It was about the sixth hour. A woman from Samaria came to draw water. Jesus said to her, "Give me a drink." (For his disciples had gone away into the city to buy food.) —John 4:6–8 ESV

Further Reading: Isaiah 40:8, 31; 2 Corinthians 2:14

Week 27, Day 183: John 5
Witnesses for the Son of God

John wrote as though he was in a courtroom and Jesus was on trial, having to prove His equality to God the Father as He is God the Son. Jesus had four witnesses give their accounts to the unbelieving: John the Baptist, Jesus' works, His Father's witness, and Scripture. The people had the choice to make between believing Jesus was who the witnesses said He was in order to have eternal life or to reject Him, choosing to disbelieve. Far too often the people, even those around Jesus, chose to disbelieve.

You are a witness to the *truth* of Jesus. When you experience Jesus display His power, mercy, or grace in your life, share it with those around you. Did you ask the Lord to provide funds for a graduating senior and He provided a scholarship in a crazy miraculous way? Tell someone! Did you ask the Lord for wisdom in buying a new home, and He provided? Tell your coworkers! Did someone pray for healing for you, and you were healed? Go and share that on social media! Were you lost in darkness, bound to sin and the ways of this world, and then received the love and light of Jesus in your life and are now walking in freedom? Share it! In doing so you will give the *glory* to God! You will allow someone else to see Jesus and His power and His glory! If you hide it and keep it to yourself, you miss out on stewarding the gift of God's power inside you. Today, go and proclaim what Jesus has done for you to anyone who will listen! Testify just how He has impacted your life!

But I have a greater testimony than John's because of the works that the Father has given Me to accomplish. These very works I am doing testify about Me that the Father has sent Me. —John 5:36

Further Reading: Psalm 71:15–16; Mark 5:19; 1 John 5:11

Week 27, Day 184: John 6
I AM the Bread of Life

After Jesus fed the five thousand with loaves and fish, He went away. The next day, the crowds went looking for Jesus and found Him on the other side of the sea. They saw Jesus performing a miracle and were hungry to see more works from God. Jesus said to them, "I AM the bread of life." Jesus' will is for everyone who believes in the Son of God to have eternal life and be satisfied in Him.

If Jesus is the bread of life, what does that mean for you today? Bread is a physical essential. You can live on just bread and water a long time. Like bread, *Jesus is essential for daily living*. Every day you need to fill up with Jesus. If you don't fill up with Jesus, you won't be satisfied in life. You will be hungry and want to fill your life with other things. So today, fill up with Jesus. Turn to Him, find your satisfaction in Him alone, and meditate on His Word. Give thanks to Him for His goodness, His beauty, and His provisions. Let Him fill you up as you go through your day so you have energy from the Lord to face whatever lies ahead. He *is* your daily bread.

"I am the bread of life," Jesus told them. "No one who comes to Me will ever be hungry, and no one who believes in Me will ever be thirsty again."
—John 6:35

Further Scripture: Psalm 107:9; John 6:40; Revelation 7:16–17

Week 27, Day 185: John 7
The Living Water

As the people gathered on the final day of the Feast of Tabernacles, Jesus said to them, "If anyone is thirsty, he should come to Me and drink! And if you believe in Me, you will have streams of living water coming from deep within."

Jesus is the answer to your thirstiness. What happens when plants need water but don't get any? They dry up and eventually die. The same is spiritually true for believers. You will dry up if you don't tap into Jesus, the source of living water. How do you know you are drying up? You become numb to the voice of the Lord. Perhaps your flesh tendencies are quicker to surface, or you find yourself turning to things of this world for satisfaction rather than setting your eyes on Jesus. You may feel down and not filled with joy. Remember, in the presence of the Lord there is the fullness of joy. Turn to Him and ask a friend to pray for you to be filled up with Jesus. Right now say out loud, "Jesus, fill me afresh with Your living water! Amen!"

"If anyone is thirsty, he should come to Me and drink! The one who believes in Me, as the Scripture has said, will have streams of living water flow from deep within him." He said this about the Spirit. Those who believed in Jesus were going to receive the Spirit. —John 7:37–39

Further Scripture: Numbers 24:7; Isaiah 58:11; 1 Corinthians 12:13

Week 27, Day 186: John 8
I AM the Light of the World

Jesus spoke to the scribes and the Pharisees in the Temple complex. After the Pharisees brought an adulteress woman to Him, Jesus told them not to condemn or judge others' sin. Jesus told this woman to go and sin no more. Soon after, Jesus proclaimed His second "I AM" statement: "I AM the light of the world."

Jesus is the light of the world. His light is for every single person in the world—no one is left out. Jesus is not judging or condemning you. He came to be your light in life. If you walk with Jesus, you will never be in the darkness. What an incredible promise from the Lord!

Today, walk in step with Jesus, following Him and allowing Him to be your light. If you feel like darkness surrounds you, press into the light of Jesus. Remember, He loves you. So don't just sit there! Walk with Him. Then go into all the world and shine the light of Jesus!

I am the light of the world. Anyone who follows Me will never walk in the darkness but will have the light of life. —John 8:12

Further Scripture: Isaiah 49:6; John 8:58; 1 John 1:5–6

Week 27, Day 187: John 9
Born Blind and then Healed

Jesus was walking with His disciples when He passed by a blind man. Jesus saw the man both physically and spiritually. Jesus stopped, talked with the man, and healed him. Now the blind man could physically see for the first time since birth. This physical healing also allowed the man to see the power and compassion of Jesus. The man testified about Jesus, calling Him, "Jesus, a prophet, Lord and Son of Man." The blind man was given the spiritual eyes to see Jesus as His Lord, and he worshipped Him.

Jesus saw the blind man and took action. Ask yourself: *Do I look at people or do I see people?* Looking can take just a moment. Seeing people like Jesus requires you to discern the situation, sympathize, and take action. This world is busy and fast-paced. Who has time to see people like Jesus? You have things to do and places to go! Today, ask the Holy Spirit to open your eyes to see people and help you discern the action to take. By taking action, you may not just help them physically but also spiritually as you open their eyes to Jesus' love for them. Embrace the faith to believe Jesus will give you the grace and strength to see people.

As He was passing by, He saw a man blind from birth. —John 9:1

Further Scripture: Psalm 119:18; Psalm 146:8; Matthew 13:13–15a

Week 27, Day 188: John 10

I AM the Door of the Sheep and I AM the Good Shepherd

In this passage, Jesus declared the third and fourth of the seven "I AM" statements found in the Book of John: "I AM the door of the sheep," and "I AM the good shepherd."

Jesus came to give eternal life to those who believe and walk through the door of salvation through Him. You don't need to look anywhere else. Come through the door of Jesus. Inside the door, He will protect you as you come and go.

Jesus is the good shepherd, and like a shepherd, He laid down His life for you. Just as a shepherd knows every sheep and brings them into the protective sheepfold, Jesus loves and cares for you. As a shepherd goes after a missing sheep, Jesus will go after you. Open your heart, release any feelings of rejection or inadequacy, and receive His love today. He loves you just as you are. He created you, knows you, and calls you by name. Allow Jesus to be your shepherd, and rest in His love and protection today. You will lack nothing.

Jesus said again, "I assure you: I am the door of the sheep. . . .
I am the good shepherd. I know My own sheep, and they know Me, as the
Father knows Me, and I know the Father. I lay down My life for the sheep."
—John 10:7, 14–15

Further Reading: Psalm 23:1; Isaiah 43:1; Acts 4:12

Week 27, Day 189: John 11

I AM the Resurrection and the Life

Jesus is in the business of bringing the dead to life. He told Martha, whose brother Lazarus had just died, "I AM the resurrection and the life." Jesus' statement foreshadowed His own resurrection, but it's also the story of the Gospel.

Seemingly dead things become alive through Jesus' power, grace, and love. Jesus miraculously brought Lazarus, who was dead for four days, back to life. *Jesus can also bring life to hopeless situations.* When you die to yourself and the sin in your life, surrendering everything you have to the Lord, His love and grace give you a new life in Christ. Jesus says to surrender it all: your life, your marriage, your kids, your finances, and pray, "Lord, my [fill in the blank] feels dead right now. I don't know how it will ever turn around and have life, but I trust in You." Jesus calls you to live this way every day. Do you believe this enough to walk this truth out in faith? Start today!

Jesus said to her, "I am the resurrection and the life. The one who believes in Me, even if he dies, will live. Everyone who lives and believes in Me will never die—ever. Do you believe this?" —John 11:25–26

Further Reading: Luke 9:24–25; Romans 6:8; 1 Corinthians 15:31

Week 28, Day 190: John 12

Die to Live

Jesus used an agricultural example to teach His disciples: "Unless a grain of wheat falls to the ground and dies, it remains by itself. But if it dies, it produces a large crop." Jesus prepared His disciples for His upcoming crucifixion and death. The hour had come for Jesus, the Son of Man, to be glorified. But from Jesus' death would come a great harvest of salvations!

In a similar way, Jesus instructed believers to make it a daily practice to die to themselves. When you die to yourself, you make room for more of the Lord to be glorified in your life, just as when wheat falls to the ground and produces a large crop. Today, say to the Lord, "Show me how to die to myself today, so that You, Jesus, may be glorified in me!" The Lord will give grace upon grace as you let go of the things He brings to mind, and new life will grow beyond what you can imagine. You may think you need to hang on to control or an area in your life, but Jesus says when you lose your life, you will gain even more. Follow Him. His love never fails.

I assure you: Unless a grain of wheat falls to the ground and dies, it remains by itself. But if it dies, it produces a large crop. The one who loves his life will lose it, and the one who hates his life in this world will keep it for eternal life. If anyone serves Me, he must follow Me. —John 12:24–26

Further Scriptures: Luke 9:23–24; Romans 8:12–13; Galatians 2:20

Week 28, Day 191: John 13
Jesus Washes the Disciples' Feet

Jesus knew the time had come for Him to depart from this world and go back to His Father. Jesus loved those around Him, and He poured into them until His final breath. He also understood His identity as God's Son. It was from this place of walking confidently in His identity that Jesus served and loved others. During dinner before the Passover Festival, Jesus served His disciples by humbly washing their feet. He even washed the feet of Judas Iscariot, whom Jesus knew would soon betray Him.

When you love and serve others in humility, do it from the place of your identity in Christ as a child of God. Accept the truth that you are fearfully and wonderfully made for a purpose and fully loved by Jesus. When you walk in this identity: loving and serving, then humility becomes natural, just as it was with Jesus. It's not about *what* you do, it's about *who* you are in Christ. Jesus modeled this for you as He washed His disciples' feet. You may be the lead pastor, a schoolteacher, the CEO, the principal, or a mom or dad raising kids, but you are still called to serve and love others. Pause for a minute and ask the Lord, *Who can I serve a glass of water to today in love? Who can I carry trash for? Whose dirty feet can I wash?* Look around you. Jesus loved you so you can love others.

Jesus knew that the Father had given everything into His hands, that He had come from God, and that He was going back to God. So He got up from supper, laid aside His robe, took a towel, and tied it around Himself. Next, He poured water into a basin and began to wash His disciples' feet and to dry them with the towel tied around Him. —John 13:3–5

Further Scripture: John 1:12; Philippians 2:3–5; 1 Peter 5:5b–6

Week 28, Day 192: John 14

I AM the Way, the Truth, and the Life

Jesus spoke directly to His disciples: "Your heart must not be troubled. Believe in God and in Me." Then after discussing all the rooms in heaven where Jesus would go away to prepare, Jesus made another "I AM" statement: "I AM the way, the truth, and the life." Jesus understood His time here on earth was coming to a close, so He didn't use many words but went right to the point.

Wouldn't you say the same is true for today? People's hearts are troubled. They look in every direction for the way, the truth, and the life. They seek success. They try to remain in control of every situation. They research countless religions and philosophies. But the Word of God says, "Jesus is the way, the truth, and the life." *Believe in Jesus, and you will be saved.* Do you know someone whose heart is troubled and searching for the way? Pray for him or her. As the Lord leads, share the message of salvation through Christ and share how you found what you were looking for in the love and grace of Jesus Christ. May the Lord lead many to His saving grace. May their hearts no longer be troubled because they have found the Way. Yes, Lord, please save the lost who need to be found by You. Amen!

Your heart must not be troubled. Believe in God; believe also in Me. . . . Jesus told him, "I am the way, the truth, and the life. No one comes to the Father except through Me." —John 14:1, 6

Further Reading: Acts 4:12; Romans 10:9; 1 Timothy 2:5

Week 28, Day 193: John 15

I AM the True Vine

Jesus introduced the seventh "I AM" statement: "I AM the true vine." In ancient Israel, grapes were a major agricultural product. So it was fitting for Jesus to use the illustration of Himself as the vine, God the Father as the vineyard keeper, and believers of Christ as the branches. The vineyard keeper knows what he wants his plant to look like and will prune it, cutting away branches, to allow it to grow in the way he knows is best. In the same way, God will cut away any branches in your life not producing fruit so that more fruit will grow.

Jesus clearly stated that if you do not abide in Him, you can do nothing. No fruit will be produced. Nothing. Period. *You must remain on the true vine in Christ to produce life-giving fruit.* Remaining or abiding in Christ means to spend time with Jesus, such as reading the Word or in prayer. Just like getting to know a friend, you must continue to spend time on your relationship with Jesus. When you abide in Christ, your fruit will resemble Christ's: love, joy, peace, patience, kindness, goodness, faithfulness, gentleness, and self-control. Those around you will want to know what is producing this fruit in you. Then you can point them to Jesus and glorify the Father.

I am the true vine, and My Father is the vineyard keeper. Every branch in Me that does not produce fruit He removes, and He prunes every branch that produces fruit so that it will produce more fruit. —John 15:1–2

Further Scripture: John 15:5; John 15:8; Galatians 5:22–25

Week 28, Day 194: John 16
The Spirit of Truth

Jesus told the disciples many things to keep them from stumbling because He knew the religious or the nonbelievers would try to throw the disciples off and make their feet stumble. But Jesus equipped His people with the Spirit of truth to guide them into all the truth.

Do you ever feel like you are being questioned for walking in the truth of Jesus? Remember, as you abide in Christ, you are being rooted and built up in Him and established in your faith. Walk in the Spirit of truth and allow Him to guide you into all truth, beyond a religious mindset or traditions. This truth will bring glory to the Lord because you are walking with what the Spirit of the truth declares to you. Today, bind up the spirit of religion and function in the Spirit of truth, allowing freedom to reign in your life.

When the Spirit of truth comes, He will guide you into all the truth. For He will not speak on His own, but He will speak whatever He hears. He will also declare to you what is to come. He will glorify Me, because He will take from what is Mine and declare it to you. —John 16:13–14

Further Scripture: Psalm 69:4; John 16:1; Colossians 2:6–8

Week 28, Day 195: John 17
Jesus' Prayer for Unity

In the time before Jesus was arrested and before He died, He went to the Father in prayer on behalf of all believers. He prayed for unity. He prayed all believers would be one, just as Jesus and the Father are one. He prayed as believers live in harmony and in unity, the world would witness how much God the Father loves God the Son and all who believe. God loves everyone unconditionally, and He longs for the world to see this love in those who follow Him and believe in Him.

How does the world see the body of Christ? Do they see believers working together in unity or believers doing their own thing? Since Jesus prayed for unity in the hours He had left on earth, clearly unity is important to the heart of Jesus. So what do you do about this? *Pray for unity in the body and for the Holy Spirit to supernaturally bring the body together.* Fix your eyes on Jesus and not on all the minor details. And today, go and ask someone from a different church to get together and talk about Jesus. Or go a step further: go together as one body to share Jesus with the lost. Just see what happens when you get outside the walls of your church. It's from the heart of Jesus for the body to be one so the world will know the great love of the Father.

I pray not only for these, but also for those who believe in Me through their message. . . . I am in them and You are in Me. May they be made completely one, so the world may know You have sent Me and have loved them as You have loved Me. —John 17:20, 23

Further Reading: Psalm 133:1; Ephesians 4:3–5; Hebrews 12:2

Week 28, Day 196: John 18
What Is Truth?

Judas Iscariot, one of the twelve disciples, betrayed Jesus to the Jewish religious leaders, leading to Jesus' arrest. Meanwhile, Peter, another disciple, denied Jesus three times. Eventually, Caiaphas and Annas, the high priest and his father-in law, passed the decision to send Jesus off to Pilate at the governor's headquarters, wanting Jesus to be sentenced to die. After all of this, Pilate had a hard time deciding what to do with Jesus. He asked Jesus the question: "What is truth?"

Like Pilate, many in the world try to figure out truth. They look to social media, government, food, sports, academics, or entertainment, trying to discover what truth is. As a follower of Christ, *you know Jesus is the Truth*. Jesus came so the world would be saved. Look no further. Jesus is truth. Today, pray for those searching for the truth. When someone asks you, "What is truth?"—share the Truth with them!

"You say that I'm a king," Jesus replied. "I was born for this, and I have come into the world for this: to testify to the truth. Everyone who is of the truth listens to My voice." "What is truth?" said Pilate. —John 18:37–38

Further Scripture: John 1:17; John 17:17; 1 John 4:6

Week 29, Day 197: John 19
The Day of Jesus' Passion

Pilate ordered Jesus to be flogged. The soldiers also mocked Him by crowning His head with thorns and clothing Him with a purple robe. Then Pilate continued to question what to do with Jesus, as he couldn't find a sufficient reason to crucify Him. Even in the midst of Jesus' pain and suffering for the sins of the world, He continued to live as an example. Pilate asked Him the question: "Where are You from?" Jesus paused. When He finally responded, He did so calmly and confident of His calling.

Have you ever been questioned about your decision to follow Christ and live for Him? Sometimes the way people ask can make you want to respond with angst, like you have something to prove. But in that moment, when you feel the need to defend your faith, don't get angry, prideful or flustered. Remember Christ's example to us, even when He was in the midst of suffering. Pause, breathe, and be slow to answer. Let the Spirit guide you and help you discern your response. Let the Spirit speak to the person questioning you. And then when the time is right, speak forth in the love and authority of Jesus.

He went back into the headquarters and asked Jesus, "Where are You from?" But Jesus did not give him an answer. —John 19:9

Further Reading: Exodus 14:14; Ecclesiastes 5:1–2; James 1:19–20

Week 29, Day 198: John 20

I Have Seen the Lord

The tomb was empty when Mary Magdalene, Simon Peter, and the other disciple went to the tomb early in the morning. Jesus had been resurrected from the dead just as He foretold! After His resurrection, the disciples spent time with Jesus and were commissioned for ministry. However, Thomas had not been with Jesus and did not believe He had indeed come back to life. Finally, after eight days, Jesus appeared to Thomas and the other disciples to physically show Thomas His nail-pierced hands and feet. Only when Thomas physically saw Jesus and His resurrected body did he believe. Jesus said to Thomas, "Because you have seen me, you have believed. Those who believe without seeing me are blessed."

Most likely you have never physically seen Jesus. When He returned to heaven, He said He'd be seated at the right hand of the Father. It is with faith you believe in the Bible. It is with faith you believe in Jesus as the Son of God—the same faith the disciples had when Jesus returned. However, your faith may be more like Thomas's; you may want to physically see Jesus. Today, ask Jesus to show up in your life, maybe not in physical form, but *allow Him to open your eyes to see His love and His special touch around you.* When you ask, have faith He will answer. He knows just what you need today.

Jesus said, "Because you have seen Me, you have believed. Those who believe without seeing are blessed. —John 20:29

Further Reading: Jeremiah 32:17; Hebrews 11:1; Romans 10:17

Week 29, Day 199: John 21
Do You Love Me?

In the final chapter of John, Jesus demonstrated His grace and love through Peter's life. Before Jesus died on the Cross, Peter denied Him three times. Now, after Jesus' resurrection, Jesus physically helped Peter by instructing him where to fish, providing even more fish than imagined, and feeding him breakfast. And then Jesus gave Peter a second chance. Even after Peter had denied Jesus, He publically restored him to ministry.

Like Peter, Jesus loves you so much. Yes, He sees your heart. Yes, He knows when you sin, when you turn away from Him, and what your weaknesses are. But Jesus is *for* you. He calls you His own. So just like Peter, if you have fallen into sin, if you have given into temptation or what seems like the easy way out, your life with Jesus is not over. Jesus is never done with you. He loves you, and He came to earth for you. Jesus gave Peter a new role. Jesus restored Peter to ministry of the Gospel and called him to pour into His people with love and care for them. Jesus will do the same for you. His mercies are new each morning, and His faithful love never ends. *Your story isn't finished.*

He asked him the third time, "Simon, son of John, do you love Me?"
Peter was grieved that He asked him the third time, "Do you love Me?"
He said, "Lord, You know everything! You know that I love You."
"Feed My sheep," Jesus said. —John 21:17

Further Reading: Lamentations 3:21–23; John 18:27; 2 Peter 3:9

Week 29, Day 200: Joshua 1—2
I Will Be with You

After Moses's death, Joshua became the leader of the Israelites. The Lord commanded Joshua to lead the people over the Jordan River and into the Promised Land. Before crossing into the new land, the Lord gave Joshua promises of His faithfulness: "I have given you every place where the sole of your foot treads. No one will be able to stand against you. I will be with you. I will not leave you. You will succeed in whatever you do. I am with you wherever you go."

As you walk with the Lord in faith, God's promises stand true for your life as well. His Word is the same yesterday, today, and tomorrow. When the Lord calls you to do something or go somewhere, whether it's to pray with someone at the park or to quit your job and begin another one, God is with you wherever you go. However, God instructed Joshua to "not depart from the book of instruction." When God leads you in faith, remember to stay grounded in the Word of God. He doesn't want you to walk in faith and then go on your own. Rather, the Lord longs for you to read and follow His Word as you walk in faith, remembering His faithful promises. It's in the truth of God's Word that you will remain strong and courageous. Today, walk in faith, knowing the Lord your God is with you wherever you go.

No one will be able to stand against you as long as you live. I will be with you, just as I was with Moses. I will not leave you or forsake you. . . . Above all, be strong and very courageous to carefully observe the whole instruction My servant Moses commanded you. —Joshua 1:5, 7

Further Scripture: Genesis 28:15; Matthew 28:20; Hebrews 13:5

Week 29, Day 201: Joshua 3—4
Breaking Camp

The Israelites looked ahead at the Promised Land and saw the Jordan River in their path. Joshua received orders from the Lord on how they would cross over. First the Israelites had to break camp, leaving a place of comfort. Then the priests had to stand in the water with both feet. When they followed these instructions, they witnessed God's miraculous hand—the Jordan River dried up, allowing thousands of Israelites to walk across the riverbed.

Breaking camp and standing in the water . . . that's what the Israelites were instructed to do as they walked in faith. What does that mean for you today? Where in your life do you need to break up what is comfortable? Has the Lord asked you to move away from the job you've held for decades? Maybe you need to say something to someone that's been on your heart for months. It's time to break camp. And then go all in. Don't just sort-of do it. Be confident to the Lord's calling. *Stand in the water with both feet.* Move to another state. Invite a friend who hasn't spoken to you out for dinner. Just go for it. If the Lord is leading you to do it, then He will be with you. As you move in obedience and in faith to His leading, you will witness God's mighty hand, His mighty power, and His mighty provision in your life. Walk it out in bold obedience! God is with you.

When the people broke camp to cross the Jordan, the priests carried the ark of the covenant ahead of the people. Now the Jordan overflows its banks throughout the harvest season. But as soon as the priests carrying the ark reached the Jordan, their feet touched the water at its edge and the water flowing downstream stood still, rising up in a mass that extended as far as Adam, a city next to Zarethan. —Joshua 3:14–16

Further Scripture: 1 Chronicles 16:8; Proverbs 3:5–6; Isaiah 42:16

Week 29, Day 202: Joshua 5—6

The Wall Fell

The Lord gave Joshua the plans for taking over Jericho, bringing victory out of destruction. Joshua listened to the Lord and, as commander, gave the plan to the Israelites. They followed the instructions from the Lord, even though they appeared to be strange, and not your average orders for taking over a city. Joshua trusted the Lord and responded with obedience.

The Lord knows the battles you face each day. While you are not likely marching around a city, it may feel as though you are facing the same kind of battle in a relationship you have had for years. You may feel as though you have dealt with the same struggle with the temptation to sin over and over. The Lord says you will face battles. Today, are you ready to stomp out anger and jealousy? Are you ready to defeat the power of drugs or alcohol in your life? Are you ready to let go of control and give it to the Lord? It is time to seek the Lord for the game plan. Ask Him how to overcome the battle you face. He promises He will fight for you. He promises victory in His name. Today, stop and seek His face, trust the plan He gives you, and respond with obedience.

The Lord said to Joshua, "Look, I have handed Jericho, its king, and its fighting men over to you. March around the city with all the men of war, circling the city one time. Do this for six days. . . . on the seventh day, march around the city seven times, while the priests blow the trumpets."
—Joshua 6:2–4

Further Scripture: Exodus 15:2; Psalm 46:10; Hebrews 11:30

Week 29, Day 203: Joshua 7—8

Blatant Sin against God

After the Israelites were struck down during the first battle with the city of Ai, Joshua discovered that "Achan son of Carmi, son of Zabdi, son of Zerah, of the tribe of Judah" had been unfaithful to the plan the Lord had given the Israelites during the destruction of Jericho. Achan had disobeyed orders and taken some of what had been set apart. Therefore, when the Israelites went to battle against Ai, they were not protected by the Lord, and men died. The Israelites became discouraged. Despite all this, the Lord instructed Joshua, "Do not be afraid or discouraged." God had a new plan for defeating Ai.

Unfortunately, sin and disobedience exist in the world. You make choices, and those around you make choices that affect the outcome of everyday life. Sometimes you just want to throw in the towel because things are just so discouraging. But God's grace is strong in your weakness. God's power is at work within you. God has a plan for good, not for calamity. When you come before Him and trust Him, He promises to work all things together for good. *So do not be afraid or discouraged.* Seek the Lord, and He will guide your next steps. Keep your head up, friend, and do not give up! God loves you and will never leave you or forsake you!

The Lord said to Joshua, "Do not be afraid or discouraged. Take the whole military force with you and go attack Ai. Look, I have handed over to you the king of Ai, his people, city, and land." —Joshua 8:1

Further Scripture: Psalm 37:24; Isaiah 41:10; Jeremiah 29:11

Week 30, Day 204: Joshua 9—10

Choose Honesty

After the Israelites conquered and destroyed both Jericho and Ai, the people of Gibeon feared for their lives. In an effort to save their lives, they carried out a crafty plan and tricked Joshua and the Israelites. The plan worked, and the Israelites, without seeking the Lord's wisdom, swore an oath to allow the Gibeonites to live in their land. Eventually, Joshua and the Israelites learned the truth, and the Gibeonites never found the freedom they desired. Instead, as a result of their deceitful ways, they served as woodcutters and water carriers for the rest of their lives.

In the moment, lying and deception can seem like the easier choice to make. Like the Gibeonites, fear of what lies ahead may overtake you to the point your flesh thinks lying is the best and only choice. Your flesh may say, "It's only a small lie. It's easier this way, and besides, no one will ever know." Eventually someone will uncover the truth, and then you will face the consequences. But if you walk in the power of the Spirit, you will not give in to the deeds of the flesh, like lying and deceiving. *When you live honestly, you live securely.* Remember, as you make choices, the Lord delights in those who are honest.

We greatly feared for our lives because of you, and that is why we did this. Now we are in your hands. Do to us whatever you think is right.
—Joshua 9:24—25

Further Scripture: Proverbs 10:9; Proverbs 12:22; Galatians 5:16

Week 30, Day 205: Joshua 11—12
Completing God's Plan

News of the Israelites' victories in battle spread throughout the northern cities of the Promised Land. As a result, Jabor, the king of Hazor, gathered all the neighboring kings and their armies to attack Israel together. The combined army was as numerous as the grains of sand on the seashore. Joshua heard of this coming attack, and the Lord reminded Joshua not to fear. Then He gave Joshua the strategy for victory. God's battle plan included both God and man. God would hand the armies over to the Israelites, but He still gave the Israelites a battle plan.

The Lord says you will face battles. You may lie in bed at night wondering how you will face tomorrow. The Lord sees you and knows the battles you face. He says do not worry about tomorrow—do not fear. He has a plan for you, and He goes before you. Trust in His plan. Even if the plan seems unusual, follow Him. The Lord told Joshua to hamstring the horses and burn the chariots, and the Israelites found victory. Follow the Lord's ways, and you will find victory in the battle.

The Lord said to Joshua, "Do not be afraid of them, for at this time tomorrow I will cause all of them to be killed before Israel. You are to hamstring their horses and burn up their chariots." . . . The Lord handed them over to Israel, and they struck them down. —Joshua 11:6, 8

Further Scripture: Deuteronomy 20:4; Proverbs 21:31; 1 Corinthians 15:57–58

Week 30, Day 206: Joshua 13—14
Caleb's Unfaltering Confidence

Forty-five years after spying out the land in Canaan, Caleb reminded Joshua about the inheritance the Lord promised him. Even after years of wandering in the wilderness without seeing the fulfillment of God's promise, Caleb remained loyal to the Lord his God. Joshua recognized Caleb's loyalty to the Lord and blessed him, giving Hebron as an inheritance.

Even at the age of eighty-five, Caleb remained strong in the Lord. You may be young or you may be growing older in years, but like Caleb, you are called to keep your eyes on the Lord. Remain steadfast and immovable. You may have hard days. You may feel as though you have giants to face. You may even be wandering in a wilderness. Continue to remain faithful to the Lord. Today, *believe God is at work*. He has not forgotten you, and His promises still stand. Great is His faithfulness.

Here I am today, 85 years old. I am still as strong today as I was the day Moses sent me out. My strength for battle and for daily tasks is now as it was then. Now give me this hill country the Lord promised me on that day, because you heard then that the Anakim are there, as well as large fortified cities. Perhaps the Lord will be with me and I will drive them out as the Lord promised. —Joshua 14:10–12

Further Scripture: Psalm 33:11; Isaiah 46:4; 1 Corinthians 15:58

Week 30, Day 207: Joshua 15—16

Asking for Inheritance

Caleb marched against the inhabitants of Debir. He promised his daughter Achsah as a wife to whoever captured Kiriath-sepher. Othniel captured and struck down Kiriath-sepher, and he received Achsah as his wife. Achsah persuaded her new husband to ask her father for a field. Achsah knew her father had more to give the newly married couple, so she asked for even more. She asked for a blessing and for springs of water. Without hesitating, her father gave her both the upper and lower springs.

In a similar way, your Heavenly Father has even more gifts for you. As you walk with Him in integrity, He will not withhold good things. He has more power, grace, wisdom, and joy to give, even beyond what you can imagine. Jesus is your daily source of living water. As you believe in Him, it lives within you. The Lord says to abide in Him, asking whatever you wish, and it will be done for you. Today, confidently ask the Lord for even more. May His living water spring up within you today!

She replied, "Give me a blessing. Since you have given me land in the Negev, give me the springs of water also." So he gave her the upper and lower springs. —Joshua 15:19

Further Scripture: Psalm 84:11; John 15:7; Revelation 21:6

Week 30, Day 208: Joshua 17—18
Go! Start Today!

The entire Israelite community came together at Shiloh. Seven tribes of Israel had not yet divided up their inheritance. Joshua wondered how long the people would delay going out and receiving what the Lord had given them. Therefore he instructed the tribes to go and survey the land, write descriptions of it, and then return to him. Joshua waited for them to return at the Tent of Meeting. Then, in the presence of the Lord, they cast lots.

As believers of Jesus, you have the opportunity to have a relationship with Him and to daily abide in Him as your source of strength, peace, joy, and guidance. But like the Israelites, you have to *go* after it. The Lord longs for you to pursue His presence daily. In order to know Jesus more, you must spend time in His presence, read His Word, observe it, and write it down. What is keeping you from this today? Why do you delay? Maybe you are busy and keep getting sidetracked. *Go!* Start today! Do not delay seeking the Lord and all He has for you in His presence!

So Joshua said to the Israelites, "How long will you delay going out to take possession of the land that the Lord, the God of your fathers, gave you? Appoint for yourselves three men from each tribe, and I will send them out. They are to go and survey the land, write a description of it for the purpose of their inheritance, and return to me." —Joshua 18:3—4

Further Scripture: Psalm 27:7—8; Romans 13:11; James 4:8

Week 30, Day 209: Joshua 19—20
Seek God in Chaos

The tribes of Israel continued to mark their inheritance of land. Each tribe had land with boundaries. Each allotment was different, and each tribe was responsible to care for their assigned land. The territory of the Danites slipped out of control. They had to fight for their plot of land and take possession of it.

When the Lord gives you land, a home, or even relationships or children, you are responsible to care for them. Sometimes, like the Danites, the things God entrusts you to steward can get out of control. *Is there anything in your life that you own or are responsible for that feels out of control?* Maybe you have a hard relationship or struggle raising children. Perhaps your home is falling apart, and you don't have the resources to keep up. You may not know what to do next. Remember, the Lord cares for you, and He has entrusted you to care for the things He has given you. Seek Him in the middle of the chaos, and trust Him to give you the wisdom to steward them well and with excellence. Don't give up! The Danites had to fight for their plot of land. You may have to press in, pray hard, and fight the battle before you. Remember, the Lord will be with you. In Him you have victory!

When the territory of the Danites slipped out of their control, they went up and fought against Leshem, captured it, and struck it down with the sword. So they took possession of it, lived there, and renamed Leshem after their ancestor Dan. —Joshua 19:47

Further Scripture: Galatians 6:9; James 1:5; 1 Peter 4:10

Week 30, Day 210: Joshua 21—22

Seek Understanding

After the tribes spread out to their inherited cities and pasture lands, word came that the Reubenites, Gadites, and half the tribe of Manasseh had built an altar on the frontier of the land of Canaan. Because of past sins and experiences, the Israelites assumed they built the altar as an act against God. However, before attacking and going to war against them, they sent Phinehas and ten leaders to seek more understanding of the altar. It turned out they built the altar with pure motives so future descendants would know about their relationship with the Lord God of Israel. When Phinehas and community leaders reported the truth about the altar to the Israelites, they were pleased and praised God. No one spoke about going to war with the decedents of Reuben, Gad, and Manasseh again.

As you have relationships with people, you will face conflict. That's part of life. As you face conflict, before responding in action, seek understanding. Listen to the person you are in conflict with. Then make your decision after you understand the entire situation. Don't just assume and take action. If the Israelites had done that, they would have found themselves at war for no reason. *Is there a situation in your life today in which you need to seek further understanding?* You may be amazed at how the Lord works it out when you take the time to understand.

When Phinehas the priest and the community leaders, the heads of Israel's clans who were with him, heard what the descendants of Reuben, Gad, and Manasseh had to say, they were pleased. . . . The Israelites were pleased with the report, and they praised God. —Joshua 22:30, 33

Further Scripture: Proverbs 15:1; Matthew 5:9; Matthew 18:15—16

Week 31, Day 211: Joshua 23—24

As for Me and My Family

Joshua spoke to the Israelites before his death, reminding them of God's powerful faithfulness over the years. Once again, he encouraged them how to live—fear the Lord, worship Him in sincerity and truth, get rid of other gods. Simply put, obey Yahweh. Then Joshua placed a memorial stone under an oak tree as witness to not deny the Lord their God, the Rock of their salvation. It's as though Joshua were saying, "Please just keep your eyes on the Rock."

Have you ever walked into a home and seen a plaque with, "As for me and my family, we will worship the Lord"? Or maybe you have these words in your own home and pass by them daily. *What does it mean for you to worship the Lord as a family?* Today, ask the Lord: "Have I gotten away from worshipping the Lord in Spirit and truth? Do I have other gods besides the one and only Jesus Christ, the Rock of my salvation? Am I obeying You?" If the Spirit brings anything to mind, turn from it and fix your eyes on Jesus. Refocus on the Lord Jesus and seek Him with all your heart, soul, mind, and strength. He loves you, and He's all you need!

Therefore, fear the Lord and worship Him in sincerity and truth.
Get rid of the gods your fathers worshiped beyond the Euphrates River
and in Egypt, and worship Yahweh. . . . As for me and my family, we will
worship Yahweh. —Joshua 24:14, 15

Further Scripture: Proverbs 4:25–27; Luke 10:27; 1 Peter 1:22

Week 31, Day 212: Judges 1—2

The Cycle of Disobedience

Despite Joshua's warnings to have no other gods and worship the Lord only, the Israelites did not listen. They did what was evil in the Lord's sight and worshipped Ba'al and other gods, abandoning the Lord, the God of their fathers. They lived in disobedience to the Lord and did not keep their eyes on Him. And as a result, they failed in battle and found themselves in chaos. However, despite their sin, the Lord raised up judges to help save the people from their enemies. The Lord rescued them from darkness.

In the same way, God the Father saw the chaos and sin of the world and sent His Son Jesus to come rescue you. Jesus came to save you from darkness and the power of sin. He came to bring life and hope, even in the midst of your chaos. *Will you turn to Jesus and allow Him to rescue you?* Or will you press on in your own strength, your own wisdom, and try it in your own power? Friend, allow Jesus to help you. Today, believe and receive His love, grace, and power. He is there for you because He loves you.

Whenever the Lord raised up a judge for the Israelites, the Lord was with him and saved the people form the power of their enemies while the judge was still alive. —Judges 2:18

Further Scripture: 1 Corinthians 10:13; Colossians 1:13–14; 1 Thessalonians 1:10

Week 31, Day 213: Judges 3—4

Facing God's Tests

Without Joshua as commander, a theme emerged among the nation of Israel. First the Israelites did what was evil in the Lord's sight, serving other gods and forgetting the Lord their God. Then an enemy would rise up and oppress the Israelites. In response, they would cry out to the Lord. The Lord would hear their cries and grant mercy by raising up a judge to deliver them in battle. This happened over and over and over. The judges did not focus on their own reputations or glory. Rather, they answered the call the Lord put on their lives so the people of Israel could walk in freedom.

The Lord loves you deeply. Even when you continue to walk in sin or seek the things of this world instead of the Lord's ways, Jesus is still there. When you cry out to Him, He will answer. Jesus will deliver you. Today, *if you feel stuck in a place of defeat, cry out to the Lord like the Israelites did.* Allow Jesus to deliver you. Then, as you walk in deliverance and freedom, the Spirit of God will use you to help others just as He used the judges in the past. The Lord is calling out followers of Christ to help deliver and bring others to victory in Jesus' name. Be ready and available!

The Israelites cried out to the Lord. So, the Lord raised up Othniel son of Kenaz, Caleb's youngest brother, as a deliverer to save the Israelites.
—Judges 3:9

Further Scripture: Psalm 32:7; Psalm 34:17; 1 Corinthians 15:57

Week 31, Day 214: Judges 5—6
An Unlikely Mighty Warrior

The Lord called out Gideon as Israel's fifth judge to deliver the people after their season of disobedience. Gideon didn't see how the Lord could use him; he was from the weakest family in the weakest tribe of Manasseh and was the youngest in his father's home. But the Lord saw Gideon as a mighty warrior. The Lord reminded Gideon that He would be with him. Along the way, Gideon asked for signs and confirmations from the Lord for this calling, and God answered his request with signs and wonders.

If you have ever felt inadequate for the Lord's call on your life, then you are in good company with Gideon. Remember, *the Lord has plans for you in His kingdom*. It's not because of your educational degrees or business success, and it's not even because of your family heritage. Rather, because He created you perfectly and wonderfully, He has plans for you. As He calls you, do not be afraid. He wants to use you daily in the kingdom of God, and He will send you as you listen to the Holy Spirit within you. He is always with you. But like Gideon, you may have times in your life when you ask the Lord for confirmation and throw out a fleece before Him. Watch the Lord confirm your steps as you seek His face. Walk it out in faith as God's mighty warrior.

He said to Him, "Please, Lord, how can I deliver Israel? Look, my family is the weakest in Manasseh, and I am the youngest in my father's house." "But I will be with you," the Lord said to him. "You will strike Midian down as if it were one man." —Judges 6:15–16

Further Scripture: 1 Samuel 17:37; Jeremiah 32:27; Hebrews 13:20, 21

Week 31, Day 215: Judges 7—8

Faith Even in Weakness

As Gideon answered the call from the Lord, he formed a mighty army and prepared to fight the Midianites. Amidst the preparations, the Lord told Gideon that his army was too large. God cut the army from 32,000 down to a mere 300 men. The Lord promised Gideon that He would deliver the Midianites into the hand of Gideon using just 300 men. Gideon walked God's promise out in faith, trusting the calling on his life. The Lord continued to confirm and equip Gideon to overcome each doubt and fear along the way. And through it all, because of Gideon's weakness, the Lord received the glory.

God's strength is made evident in your weakness. He promises that in your weakness, He is strong. Therefore you can boast in His strength and not in your own. Remember as you walk out your calling for the day, no mountain is ever too large for the Lord. There is no marriage too broken, no job is too difficult, and no sickness too far gone for the Lord. Like Gideon, the Lord wants you to trust Him. In your weakness, have faith in the impossible, and follow His ways. Draw near to Him, and He will deliver you from your situation. Trust. Trust. Trust.

The Lord said to Gideon, "You have too many people for Me to hand the Midianites over to you, or else Israel might brag: 'I did it myself.'"
—Judges 7:2

Further Scripture: Judges 7:7–8; 2 Corinthians 12:9; Hebrews 11:6

Week 31, Day 216: Judges 9—10
Taking a Stand against Evil

Gideon's son Abimelech did not receive the power he thought he deserved over the people. As a result, he reacted out of bitterness and jealousy toward his family. He murdered seventy of Gideon's sons (and Abimelech's own brothers) minus Jotham, who escaped. Even though Abimelech continued to do evil and turned away from God, God is sovereign, and His hand was and is upon Israel. In the midst of battle, Abimelech was fatally struck by a millstone. The Lord was present in the battle and delivered the Israelites to victory.

This is a story about a man losing his mind and acting completely apart from the Lord's plan. But even so, the Lord remained in control. The crazy, selfish plans of man cannot overcome God's sovereignty. He is always there, showing His grace and mercy. You may need to hear this today. *God will not give up on you*, just as He never gave up on the Israelites. He is there even in the unseen, hard moments of battle. And He is victorious. Even when crazy surrounds you, you are surrounded by the Lord God Almighty. Praise His name!

In this way, God turned back on Abimelech the evil that he had done against his father, by killing his 70 brothers. And God also returned all the evil of the men of Shechem on their heads. So the curse of Jotham son of Jerubbaal came on them. —Judges 9:56–57

Further Scripture: Psalm 135:6; Proverbs 16:4; Colossians 1:17

Week 31, Day 217: Judges 11—12

You Are Defined by Christ

Jephthah became a great warrior and leader for the Israelites. The Book of Hebrews even mentions his faith. He boldly and uniquely led the Israelites to defeat the Ammonites. Even though Jephthah was the son of a prostitute, he did not let his past define him. He honored his vow to the Lord during difficult and unlikely circumstances and led the Israelites through battle as he walked by faith.

Your past does not define you. You may have experienced abuse or come from a broken family. But praise God! Your family history does not define you. As you trust Jesus and walk with Him, remember, *you are a child of God.* You are a new creation—the old things have passed away and new things have come. He formed you in your mother's womb, and He has plans for you. He will work all things together for good for those who trust in Him. Today, walk in who you are in Christ!

Jephthah the Gileadite was a great warrior, but he was the son of a prostitute, and Gilead was his father. —Judges 11:1

Further Scripture: Romans 8:28; 2 Corinthians 5:17; Hebrews 11:32–34

Week 32, Day 218: Judges 13–14
Ask the Lord to Confirm

The Israelites once again did what was evil in the Lord's eyes, so the Lord handed them over to the Philistines for forty years. During that time, a man named Manoah and his wife were unable to conceive a baby. But then the Angel of the Lord appeared to his wife, telling her she would have a son and giving her clear instructions on how to raise the son as a Nazarite. The Angel of the Lord said to her, "This child will begin to save Israel from the power of the Philistines." When his wife shared everything the Angel of the Lord said, Manoah turned to the Lord, asking Him to confirm and teach them how to raise their baby. God answered Manoah's request and sent the Angel of the Lord to visit this couple. Soon after, the couple gave birth to Samson, the last judge.

Manoah turned to the Lord for confirmation and clarity. He heard the news and instructions from the angel through his wife and believed it, but he wanted more confirmation. When you know the Lord has called you to something but you still have questions, *turn to Him and ask for even more wisdom.* Sometimes you may want to turn to a media source, see what your friends are doing, or look to the latest book. Instead, ask the Lord. The Lord will answer you and will direct your path. He promises that if anyone asks Him for wisdom, He will give generously without judgment. He will counsel you even through the night and make known His plans for you, teaching you along the way. Then it's your turn to step out in faith and walk out what He is leading you to do.

Manoah prayed to the Lord and said, "Please Lord, let the man of God you sent come again to us and teach us what we should do for the boy who will be born." God listened to Manoah, and the Angel of God came again to the woman. —Judges 13:8–9

Further Scripture: Psalm 16:7–8; Psalm 25:4–5; James 1:5

Week 32, Day 219: Judges 15—16
The Strength of the Spirit

The Lord's hand was upon Samson's life. Even though the men of Judah were determined to hand him over to the Philistines, Samson's God-given strength brought him victory. He was a one-man army, killing one thousand men with the jawbone of a donkey. Even though Samson did not walk closely with the Lord, the Lord gave him victory in battle. After the victory, he was tired and thirsty. In that moment of weakness, he asked the Lord for water. The Lord provided the water, Samson drank, his strength returned, and he was revived. He went on to judge for twenty more years in the days of the Philistines.

The Lord waits for you to turn to Him, so He can strengthen you. No matter how far you've gone astray or how long you have done life on your own, God never leaves you. He has a plan for you, and He waits for you to turn to Him for help. You may be thirsty and weary from the weight of life. Turn to Him for refreshment. He is your source for strength and living water. He will restore your soul. He will revive you. *Just ask Him.*

He became very thirsty and called out to the Lord . . . So God split a hollow place in the ground at Lehi, and water came out of it. After Samson drank, his strength returned, and he revived. That is why he named it En-hakkore, which is in Lehi to this day. —Judges 15:18–19

Further Scripture: 2 Samuel 7:1; Psalm 119:93; John 7:38

Week 32, Day 220: Judges 17—18

The Progression of Sin

The Danites sent five brave men out to scout the land and explore it. They came to the hill country of Ephraim near the home of Micah and spent the night there. During their scouting journey, they discovered idolatry, lies, and deception. The spies of Dan did not have their eyes on God as Joshua had commanded. But even in their waywardness, they knew the truth. They knew to inquire of God, and they knew God was watching over everything on their journey.

What would someone discover if he or she looked into your life? Do you appear to glorify the Lord but have hidden sins behind closed doors? Rest assured, no matter what is discovered in your life, the Lord will always watch over your journey. That's the beauty of the Lord. He is with you, and He loves you unconditionally. No matter how far you may stray, no matter how deep into other false gods and idols you may go, the Lord is with you and watching over you. The Danites knew the Lord was with them but continued in bondage to false idols. Don't live like a Danite. *Ask the Lord for freedom.* Ask Him to help you on your journey and set you free from the temptation to bow down to other gods and live in sin.

Then they said to him, "Please inquire of God so we will know if we will have a successful journey." The priest told them, "Go in peace. The Lord is watching over the journey you are going on." —Judges 18:5–6

Further Scripture: Exodus 20:23; Psalm 91:11; 3 John 1:6

Week 32, Day 221: Judges 19—20

The Horrific Sin of Benjamin

A Levite traveling with his concubine sought hospitality in the city of Gibeah in Benjamin. When no one offered the Levite a place to stay, an older man took them in for the evening. But the Benjaminites of Gibeah surrounded the house and threatened the Levite. They took his concubine and raped her through the night. As a result of the abuse, she died. The Levite gruesomely cut her body up into twelve pieces and sent the pieces to each of the twelve tribes of Israel. This alerted the Israelites of the deep sin occurring in the tribe of Benjamin. The Israelites grieved and wept over how they had taken their eyes off the Lord. They knew they were in need of a judge to deliver them from the evil. The Lord gave them orders to fight because once again He would give them victory.

Lack of hospitality, homosexuality, rape, abuse, murder—you may find it difficult to read this list of sins from the Benjaminites as they took their eyes off the Lord. They did what was right in their own eyes, and it led to a corrupt, evil culture. Would you agree that the culture you live in today sounds alarmingly similar to the Benjaminites? Many in this generation have taken their eyes off Jesus and gone their own way. And yet hope remains because Christ's love remains. The same victory and saving grace for the Benjaminites is available to you and to all those around you. Jesus restores all who turn to Him. Today, pray for this generation to turn their eyes back to Jesus and walk in His victory!

Phinehas son of Eleazar, son of Aaron, was serving before it. The Israelites asked: "Should we again fight against our brothers the Benjaminites or should we stop?" The Lord answered: "Fight, because I will hand them over to you tomorrow." —Judges 20:28

Further Scripture: Psalm 44:6–8; Isaiah 40:28; James 4:9–10

Week 32, Day 222: Judges 21
Under the Spirit of the Lord

The Lord used judges to deliver and save the Israelites. It was only by God's hand that His people, the Israelites, were not wiped out. Four times in the Book of Judges, Israel did what they wanted because there was no king in Israel. Because God had a plan, purpose, and promise for Israel, He continued to appoint a judge to step in and lead the nation. Even so, every judge fell short to the *One True King*: Jesus Christ—the King of kings and Lord of lords.

There's a good chance you have fallen a few times in life. Fallen back into that addiction to pornography. Fallen back to one more round of pain medication, promising this will be the last. Fallen into a pit of worry, anxiety, or self-pity. Fallen into the trap of gossip or deception. But just as God spared the tribe of Benjamin when He could have destroyed them for good, He sent Jesus to come and save you. Regardless of how far you have fallen, Jesus came to save you because He loves you. Give your life fully to Jesus saying, *"Jesus, take over my life. I surrender, and I want You to be the King of my life forever."*

In those days there was no king in Israel; everyone did whatever he wanted.
—Judges 21:25

Further Scripture: John 18:37; Galatians 2:20; Revelation 17:14

Week 32, Day 223: Ruth 1—2

Naomi and Ruth

During the time of the judges, Naomi, a widow living in Moab, moved back to her native Bethlehem with her two widowed daughters-in-law. At Naomi's urging, one daughter-in-law returned to her own family, but Ruth was committed to staying with Naomi. Despite Naomi's negative and bitter attitude about her circumstances, Ruth made a commitment to go wherever Naomi went, live where she lived, and even serve Naomi's God. Ruth committed to the Lord, and she never turned back. The Lord honored Ruth's sincere commitment, and through her faith, He began to turn their circumstances around.

Have you made a commitment to the Lord? Have you told Him, "You have my life. You are my all. I will go wherever You lead me"? Where do you stand with that commitment? Today is the day to think through it. You may have wandered or gotten sidetracked, but Jesus is always there for you. May you be reminded of your first love in Jesus and your commitment to Him. Today, recommit yourself to Jesus. Tell Jesus you love Him and will have no other gods before Him. Tell Him that you will go wherever He leads you, and you will follow Him by putting others before yourself. The Lord your God will honor you for your commitment to Him.

But Ruth replied: Do not persuade me to leave you or go back and not follow you. For wherever you go, I will go, and wherever you live, I will live; your people will be my people, and your God will be my God.
—Ruth 1:16

Further Scripture: Psalm 31:14; Zachariah 13:9; John 12:25–26

Week 32, Day 224: Ruth 3—4
The Kinsman Redeemer

After Ruth spent time in the fields working, Naomi encouraged her to find security for her future. Naomi understood Boaz's role in Ruth's life as her kinsman redeemer. According to the laws of the Pentateuch, a kinsman redeemer is one who redeems or rescues a person or property. Boaz was the male relative who had the privilege or responsibility to act on behalf of Ruth—his relative in need. Boaz showed honor and respect toward Ruth in this process. In time, Boaz and Ruth married and gave birth to a son, Obed. In God's sovereignty, Obed became the grandfather of David. David was not only a great king for Israel, but he was also a part of the genealogy of your New Testament redeemer, Jesus Christ.

This example of Boaz and Ruth serves as a reminder of God's plan to provide a kinsman redeemer for you through His Son. Jesus meets your needs and rescues you. Jesus encourages fellow believers to meet the needs of one another, just as Boaz helped meet the needs of Ruth. Jesus purchased the life of every believer through His blood on the Cross, paying a high cost. Jesus graciously showed you kindness, hope, and joy through redemption, something you cannot earn. *Redemption is Jesus loving you through grace.* Redemption is God's ultimate plan for His people. Today, give thanks for your life in Christ through redemption.

Boaz took Ruth and she became his wife. When he was intimate with her, the Lord enabled her to conceive, and she gave birth to a son. Then the women said to Naomi, "Praise the Lord, who has not left you without a family redeemer today. May his name become well known in Israel."
—Ruth 4:13–14

Further Scripture: Ruth 4:17; Galatians 4:4–5; Ephesians 1:7–8

Week 33, Day 225: 1 Samuel 1—2

Hannah's Vow to God

Elkanah, a man from Ramathaim-zophim in Ephraim, had two wives: Peninnah and Hannah. Peninnah had children, but Hannah was childless. Elkanah loved Hannah despite her barrenness. Even so, Hannah longed for a child. She went to Eli, the priest at the Lord's Tabernacle. She made a vow to the Lord, and, with a broken heart, she prayed from the depth of her soul, requesting a child from the Lord. In God's timing, Hannah received the whom cried out for.

Have you ever desired something so deeply it broke your heart? Have you ever found yourself pouring your heart out to the Lord? Hannah exemplified this heart of brokenness and longing. When you are at the point of brokenness, remember who God is, and remember His faithful works. The Lord desires for you to pour out your heart to Him. He desires for you to make your requests known to Him. Ask Him for help, and receive the Lord's peace. Trust God's timing and worship Him.

"No, my lord," Hannah replied. "I am a woman with a broken heart.
I haven't had any wine or beer; I've been pouring out my heart before the
Lord. Don't think of me as a wicked woman; I've been praying from the
depth of my anguish and resentment." —1 Samuel 1:15–16

Further Scripture: Psalm 62:8; John 14:27; Philippians 4:6

Week 33, Day 226: 1 Samuel 3—4
Speak, Lord

Samuel, Hannah and Elkanah's son, grew up in the presence of Eli the priest just as Hannah had promised he would in her vow to the Lord. While Samuel was lying down to rest in the Tabernacle of the Lord, the Lord spoke to him. However, it took a few times for Samuel to understand it was God, not Eli, speaking to him. At last, after the counsel of Eli, Samuel replied to the Lord, "Speak, for Your servant is listening!"

The Lord, your great Shepherd, speaks to those who believe in Him. His sheep know His voice. Are you at a place where you can hear the voice of the Lord? Today, take ten minutes to rest in the Lord. Say to Him, "*Speak, for Your servant is listening.*" You must be intentional to open your ears to hear His voice. Ask Him to show you a broader picture than you can see at the moment. Then, when you hear from the Lord, act on the things He says. The Lord gave Samuel a bold word to deliver to Eli, and Samuel obeyed. The Lord may want to speak to others through you. Don't get in the way of listening to His voice.

The Lord came, stood there, and called as before, "Samuel, Samuel!"
Samuel responded, "Speak, for Your servant is listening." —1 Samuel 3:10

Further Scripture: John 10:27; 1 Corinthians 10:11; Revelation 3:20

Week 33, Day 227: 1 Samuel 5—6
Stop, Surrender, and Turn to the Lord

After the Philistines captured the Ark of the Lord from Israel, the Philistines began to experience God's hand against them. They moved the Ark to Ashdod, then Gath, and then Ekron, and God's wrath followed. The Philistines experienced God's hand so strongly against them that the Ekronites called out to the Philistine rulers, "Send the ark of Israel's God away. It must return to its place so it won't kill us and our people!" They realized they were not within the will of God. They needed to get back to His will and original plan for the Ark of the Lord.

Have you ever had a season in which everything went wrong? You may have experienced strife or pain and exhausted every effort to fix the situation. Finally you realized the one thing left to do: turn the situation over to God and follow His ways. That's what happened to the Philistines. Maybe that's where you are today. You made a poor choice and kept on going, trying to fix it. Today, *stop running*. *Surrender* and lift your heart to the Lord, releasing the burden you have carried. Confess your wrongdoing, and if there is anything you need to do to make right, do it. In the Lord's will there is perfect peace. You are longing for that peace. So *turn around* and run into God's loving, gracious arms. Let His love wash over you.

The Ekronites called all the Philistine rulers together. They said, "Send the ark of Israel's God away. It must return to its place so it won't kill us and our people!" For the fear of death pervaded the city; God's hand was oppressing them. —1 Samuel 5:11

Further Scripture: Isaiah 26:3; Joel 2:13; Matthew 7:13–14

Week 33, Day 228: 1 Samuel 7—8
Struggling to Rely on God

Samuel served the Israelites as judge throughout his life. However, the elders came to Samuel and said they were done with the season of judges. They were not satisfied with God as their heavenly King, and instead, they wanted an earthly king to rule their land. Samuel listened to their request, knowing it was sinful. Then he sought the Lord for counsel. The Lord told Samuel, "Listen to the people, everything they say to you." The Lord assured Samuel not to worry. The people were rejecting God, not Samuel.

It's so hard to see people walk in the ways of the world. You share truth with them, but they don't listen. They want what others have. Sometimes they have to learn the hard way, figuring it out for themselves. It can be difficult to stand by and watch. Sometimes God allows people to have the answer they think they want. Remember the truth that God has a plan, and His plan will prevail. You can't force people to follow God, but you are called to love them like Jesus. And give thanks for God's promise to work all things together for the good of those who trust in the Lord.

When they said, "Give us a king to judge us," Samuel considered their demand sinful, so he prayed to the Lord. But the Lord told him, "Listen to the people and everything they say to you. They have not rejected you; they have rejected Me as their king." —1 Samuel 8:6–7

Further Scripture: Psalm 81:11–12; Proverbs 1:29–31; Romans 8:28

Week 33, Day 229: 1 Samuel 9—10
The Anointing of King Saul

The Lord revealed to Samuel that Saul, an unassuming yet impressive young man from the tribe of Benjamin, would be king over Israel. Samuel anointed Saul with oil for this specific calling. Then the Lord confirmed His choice by allowing Saul to experience the Spirit of God taking control of him, and he prophesied with the prophets. Later as Saul was presented to the people as their king, he walked in humility and let the Lord unfold the timing of His plan.

As a follower of Christ, you have an anointing on your life. Another meaning for the word *anointed* is "chosen one." Today, you are a chosen one for a specific purpose in furthering the kingdom of God. This means you have been enabled, entrusted, and empowered to accomplish God's will. Anointing is not just for Christian speakers or leaders. It is for every believer because of the Holy Spirit's dwelling within you. No matter the tasks your walk with Jesus brings, in humility, *walk in the power of your anointing.* You were chosen. Whether it's parenting or teaching the Word of God, managing a company or working at a factory, the Holy Spirit empowers you to further His kingdom. Praise the Lord for this mighty truth!

*At this time tomorrow I will send you a man from the land of Benjamin. Anoint him ruler over My people Israel. He will save them from the hand of the Philistines because I have seen the affliction of My people, for their cry has come to Me. —*1 Samuel 9:16

Further Scripture: 1 Samuel 10:16; 2 Corinthians 1:22–23; 1 John 2:27

Week 33, Day 230: 1 Samuel 11—12

A Brand-New King

After Saul and Samuel led the Israelites in a united battle against the Ammorite forces, the Israelites agreed Saul should be their king. Now was the time for Samuel to step down and for Saul, the requested king, to begin his reign as leader. In his final public speech, Samuel warned the Israelites to fear the Lord, worship Him faithfully with all their heart, and consider all the great things the Lord had done for them. Even though an earthly king was not God's plan for His people, the Lord promised to never abandon them.

Throughout the years, the Lord reminded His people to keep their eyes on Him. How about you? Are your eyes on Jesus, the King of kings and Lord of lords? Or are you living as ruler of your own life? The enemy creates schemes to sidetrack you. The world is full of distractions, and life brings battles. In the midst of these distractions and battles, God is always there. He will never abandon you. Even when you make decisions in your flesh, He will never abandon you. There is nothing you can do to drive God away. Today, *turn your eyes to Jesus the King*, and tell Him you love Him and Him alone. Don't wait to turn to Him only when fear or trials overcome you. Turn to Him today!

The Lord will not abandon His people, because of His great name and because He has determined to make you His own people. . . . Above all, fear the Lord and worship Him faithfully with all your heart; consider the great things He has done for you. —1 Samuel 12:22, 24

Further Scripture: Psalm 29:10; Hebrews 13:5; Revelation 15:3

Week 33, Day 231: 1 Samuel 13

Losing the Royal Dynasty

Saul reigned as king over Israel for forty-two years. He formed a standing military presence and reigned from Gilgal. During this time, Saul's son Jonathan attacked a Philistine garrison in Geba that threatened Gilgal. In response, the Philistine army gathered again and was as numerous as sands on the seashore. Remembering Samuel's prophetic words to wait seven days for the appointed time, Saul remained in Gilgal. Saul waited day after day, but Samuel didn't come. His troops were gripped with fear and began to desert him. Therefore Saul made the choice to go ahead and offer the burnt offerings without Samuel. And then Samuel showed up on the seventh day, just as Saul had anticipated. Saul lost hope in Samuel coming and didn't wait. He chose to take the situation into his own hands without seeking the Lord. He forced it, and, when Samuel arrived right on time, he called Saul foolish. As a result of Saul's lack of patience, Samuel told Saul that his reign as king would not endure.

Have you ever grown impatient waiting on the Lord for a new job, a new home, a child, or a relationship? Even though you knew the Lord wanted you to wait, you were afraid of what waiting would do, so you forced the situation. And then, suddenly, you knew you made the wrong choice. *Ugh.* If only you could go back and wait on the Lord. Today, take a deep breath. Remember to wait on the Lord and His timing. *Wait until you can respond in peace, not panic.* Believe the Lord's promise that He is for you, not against you. He has plans to prosper you, giving you hope and a future. Don't force the matter. Wait upon the Lord.

Samuel said to Saul, "You have been foolish. You have not kept the command which the Lord your God gave you. It was at this time that the Lord would have permanently established your reign over Israel."
—1 Samuel 13:13

Further Scripture: 1 Samuel 13:10–11a; Psalm 27:14; Jeremiah 29:11

Week 34, Day 232: 1 Samuel 14
The Victory Is God's

Though Jonathan and his father Saul were both aware of the Philistine garrison, Saul remained with his six hundred troops on the outskirts of Gibeah while Jonathan and his armor bearer, in contrast, stepped out in faith to pursue an attack against the Philistines as the Lord confirmed their actions. Jonathan didn't just talk about it. He said to his loyal armor bearer, "Come on, let's go!" Jonathan believed if God was in it, they would find victory. With God by their side, the two men stepped out in faith and found victory, striking down twenty men. Saul remained trapped in fear while Jonathan experienced freedom, walking in faith and obedience.

Is there an area in your life in which you need to step out in faith? Is that still, small voice saying, "Come on, let's go"? You believe in the power of the Lord, and now it's time for you to take a step of faith. While stepping out, ask the Lord to confirm your steps, one at a time. Just as He confirmed Jonathan's steps, *He will confirm yours*. Today is the day to get over the fear of the unknown. The choice is yours—step out in faith and experience freedom and even more than you can imagine or remain and only watch others experience the adventure of walking in faith.

Jonathan said to the attendant who carried his weapons,
"Come on, let's cross over to the garrison of these uncircumcised men.
Perhaps the Lord will help us. Nothing can keep the Lord from saving,
whether by many or by few." —1 Samuel 14:6

Further Scripture: Ephesians 3:20; Hebrews 11:1; James 2:14–17

Week 34, Day 233: 1 Samuel 15—16
God's Anointed King

In a battle against the Amalekites, Saul sinned and disobeyed the Lord's complete instructions. Because of his disobedience, the Lord rejected Saul as king of Israel. In the midst of Samuel's mourning and grief over Saul's sin and rejection as king, the Lord instructed Samuel to prepare to anoint the new king of Israel. The Lord selected David, who attended sheep and was the youngest, unassuming son of Jesse. The Lord chose David because of what He saw underneath that humble identity—David's heart. Samuel obediently anointed David, and the Spirit of the Lord took control of David from that day forward.

The Lord saw something in David no one else saw. Whereas people look at the visible, *the Lord sees the heart.* Jesus said life comes from the heart, and those with pure hearts will see God. If all you do is worry about your outward appearance, you are missing the point. Beauty can come and go, but the Lord praises a person who fears Him. Real beauty comes from within. Child of God, like David, you are anointed for the kingdom of God. The Lord just wants your heart. May the Lord renew your heart today as you seek Him.

But the Lord said to Samuel, "Do not look at his appearance or his stature, because I have rejected him. Man does not see what the Lord sees, for man sees what is visible, but the Lord sees the heart." —1 Samuel 16:7

Further Scripture: Proverbs 4:23; Proverbs 31:30; Matthew 12:34

Week 34, Day 234: 1 Samuel 17

Face the Giants

David had been anointed by Samuel to be the king of Israel, but he remained in the pasture tending the sheep. While bringing food to his brothers who served in the army, David heard about Goliath, and he saw the Israelites retreat in fear of him. However, David was not afraid of battling this giant warrior. David knew the same God who rescued him from the paw of a lion and the paw of a bear would rescue him from the hands of this Philistine. He walked in faith, he walked in his anointing, and he walked as God created him, trusting the Spirit of God to be with him. Using weapons he was familiar with—ones he had used for years while tending sheep, David found victory by defeating Goliath with just a slingshot and a stone.

Like David, it's time to face your giants. What is the overwhelming concern, or giant, you face that seems to get more difficult as time passes? It's time to recognize the Lord is with you and the victory belongs to Him. You are anointed with the power of the Holy Spirit, and through His power, you are able to overcome your giants. Stop standing on the sidelines. Go after it. The battle belongs to the Lord.

"The Lord who rescued me from the paw of the lion and the paw of the bear will rescue me from the hand of this Philistine." Saul said to David, "Go, and may the Lord be with you." —1 Samuel 17:37

Further Scripture: 1 Samuel 17:45–47; Psalm 18:39; 1 John 2:27

Week 34, Day 235: 1 Samuel 18
The Lord Was with David

Even though Saul was still king over the Israelites, he jealously watched David's success. This jealousy drove Saul's actions and decisions in dealing with David. He even attempted to kill David . . . not once but twice! Despite Saul's efforts, David continued to find success because the Lord's hand was upon him.

Envy is the pain you feel when someone achieves something you think belongs to you. Pause for a moment and think about that statement. Do a heart check for yourself for envy and jealousy. Is there someone in your life who, when you think about his or her situation, causes your heart to stir up with emotion? When you walk in the flesh, jealousy is a natural emotion. Confess this jealousy to the Lord. Let it go. Ask the Lord to fill you anew with His Spirit. As you walk in the power of the Spirit, the Spirit gives you the strength to overcome the flesh and experience freedom. Rather than experience jealousy, you experience joy for the other person and delight in others' success. *Lord, fill me anew with your Spirit, bringing me freedom to build up your kingdom.*

So Saul watched David jealously from that day forward.
—1 Samuel 18:9

Further Scripture: Psalm 25:4–5; Galatians 5:16, 19–20, 22–23; James 3:16

Week 34, Day 236: 1 Samuel 19—20
Covenant Relationships

Saul repeatedly attacked David, attempting to end David's life. But the Lord spared David. Saul's own son, Jonathan, loved David like a brother and helped protect him, even though it put his own life and his relationship with his father in danger. Jonathan even devised a plan to help David flee from Saul. Before parting ways, Jonathan and David made a covenant to watch over each other, even their future generations. Jonathan told David to go with the assurance (literally: "go in peace") because the Lord was with them. The two would always be friends.

The Lord sends you out with that same peace. The Lord watches over you in peace because you are in a covenant with Him. No matter what comes your way, *Jesus will give you peace*. He has already conquered the world, so His sons and daughters may be strong and courageous, even in the midst of suffering. He loves you, and He wants you to walk in the assurance of His love. There is so much in this world that is uncertain, but in Christ, you have assurance, no matter what.

Jonathan then said to David, "Go in the assurance the two of us pledged in the name of the Lord when we said: The Lord will be a witness between you and me and between my offspring and your offspring forever."
Then David left, and Jonathan went into the city. —1 Samuel 20:42

Further Scripture: John 16:33; Romans 5:1–3; Colossians 3:15

Week 34, Day 237: 1 Samuel 21—22
David's Journey through Israel

Knowing Saul wanted to kill him, David began a journey of fleeing from Saul in order to save himself. The Lord used specific people to speak into his life and direct him to the next location as he traveled from Nob to Gath, to the cave of Adullam, and to the land of Judah. David had an anointing on his life to be the king, but it wasn't an automatic, straight walk to the throne. It was quite the journey.

Have you ever thought about your own journey? The Holy Spirit guides the anointed and the Lord uses people to speak into your life. The journey may not always look like you expect. It will be filled with interesting stops and detours along the way. Remember to keep your eyes on Jesus. He will lead you where He desires you to serve in His kingdom. Talk with Him and trust Him as you go!

Then the prophet Gad said to David, "Don't stay in the stronghold. Leave and return to the land of Judah." So David left and went to the forest of Hereth. —1 Samuel 22:5

Further Scripture: Psalm 119:105; Proverbs 3:5–6; Hebrews 12:1–2a

Week 34, Day 238: 1 Samuel 23—24
Cutting Saul's Robe

Saul and his men were in pursuit of David when Saul needed to relieve himself. In God's sovereignty, out of all the caves available, they stopped by the cave in which David and his men were hiding. While Saul was inside the cave without his guards, he never realized David was there as well. At the encouragement of his men, David went to Saul and secretly cut off a corner of his robe. However, as soon as David took this action, his conscience bothered him because he lifted his hand against the Lord's anointed. In response, David told the men not to rise up against Saul, even though the king was right there in front of them. Rather, after Saul left the cave, David went out to him and honestly shared with Saul what he had done. He cleared his conscience, and, for a time, Saul and David were at peace with each other.

The Lord instructs His followers to live with a clear conscience—meaning to live free of guilt, without any hindrance in your relationship with God or anyone else. Stop for a minute and ask the Lord if there are any actions or words you need to confess. Ask the Lord to reveal to you how to make a situation right. He may lead you to go and ask for forgiveness. When you have the courage to clear your conscience, the Lord will relieve the weight you have been carrying. He brings freedom and has a way of working the situation out for good as you trust Him. God will meet you in that place of honesty with His unconditional love and grace.

Afterward, David's conscience bothered him because he had cut off the corner of Saul's robe. —1 Samuel 24:5

Further Scripture: Isaiah 53:7; 1 Peter 3:16; Acts 24:16

Week 35, Day 239: 1 Samuel 25
Rejection, Retaliation, and Refocus

After Israel mourned the death of Samuel, David went down to the Wilderness of Paran where he met a rich businessman named Nabal, who was probably at the peak of his sheep-shearing season. Yet Nabal refused to bless and provide food for David and his men, even after they had been kind to Nabal's shepherds. Nabal completely rejected David's request. David reacted to Nabal's rejection by organizing his men in an effort to retaliate and attack Nabal. However, the Lord intervened through Nabal's wife, Abigail. The Lord used Abigail's wisdom and determination to refocus David's attention back on the Lord. The Lord reminded David of His faithfulness and provided for all of David's needs.

Have you ever felt the gut-wrenching feeling of *rejection*? It's upsetting. You may feel as though you need to *retaliate* to prove a point, make it right, or even give the person what they deserve. Next time you feel like this, take a deep breath and *ask the Lord to help you refocus*. The Lord sees and knows the situation. He may send someone to help you or even turn the heart of the other person around. Instead of responding in anger and taking matters into your own hands, rest in the Lord, and peace will cover you as you wait. God has a way of working things out for good and not for evil when you wait upon Him. He will rescue you.

Then David said to Abigail, "Praise to the Lord God of Israel, who sent you to meet me today! Your discernment is blessed, and you are blessed. Today you kept me from participating in bloodshed and avenging myself by my own hand." —1 Samuel 25:32–33

Further Scripture: Proverbs 20:22; 1 Thessalonians 5:15; 1 Peter 3:9

Week 35, Day 240: 1 Samuel 26—27

God Is Faithful

Once again David found himself in a situation in which he could kill Saul. David knew that if he eliminated Saul, he would immediately ascend as king over Israel. Even so, David chose not to take God's plan into his own hands. David told his men not to destroy Saul, displaying his trust in God because he believed God's plan would prevail in God's timing. However, David did take Saul's jug of water and spear, proving to Saul his life had been spared. In taking the high road, David's actions brought forth Saul's conviction and confession. In turn, Saul blessed and honored David.

What is the "Saul" in your life? Is there something you could force to happen, knowing then you'd see God's promise happen quickly? In the moment, it may seem easier to take matters into your own hands. However, the Lord has a plan and timing for your life. If there is any question in your heart, then pause. As you walk in integrity, your plans will succeed with the Lord. Seek Him for direction. If the Lord has given you a promise for what is to come, then He has a plan for good. *He will bring to it to pass.* The Lord will bless the integrity of your heart.

May the Lord repay every man for his righteousness and his loyalty. I wasn't willing to lift my hand against the Lord's anointed, even though the Lord handed you over to me today. Just as I considered your life valuable today, so may the Lord consider my life valuable and rescue me from all trouble.
—1 Samuel 26:23–24

Further Scripture: Psalm 41:12; Proverbs 4:24–26; Hebrews 10:23

Week 35, Day 241: 1 Samuel 28–29
When Faced with a Dilemma

The Philistines came together as one army to fight against Israel and King Saul. When Saul saw them, he trembled with fear and inquired of the Lord. But the Lord was quiet and didn't answer him. In his fear and distress, Saul continued to search for direction. He disguised himself and, in the middle of the night, visited the home of a medium. He knew it was against the Lord to seek a medium, but he did it anyway. And what he heard did not make him feel any better. It actually brought him into even greater despair.

There are times in life when the Lord allows for quietness and does not give immediate answers. Even in quietness, even in the stillness, the Lord is with you. He has something for you to learn through the quiet seasons. Trust the Lord's timing and continue to seek Him. Like Saul, you may be tempted to look elsewhere for answers. Resist this temptation by standing firm in the Lord. However, if you find yourself disguised in the middle of the night seeking something or someone other than the Lord, *it is time to take off your mask.* Confess to the Lord. He will wash away every sin as far as the east is from the west. He will set you free. He is there to fight your battle because His love for you never ends. His mercies are new each morning.

When Saul saw the Philistine camp, he was afraid and trembled violently. He inquired of the Lord, but the Lord did not answer him in dreams or by the Urim or by the prophets. Saul then said to his servants, "Find me a woman who is a medium, so I can go and consult her." His servants replied, "There is a woman at En-dor who is a medium." Saul disguised himself by putting on different clothes and set out with two of his men. They came to the woman at night. —1 Samuel 28:5–8

Further Scripture: Lamentations 3:22–23; Psalm 103:12; James 1:14–15

Week 35, Day 242: 1 Samuel 30—31

The Shift in David's Leadership

David and his men arrived in Ziklag to discover that the Amalekites had raided the Negev and attacked and burned down Ziklag. Not only was everything destroyed, but their wives, sons, and daughters had been kidnapped. David and his men wept until they had no strength left to weep anymore. In David's deep grief over his loss, David found strength in the Lord. He turned to the Lord for direction and wisdom on what to do next. The Lord was faithful to give David clear direction and the promise of victory and restoration.

As you read David's story of loss, there's a good chance you can feel the pain in these words because you have walked through similar pain and loss. You can recall a time you wept so loudly and for so long that you got to a point you had no more tears. You may be going through a season of intense pain right now. Even in your misery, turn to the Lord for strength. He promises to strengthen you in your weakness. He promises to be near to the brokenhearted. He will comfort those who mourn. Ask Him for direction. He will give you the steps to take. In Jesus, He promises victory and restoration. Lift your head up and seek His face.

But David found strength in the Lord his God. . . . and David asked the Lord: "Should I pursue these raiders? Will I overtake them?" The Lord replied to him, "Pursue them, for you will certainly overtake them and rescue the people." —1 Samuel 30:6, 8

Further Scripture: Psalm 23:4; Psalm 32:8; Psalm 73:26

Week 35, Day 243: 2 Samuel 1—2
David's Second Anointing

After grieving, fasting, and mourning the death of Saul, even composing a song in his honor and teaching it to the Judahites, David went to Hebron as directed by the Lord. It was in Hebron that the men of Judah came to anoint David king over the house of Judah—over David's tribe only. Although David knew the Lord promised he would be king over all Israel, David waited with humility that honored Saul and trusted the Lord's timing for his appointed reign.

Waiting . . . no one likes to wait for anything. However, everything has a season. Every season has a purpose. The Lord doesn't waste the waiting season. *Growth happens when you wait.* You tend to want to rush or get immediate satisfaction. Yet the Lord's ways can often be slow and take time. Let the Lord's plan unfold in His way and in His time. Enjoy the process as you hold fast and trust His promises.

Therefore, be strong and courageous, for though Saul your lord is dead, the house of Judah has anointed me king over them. —2 Samuel 2:7

Further Scripture: Psalm 21:7; Psalm 27:14; Psalm 37:34

September 1

Week 35, Day 244: 2 Samuel 3—4

The Assassinations of Abner and Ish-Bosheth

Joab killed Abner. Rechab and Baanah killed Ish-bosheth. Then the three of them approached David, expecting him to be grateful these men were dead and no longer served as threats to the king. Instead, David had the opposite reaction. He was not grateful, and he grieved over the shedding of innocent blood. David sensed their motives. He cursed Joab's house and ordered Rechab and Baanah to be killed.

Why did they choose to murder? David knew these men had heart wounds from previous experiences and hadn't sought the Lord to heal their hurt, nor did they seek David's counsel.

You may find people rub you the wrong way and even hurt your feelings. If someone hurts you, do not let your wounded heart go untended. If you had a physical scrape from falling down, you would be certain to clean it out, treat it, and ensure no infection would manifest or grow larger. The same is true when others wound your heart. If a heart wound is left untreated, envy and bitterness can build up like an infection. In Joab, Rechab, and Baanah's case, their festered hearts led to murder. The Lord's love can heal your pain and bring hope to any situation. Today, if you have a heart wound you haven't tended to, ask the Lord to help you heal.

How much more when wicked men kill a righteous man in his own house on his own bed! So now, should I not require his blood from your hands and wipe you off the earth? —2 Samuel 4:11

Further Scripture: 2 Chronicles 7:14–15; Jeremiah 33:6; James 3:14–16

Week 35, Day 245: 2 Samuel 5—6

Bringing the Ark to Jerusalem

David brought the Ark of the Covenant to Jerusalem. As the Levites carried the Ark on their shoulders, David and the whole house of Israel celebrated with songs, instruments, lyres, harps, tambourines, and cymbals. David danced before the Lord with all his might. David's wife, Michal, saw her husband dancing in the Lord's presence and judged him as being a vulgar person. But David was not ashamed of his celebration in the Lord's sight.

The Lord longs for you to worship Him, not concerning yourself with what others may think. The Lord says that in His presence is fullness of joy. If worshipping the Lord makes you want to pick up your feet and twirl around, then do it! Worship the Lord because He has turned your lamenting into dancing! Don't worry about what others may think. He is worthy of it all and worthy to be praised! Offer your life to the Lord because He has removed your sackcloth and clothed you with gladness! You can sing and not be silent! Today, freely worship the Lord!

David replied to Michal, "I was dancing before the Lord who chose me over your father and his whole family to appoint me ruler over the Lord's people Israel. I will celebrate before the Lord, and I will humble myself even more and humiliate myself. I will be honored by the slave girls you spoke about."
—2 Samuel 6:21–22

Further Scripture: Psalm 16:11; Psalm 30:11–12; 2 Corinthians 3:17

Week 36, Day 47: 2 Samuel 7—8

David's Kingdom Is Forever

While King David reigned over Israel, he enjoyed rest inside the palace walls and began to make his own plans. However, the Lord used the prophet Nathan to share a vision and speak a word of counsel to David. After David received the word from Nathan, he spent time in the Lord's presence, remembering God's faithfulness and giving thanks. David heeded the words and direction from the Lord. He understood the eternal covenant with the Lord. Rather than pursuing his own plans, David followed the will of the Lord.

The Lord promises that when you trust in Him, He will direct your path. You may have an idea and begin to walk it out, but then God puts people or situations along your path to redirect or even postpone your plans. The Lord desires for you to be teachable and moldable. Don't be stubborn and set in your ways. Allow the Spirit of God to guide and direct you. And if you are questioning the change of plans, ask the Lord for confirmation. Then walk without wavering in confident faith. The Lord will determine your steps. His plans will prevail because His ways are higher than your ways, and His thoughts higher than your thoughts. Be assured through Christ you will have victory.

The Lord made David victorious wherever he went. So David reigned over all Israel, administering justice and righteousness for all his people.
—2 Samuel 8:14–15

Further Scripture: Proverbs 16:9; Isaiah 55:8–9; James 1:6

Week 36, Day 247: 2 Samuel 9—10

David's Grace to Mephibosheth

David wondered if anyone was left in Saul's family to show kindness to because of his dear friend Jonathan. Saul's servant, Ziba, remembered Saul's crippled grandson Mephibosheth, who lived far away in Lo-de-bar. David had Mephibosheth brought to him, and Mephibosheth arrived afraid of why David had requested his presence. David assured him to not be afraid and welcomed Mephibosheth to eat every meal at his table and promised to restore Saul's fields to him. These were unexpected and untypical gifts to give a crippled person like Mephibosheth.

David offered Mephibosheth unmerited favor—God's grace. Mephibosheth did nothing to deserve it, and yet David sought him out, lavishing upon him lovingkindness. Friends, the same is true for you. The Lord chased after you and drew you to His love. The Lord's love is not based on your good works but because God the Father sees you and calls you His child. You are freely and wholly adopted into His kingdom and welcomed at the Lord's table. *He loves you just as you are*, imperfections and all, and He will lavish upon you good and perfect gifts. Today, receive His grace. He has a seat ready for you at His table, just sit down and enjoy His presence day after day!

David said, "Mephibosheth!" "I am your servant," he replied.
"Don't be afraid," David said to him, "since I intended to show you
kindness because of your father Jonathan, I will restore to you all your
grandfather Saul's fields, and you will always eat meals at my table."
—2 Samuel 9:6–7

Further Scripture: Romans 8:15; Ephesians 1:5; Titus 3:4–5

September 5

Week 36, Day 248: 2 Samuel 11—12

David's Progressive Slide into Secret Sin

While David's men were in battle, David chose to remain in Jerusalem. He was away from his army, his team, and his routine. In this situation, David committed adultery with Bathsheba, Uriah's wife. As a result, Bathsheba conceived a child, causing David to devise plans to cover up his sin of adultery. However, those plans didn't work. So David plotted for Uriah to be killed on the front lines of battle. One sin led to another. David may have thought he had deceived those around him, as he ended up marrying Bathsheba and having a son, but the Lord saw it all. The Lord saw exactly what David was doing in secret, and although David's eternal covenant would not change with the Lord, David would face consequences of his sin.

Secret sin. You may think no one knows. You take a break from your regular routine, step away from your team, your group, your people … and temptation hits you. The enemy knows your weaknesses, and he wants to disarm your power in the kingdom. If you are in the middle of a secret sin, you need to know the Lord sees you. You may think you are hidden, but the Lord knows. However, despite your sin, He loves you. Just as He did not break covenant with David, He does not break covenant with you. However, *it is time to stop hiding*. God's grace is always available, and His mercies are new each morning. Allow light to shine in the secret places of your life. Confess to the Lord, then share with a trusted person in your life, and turn away from the wicked ways. Free yourself of secrets, and you will find an abundant life with Christ!

"You acted in secret, but I will do this before all Israel and in broad daylight." David responded to Nathan, "I have sinned against the Lord." Then Nathan replied to David, "The Lord has taken away your sin; you will not die." —2 Samuel 12:12–13

Further Scripture: Psalm 69:5; James 5:16a; 1 John 1:9

Week 36, Day 249: 2 Samuel 13—14
The Sins of David's Sons

David's son, Amnon, had lustful desires for his half-sister, Tamar. Rather than seeking the counsel of someone who walked uprightly with the Lord, Amnon shared his feelings with his shrewd cousin, Jonadab. Then Jonadab devised a plan for Amnon to be alone with Tamar. The plan worked, enabling Amnon to act on his lustful feelings by raping his sister. As things unfolded, Amnon was later murdered by his brother Absalom in revenge. David's family found themselves in chaos. Rather than flee the temptation to sin, Amnon gave into it, and its effects cascaded through several families.

Believers are to stand firm and not give into temptation. You are instructed to *flee* from your fleshly desires. Fleeing involves speed and effort. You flee when a situation is dangerous and you need to get away quickly. Fleeing sexual immorality may mean quickly leaving a room to get away from someone you know may lead to lustful thoughts or actions. It may mean leaving your computer, TV, or phone if you have a temptation to view pornography. You resist the temptation. Then you align yourself with people who will encourage you to stand strong and seek the things of Christ. *The Lord has given you strength and power to stand strong, and His Spirit is great within you for help and guidance.* Call upon the name of the Lord. You will be stronger when you flee.

When she brought them to him to eat, he grabbed her and said,
"Come sleep with me, my sister!" —2 Samuel 13:11

Further Scripture: 1 Corinthians 6:18; 2 Timothy 2:22; 1 Peter 2:11

Week 36, Day 250: 2 Samuel 15—16
Exhausted from the Enemy Attacks

As David and his men journeyed away from the palace, a man named Shimei, son of Gera, began to yell curses at David. He even threw stones and dirt at David. David and his men were exhausted from the journey and from the stress Shimei caused them, so they stopped to rest.

Can you imagine having stones and dirt thrown at you or curses yelled at you while on a journey? If you stop for a minute and think about it, you probably can relate. Think about your own walk with the Lord and the insults or the lies from the enemy that have come your way. These lies can beat you down to the point of exhaustion, leaving you with no strength to stand. However, the Lord promises that, in your weakness, you are made strong through His sufficient grace. So in the midst of any attack thrown at you, draw strength from the Lord and His truth. Remember your anointing from the Lord. When you embrace your anointing, no matter what comes your way, you will be able to stand strong. The Lord triumphs over the enemy and has the victory!

So David and his men proceeded along the road as Shimei was going along the ridge of the hill opposite him. As Shimei went, he cursed David, and threw stones and dirt at him. Finally, the king and all the people with him arrived exhausted, so they rested there. —2 Samuel 16:13–14

Further Scripture: 2 Corinthians 12:7b–10; Colossians 2:15; 1 John 2:20

Week 36, Day 251: 2 Samuel 17—18

Run to Deliver Good News

Absalom, the son of King David, died in battle as David's troops pursued Israel. In response, Joab blew the ram's horn to assemble the troops, signaling the battle was over. Afterwards, the men gathered to discuss who would go and share the news with King David. Two men wanted to run to share the "good news." Each man ran a different route, arrived at different times, and conveyed the same "good news" but did so in different ways. Neither runner shared the "good news" directly or truthfully to King David. Although David's kingdom was restored because of the victory in battle, he was deeply grieved by the "good news" his son had died.

As followers of Christ, the Good News you carry is about the death of *the* Son. Even though Jesus' death grieved God the Father, it brings victory and hope as it covers the sins of those who believe. Will you deliver the good news directly and truthfully? The truth is God loved the world so much He gave His one and only Son so that everyone who believes in Him will not perish but have eternal life. This is the good news about the death of *the* Son you are called to deliver for the glory and honor of God's kingdom! Today, put on your running shoes and deliver the good news of the Gospel!

The watchman saw another man running. He called out to the gatekeeper, "Look! Another man is running alone!" "This one is also bringing good news," said the king. —2 Samuel 18:26

Further Scripture: John 3:16; Romans 10:15; 1 John 4:10

Week 36, Day 252: 2 Samuel 19—20

Reasserting His Kingship

As David began to walk out his calling as king, not only was his kingdom restored, but so were his relationships. Joab, the commander of David's army, spoke truth into David, rebuking him in the midst of grief over the loss of his son. Then Shimei, son of Gera, apologized for the curses and insults he made. In humility, David showed forgiveness to both men. Mephibosheth, whom David believed had betrayed him, came forward and shed the light of truth onto the false reality portrayed by his own servant, Ziba. David showed Mephibosheth understanding. David showed appreciation toward an eighty-year-old man named Barzillai for his support. In all these interactions, David displayed grace and truth, bringing restoration to each relationship as he walked forward in his calling as king. The Lord blessed him for his obedience.

God is a God of restoration. He has restored you, a sinner, into a right relationship with His Son Jesus. As you walk into your calling as a child of God, an heir in the kingdom of God, who has been anointed for such a time as this, the Lord will restore those things in your life that were once broken. Walk out your calling with humility and love. Today, pause and ask the Lord for restoration in your own heart, in your relationships with others, or even in your relationship with Jesus. He will personally *restore, establish, and strengthen you.* May your life be a testimony of the Lord's restoration power of making all things new!

They forded the Jordan to bring the king's household across and do whatever the king desired. —2 Samuel 19:18

Further Scripture: Galatians 6:1; Ephesians 4:1; 1 Peter 5:10

Week 37, Day 253: 2 Samuel 21—22

God Answered David's Prayers

For three years during David's reign, Israel experienced famine. David inquired of the Lord as to why they had to endure this season of suffering. The Lord explained it was because Saul and his family killed the Gibeonites. In response, David humbly went to the Gibeonites, asking what he could do to make the situation right. David agreed to do what the Gibeonites requested. After this act of atonement from David, the Lord answered David's prayer for the land, and the famine ended.

Have you ever asked the Lord why you are experiencing a season of suffering? Or why a loved one is enduring such pain? Or why your child has to walk a particularly difficult road? The key to remember during times of suffering is to ask the Lord for guidance and help *immediately*. Jesus promises to work all things together for the good of those who place their trust in Him. When you turn to the Lord, He will help you and give you the strength to endure. He may lead you to repent or to rely more on Him and not on yourself, but He will always be there to help you. If you are facing a time of suffering today, may you hold on to the hope that the Lord is with you and that you are not alone in your suffering.

During David's reign there was a famine for three successive years, so David inquired of the Lord. The Lord answered, "It is because of the blood shed by Saul and his family when he killed the Gibeonites." —2 Samuel 21:1

Further Scripture: 2 Corinthians 1:8–9; Philippians 3:10; Hebrews 12:7a, 11

Week 37, Day 254: 2 Samuel 23—24

David's Anointed Mighty Men

David was safe and surrounded by his thirty-seven mighty men. He was older in years, and he had found victory in battle. Yet for some reason David foolishly gave into the temptation to take a census of all people in Israel and Judah. This brought about God's anger, and David knew it. David's conscience troubled him, and he had great anxiety. In response, David went before the Lord in repentance, asking how to make things right again. As a consequence, the Lord brought about a nationwide plague that killed seventy thousand people. In the end, the Lord finally answered David's request, and the plague ended.

Have you ever had that feeling that you knew something just wasn't right? Are you overcome with anxiety or having a hard time sleeping at night? Are you replaying the same situation in your mind over and over? Stop and seek the Lord. Ask the Lord if you have you gone astray and have troubled Him. If so, the Holy Spirit will convict you of your sin. Your sense of conviction won't go away until you repent. However, the Lord is all-knowing and all-loving. Turn to the Lord to make things right and ask for forgiveness. He will clear your mind from the heaviness you feel and lighten your load. Today, give thanks for His forgiveness and mercy. And remember, nothing will ever separate you from His love.

David's conscience troubled him after he had taken a census of the troops. He said to the Lord, "I have sinned greatly in what I've done. Now, Lord, because I've been very foolish, please take away Your servant's guilt."
—2 Samuel 24:10

Further Scripture: Romans 9:1; Ephesians 2:4–5; 1 Peter 3:16

Week 37, Day 255: 1 Kings 1
Solomon's Anointed Reign

King David was confined to his room due to old age. It was here the prophet Nathan and Bathsheba visited him to share the news about Adonijah, David's son, who was exalting himself as David's successor and conspiring and gathering people to support him as king. Without hesitating, King David swore an oath that it was Solomon who would become king after him. He ordered Nathan and Zadok the priest to anoint Solomon. The people celebrated Solomon, their new king, as he rode through town on David's mule. That is, everyone celebrated but Adonijah, who now feared for his own life. However, Solomon granted mercy and forgiveness towards Adonijah for the prideful actions taken against him. The Lord's hand was upon Solomon.

In many ways, Solomon can be compared to Jesus. Solomon was celebrated while riding on a mule, was anointed as king, had great wisdom, and showed mercy and forgiveness. Even so, Jesus is *greater* than Solomon. Jesus came riding on a donkey as the people shouted, "Hosanna." Jesus, the Anointed One, forgives all your sins, offering grace, mercy, and eternal life. Jesus is the King of kings and the Lord of lords. Today, worship the Lord. Bow down before Him. Step away from the things of this world and pour your heart out to the one who saved you from death. He is worthy of your praise. He is the Almighty One!

The king swore an oath and said, "As the Lord lives, who has redeemed my life from every difficulty, just as I swore to you by the Lord God of Israel: Your son Solomon is to become king after me, and he is the one who is to sit on my throne in my place, that is exactly what I will do this very day."
—1 Kings 1:29–30

Further Scripture: Matthew 12:42; John 14:12; 1 Timothy 6:15–16

◇

Week 37, Day 256: 1 Kings 2
David's Last Words

In King David's final days, he gave Solomon instructions as king from the Law of Moses: "Be strong and courageous, keep your obligation to the Lord, walk in His ways, and keep His statutes, commands, ordinances, and decrees. If you follow the Law of Moses, you will have success in everything you do and wherever you turn." Then David gave an account of a few men and their past actions towards him, instructing Solomon to keep an eye on them. After David died, Solomon heeded his father's words, walking in authority and wisdom as king while keeping his heart set the Lord.

Like Solomon and the Israelites, you know the Word of God. You know His truth and His instructions to walk in the ways of the Lord. And now, through believing in Jesus, you have eternal life. You have received His grace, and you are able to walk daily in the power of the Holy Spirit who is inside you. Are you walking in His Truth? At times, it can be easy to let the truth go in one ear and out the other. But before you know it, you have conformed to the ways of the world. Slowly, other gods become more important than the one true God, your Messiah, Jesus Christ. Your Heavenly Father has instructed you, like David did to Solomon—*walk in His ways.*

As for me, I am going the way of all of the earth. Be strong and be courageous like a man, and keep your obligation to the Lord your God to walk in His ways and to keep His statutes, commands, ordinances, and decrees. This is written in the Law of Moses, so that you will have success in everything you do and wherever you turn. —1 Kings 2:2–3

Further Scripture: Psalm 119:1; Proverbs 23:26; Romans 12:2

Week 37, Day 257: 1 Kings 3–4
Solomon's Wisdom

The Lord appeared to Solomon in a dream and said, "Ask. What should I give you?" Solomon asked for wisdom, explaining he desired to have an obedient heart to judge the people and to discern between good and evil. The Lord was pleased with Solomon's request. As Solomon walked out his calling as king, it became evident to all Israel that the Lord gave him the wisdom he requested. Because he humbly asked for wisdom, the Lord also granted Solomon riches and honor and blessed him abundantly.

Today, if you could ask God for anything, what would you ask for? A new house? A mended relationship? Healing from a disease? The possibilities could go on and on. But have you ever asked the Lord for wisdom? Start today. As you approach the moments of your day, ask the Lord for wisdom in making decisions both large and small. From what to eat, where to work, how to parent your teenager, what to say to a friend in a troubled marriage, or who to share the Gospel with—*ask Him.* The Lord wants to bless you generously with wisdom.

So give Your servant an obedient heart to judge Your people and to discern between good and evil. For who is able to judge this great people of Yours?
—1 Kings 3:9

Further Scripture: Proverbs 4:6–7; James 1:5; James 3:17

Week 37, Day 258: 1 Kings 5—6
Solomon's Temple

When a season of rest came for King Solomon and Israel, he began to build a temple so the presence of God could have a permanent dwelling place. Solomon used craftsmen and a gifted work force to create the temple. In the midst of construction, the word of the Lord came to Solomon, reaffirming the Lord's desire: "If you walk in My statutes, observe My ordinances, and keep all My commands by walking with them, then I will fulfill My promises to you." God did not say only that if the temple had ornate paneling and gold floors, then He would keep His promises. No, the Lord reaffirmed that His desire was for Solomon to walk in His ways.

The Lord said your body is now the temple of the Holy Spirit. The Spirit of God dwells within you. The Lord has not asked you to fix yourself up beautifully on the outside to be pleasing to Him. The Lord asks you to follow His ways. True beauty comes from within. Today, ask yourself, *"Am I focusing more on the construction on the outside of my temple or on following the Spirit of God who resides on the inside?"* As you walk in His ways, beauty from the inside will shine to the outside.

The word of the Lord came to Solomon: "As for this temple you are building—if you walk in My statutes, observe My ordinances, and keep all My commands by walking in them, I will fulfill My promise to you, which I made to your father David. I will live among the Israelites and not abandon My people Israel." —1 Kings 6:11–13

Further Scripture: Isaiah 66:2; 1 Corinthians 3:16; 1 Corinthians 6:19–20

Week 37, Day 259: 1 Kings 7
Extravagant Distraction

Not only did Solomon spend seven years building the Temple, he also took thirteen years building an elaborate palace complex for himself and his family. In the middle of discussing the details of the Temple, the resting place for the presence of the Lord, details of the palace complex are intricately described. And then the final details of the Temple are outlined and the construction was completed. Solomon was assigned by God to build a Temple for the presence of the Lord to reside, and then, in the midst of Temple construction, he built an even larger and extensive palace complex.

Do you ever get sidetracked while in the presence of the Lord? You may be having prayer time or reading His Word, when suddenly you click on social media or you find yourself dreaming about where to go shopping or wondering who won the latest football game? The world has so many things to distract you that it can be hard to stay focused on the Lord. The Lord says to set your mind on things above, not on earthly things. Seek first the kingdom of God and His righteousness, and then all these things will be added to you. As you rest and focus in His presence, you will experience the fullness of joy. You may look to the things that sidetrack you for peace, but when it comes down to it, *it's only when you focus your mind on Christ that He will keep you in perfect peace.* Today, stay focused on Christ.

Solomon completed his entire palace complex after 13 years of construction.
—1 Kings 7:1

Further Scripture: Proverbs 5:1–2; Isaiah 26:3; Colossians 3:1–2

Week 38, Day 260: 1 Kings 8
The Dedication of the House of God

Solomon dedicated the newly constructed Temple to the Lord. On his knees, Solomon testified and praised the Lord for His faithfulness and petitioned for the Lord to restore His people. With his hands spread out toward heaven, Solomon stood before the Lord, blessed the Temple, and experienced fellowship in the Lord's presence.

As you come before the Lord in prayer, think about your posture. It is okay to physically kneel or physically stand, expressing your devotion to the Lord. Today, take a minute to kneel or bow your head to the ground in adoration. Perhaps you feel led to walk outside and look at His mighty creation with your hands stretched toward heaven. Thank Him for His faithful promises in your life. Just as there are times when you need to get down on the floor to talk with small children, something happens in your heart when you lower yourself before the Lord and talk with Him. Don't worry about what others may think. Enjoy this fellowship with your Heavenly Father.

When Solomon finished praying this entire prayer and petition to the Lord, he got up from kneeling before the altar of the Lord, with his hands spread out toward heaven, and he stood and blessed the whole congregation of Israel with a loud voice: "May the Lord be praised! He has given rest to His people Israel according to all He has said. Not one of all the good promises He made through His servant Moses has failed." —1 Kings 8:54–56

Further Scripture: Psalm 134:1–2; Daniel 6:10; Revelation 7:11

Week 38, Day 261: 1 Kings 9—10

Jesus Is Greater than Solomon

The Temple and King Solomon's palace were completed and dedicated. Now Solomon grew his kingdom with wisdom from the Lord. He so surpassed all the kings of the world in riches and wisdom that the Queen of Sheba came to confirm that what she had heard about King Solomon was true. Solomon's kingdom took her breath away because, yes, the things she had heard were true. Solomon's kingdom was great indeed, and even his servants were happy.

What if you received a visit from someone to see if the things said about you were true? Would their visit make you nervous or would you be free to say, "Come on in!"? The Lord desires for you to live your life with integrity and a clear conscience so when a surprise visit happens, your life will reflect the words of your mouth. But what if the "surprise visitor" finds something you'd rather he or she not know about? Take a deep breath. It's okay. Because someone greater has come since King Solomon—someone named Jesus. Yes, Jesus knows everything about your life. He knows where you struggle, and He is there to walk with you. He loves you through it. When you surrender your life to Christ, He provides the grace you need to press on and keep walking. Rest in His greatness today. There is no reason to strive in your own power for perfection in this world because His grace is great within you!

She said to the king, "The report I heard in my own country about your words and about your wisdom is true. But I didn't believe the reports until I came and saw with my own eyes. Indeed, I was not even told half. Your wisdom and prosperity far exceed the report I heard. How happy are your men."—1 Kings 10:6–8

Further Scripture: Matthew 12:42; 2 Corinthians 8:9; 1 John 4:4

Week 38, Day 262: 1 Kings 11—12

Solomon Sinned against God

Solomon appeared to be at the peak of his reign. He had more wisdom and riches than anyone else in the world. But then his heart got sidetracked, and he willingly disobeyed the Lord. He accumulated seven hundred wives and three hundred concubines who seduced Solomon to follow other gods and turned his heart away from the Lord. Solomon did evil in the Lord's eyes, and the Lord became angry with him. Solomon's kingdom began to fall apart. The Lord asked Solomon to keep his eyes on Him alone, but as time went on, Solomon strayed, wanting more and more of that which wasn't of the Lord.

The things of this world will seduce you into wanting more. But it doesn't just happen overnight. Daily, small choices you make against the Lord's way will sidetrack your heart. Before you know it, you have built your own kingdom, your own ways, and your own people. Be careful! Allow Solomon's life to be a warning to you. The gate leading to life is narrow and difficult. In order to keep walking through the narrow gate, renew your mind in Christ. Meditate on His Word. Find fellowship with other believers. Remember, you are anointed to walk in the truth, not the lies of this world. Jesus is enough to satisfy your soul.

He had 700 wives who were princesses and 300 concubines, and they turned his heart away from the Lord. When Solomon was old, his wives seduced him to follow other gods. He was not completely devoted to Yahweh his God, as his father David had been. —1 Kings 11:3—4

Further Scripture: Matthew 7:13—14; Romans 12:2; 1 John 2:27

Week 38, Day 263: 1 Kings 13—14
The Deception of the Man of God

During Jeroboam's reign as king, a man of God came to Jereboam with a revelation from the Lord. When this word actually happened, King Jeroboam invited the man of God to his home, offering the man refreshment and a reward. However, the man of God refused because God told him not to eat bread or drink water. In this instance, the man of God was obedient to the Lord's specific direction and was steadfast in his walk. But later, when an old prophet went after the man of God and also asked him to come back with him for bread and drink, the man of God returned. At this point, he disobeyed the voice of the Lord, and as a result, he faced deadly consequences.

As you walk with the Lord, you need to trust His voice in your life and stick to it. Jesus says, "My sheep hear Me and know My voice." Others may speak into your life, *but if you know what you heard from the Lord, don't be easily persuaded by others.* If someone tells you to do something or has a word for you, listen to it. But before you react or respond, take some time to ask the Lord to confirm it through His Word, through others, and by giving you peace. If it goes against what the Lord is saying to you, don't compromise or let it persuade you. The Lord will honor your obedience to His voice in your life.

But he answered, "I cannot go back with you, eat bread, or drink water with you in this place, for a message came to me by the word of the Lord: 'You must not eat bread or drink water there or go back by the way you came.'" —1 Kings 13:16–17

Further Scripture: Isaiah 30:21; John 10:27; Galatians 5:7–8

Week 38, Day 264: 1 Kings 15—16
Good or Evil in God's Sight

Following the reign of several kings who did what was evil in the eyes of the Lord, King Asa took the throne. King Asa reigned for forty-one years and did what was right in the Lord's sight. He banished male cultic prostitutes, removed all idols, and even dealt with generational sin by removing his grandmother as queen mother, by chopping and burning down her obscene images. In other words, King Asa removed anything not pleasing to God, except for the high places. King Asa's heart was devoted to God his entire life.

King Asa went into his grandmother's home and found obscene images. Would the King of kings find anything in your home that needs to be removed? As you reflect, think about items or activities that may have become idols in your life: a TV show, gaming for long hours, an app on your phone, or clothes in your closet. Maybe there is an activity you partake in because all the generations of your family have, but you know it is evil in the eyes of the Lord. Ask the Lord today: *"Is there anything in my home I need to remove in order to keep my heart completely devoted to You?"* Then, in obedience, remove whatever the Lord reveals to you.

Asa did what was right in the Lord's eyes, as his ancestor David had done.
—1 Kings 15:11

Further Scripture: Romans 6:1–2; Matthew 6:21; 1 Corinthians 8:5–6

Week 38, Day 265: 1 Kings 17—18

The Coming of Revival

After three years of hiding during a famine, the Lord sent Elijah to present himself to Ahab, saying God would finally send the rain. Before King Ahab and all the people of Israel, Elijah courageously prayed to the God of Abraham, Isaac, and Jacob to send rain so the people would know Yahweh was God. First the people prayed to Baal for it to rain, but Baal did not answer. The Lord, however, answered in a mighty way. Yahweh sent fire to fall and consume the burnt offering. When the people saw this, they exclaimed, "Yahweh, He is God! Yahweh, He is God!" And then, after Elijah bowed before the Lord on his knees, the Lord answered with a downpour of rain throughout the land! After three years, water returned, and the people witnessed a mighty act from Yahweh!

The Lord calls you to live courageously and boldly for Him. He desires for you to live with His power, not in your own strength, but instead fully relying on God. This begins with prayer. It begins with asking the Lord to show His power in your life. *What are you praying boldly about today?* You can ask God because you know God hears you. Be courageous and believe the Lord will answer your prayer. And when He answers your God-sized prayer, testify to others how great God is in your life! There is no other God like your God.

Then Yahweh's fire fell and consumed the burnt offering, the wood, the stones, and the dust, and it licked up the water that was in the trench. When all the people saw it, they fell facedown and said, "Yahweh, He is God! Yahweh, He is God!" —1 Kings 18:38–39

Further Scripture: Isaiah 45:5–6a; Micah 7:7; 1 John 5:14–15

Week 38, Day 266: 1 Kings 19—20

Get Up and Eat!

Though the prophet Elijah saw the Lord move in a miraculous, powerful way when it finally rained after three years of drought, the enemy was able to discourage him. He became afraid and ran for his life. Elijah journeyed to the wilderness alone, sat under a tree, and prayed he would just die. He said to the Lord, "I have had enough!" But then an angel showed up and told him, "Get up and eat or the journey will be too much for you." The angel provided food and water for Elijah to eat and drink. Elijah regained strength and began the new journey the Lord called him to.

Have you ever found yourself at the point in your ministry, your job, your family, or your marriage where you've said, "I have had enough!" When you do, here's the promise to remember: Even when you think you are at the end and the enemy has convinced you there's no way out, *do not give up. There is always hope.* In Elijah's weakness, the Lord provided truth, food, water, and an angel to say, "Get up!" Today, you may need to hear these words: *Get Up!* Or maybe, you need to say those words to a friend who is in despair. The Lord will provide even when you think you are at the end of your rope. Don't lose hope. The Lord will lift you up and help you regain your strength to stand strong again. You can do this through Christ who gives you strength.

But he went on a day's journey into the wilderness. He sat down under a broom tree and prayed that he might die. He said, "I have had enough! Lord, take my life, for I'm no better than my fathers." Then he lay down and slept under the broom tree. Suddenly, an angel touched him. The angel told him, "Get up and eat." —1 Kings 19:4–5

Further Scripture: Psalm 28:7; Psalm 73:26; Isaiah 40:31

Week 39, Day 267: 1 Kings 21–22

Godly Alignment

Judah's King Jehoshaphat walked in the ways of his father King Asa and did what was right in the eyes of the Lord. However there were times when Jehoshaphat would make a decision on his own and then include the Lord in His plan. When facing battle, King Jehoshaphat first aligned with King Ahab, who was not a man of God and then, afterwards, sought the Lord for direction. King Jehoshaphat lacked care in determining with whom to align himself, ultimately compromising what he believed.

As you walk with Christ, the enemy wants to distract you and entice you to walk away from the Lord. Be careful with whom you align yourself. When you align yourself with people who are not seeking the Lord, they can distract you and point you away from Christ. However, when you take the time and align yourself with like-minded believers, you sharpen one another. Today, take a minute to think about the people in your life you turn to for counsel. Are they walking with the Lord or walking in their own ways? If you are walking with Christ, be sure to hold on to His truth and His ways.

The king of Israel said to Jehoshaphat, "There is still one man who can ask Yahweh, but I hate him because he never prophesies good about me, but only disaster. He is Micaiah son of Imlah." "The king shouldn't say that!" Jehoshaphat replied. —1 Kings 22:8

Further Scripture: Proverbs 27:17; 2 Corinthians 6:14; 1 John 4:1

Week 39, Day 268: 2 Kings 1—2

Passing the Mantle

Elisha never left the side of his mentor Elijah. Even when Elijah told him over and over to "stay here," Elisha remained by his side, traveling with him. Finally Elijah looked at Elisha and said, "Tell me what I can do for you before I am taken from you?" Elisha could have asked for anything from Elijah, and he asked for a double portion of God's power that was evident in Elijah. After the Lord took Elijah to heaven in a whirlwind, Elisha picked up his predecessor's mantle and began walking out the miraculous power of God. It became evident the Lord answered Elisha's request.

Everyone who believes in Jesus has received His mantle—the full anointing of the Holy Spirit. As you walk by Jesus' side daily, remember you are anointed for the kingdom of God, and *His power resides in you.* When you hunger and thirst for righteousness, *the Lord promises you will be filled.* As you are filled up with Him, your life will display His power. Walk out His power with confident trust in the Lord.

---

*After they had crossed over, Elijah said to Elisha, "Tell me what I can do for you before I am taken from you." So Elisha answered, "Please, let me inherit two shares of your spirit." —*2 Kings 2:9

Further Scripture: Psalm 63:1; Matthew 5:6; 1 John 2:20

Week 39, Day 269: 2 Kings 3

Ready with a Word

Elisha walked with the Lord and was therefore ready with a Word when called upon by the kings of Judah, Israel, and Edom as they headed into battle with Moab. The Lord's hand came on Elisha, and he spoke out confidently. However, the armies did not listen to the Word from the Lord completely. As a result, not only did they not receive the complete benefit, but the Lord chose to show His wrath to them.

Are you walking with the Lord so that when you need to make a decision or talk with someone about Jesus, you are ready to proclaim the truth? Like Elisha, the Lord's hand will be on you. He is always with you, and His power is within you. In Christ, you are to be alert at all times. Today, take the time to spend with the Lord and read His Word so you will be ready. Then, be confident as the Lord guides you and opens opportunities for you to speak for Him.

But Jehoshaphat said, "Isn't there a prophet of the Lord here? Let's inquire of Yahweh through him." One of the servants of the king of Israel answered, "Elisha son of Shaphat, who used to pour water on Elijah's hands, is here." Jehoshaphat affirmed, "The Lord's words are with him." So the king of Israel and Jehoshaphat and the king of Edom went to him.
—2 Kings 3:11–12

Further Scripture: Isaiah 64:8; Luke 21:36; 1 Peter 3:15

Week 39, Day 270: 2 Kings 4
Limited Only by Faith

The Lord used the prophet Elisha to display His miraculous power. The Lord filled jar after jar after jar of oil, delivering a miraculous provision for the widowed woman and her sons. The Lord recognized the hospitality of the Shunammite woman, allowing her and her older husband to conceive their first son. And even when the son died, Elisha called upon the Lord to breathe life back into the boy and raise him from the dead. Then through God's power, Elisha turned a deadly stew into a healthy, life-giving stew. Through the Lord, Elisha multiplied bread for one hundred men to eat and even had leftovers. In all of these situations, the Lord provided when there seemed to be no way.

God is a God of miracles—yesterday, today, and tomorrow. Believers are able to call upon His name and believe for His power to work in ways you cannot imagine, in His time and in His way. Hold fast to the faith and believe He is at work, even if you don't see evidence of it. Maybe today, you need to hear this truth so your hope remains steadfast. Continue to press in and believe that He is able to heal, provide, comfort, and strengthen you. He promises He will never leave you, so keep on holding on to Him by faith.

The woman conceived and gave birth to a son at the same time the following year, as Elisha had promised her. —2 Kings 4:17

Further Scripture: Jeremiah 32:27; Matthew 17:20; Acts 3:16

Week 39, Day 271: 2 Kings 5—6

Humble Obedience Leads to Radical Transformation

Naaman, the commander of the army for King Aram and a brave warrior, had a skin disease. In faith, Naaman's wife's Israelite servant girl boldly spoke up and shared about a prophet in Samaria who could heal Naaman. So Naaman traveled to see this prophet named Elisha. Elisha instructed Naaman, "Go wash seven times in the Jordan and your flesh will be clean." After refusing to follow Elisha's instructions at first, Naaman humbled himself, got over his pride, and walked in obedient faith. In doing so, he was completely healed. Elisha told him to go in peace. Naaman didn't have to pay Elisha for the healing; he only had to walk in humble obedience.

Are there any areas in your life where you need to swallow your pride, walk in humility, and obey the Lord? Today, you may need to hear, "Humble yourself and just do it." Whatever you feel the Lord asking you to do, walk it out in faith. It may not be hard, heroic, or complicated. *The Lord doesn't ask you to be fancy, He just asks for humble obedience.* When you walk in faith and in obedience to the Lord, His peace will wash over you, and He will receive the glory.

But his servants approached and said to him, "My father, if the prophet had told you to do some great thing, would you not have done it? How much more should you do it when he tells you: 'Wash and be clean'?" So Naaman went down and dipped himself in the Jordan seven times, according to the command of the man of God. Then his skin was restored and became like the skin of a small boy, and he was clean. —2 Kings 5:13–14

Further Scripture: Psalm 25:8–9; Psalm 115:1; Micah 6:8

Day 272: 2 Kings 7—8
Sit and Die or Go and Discover

Four lepers sat outside the wall of Samaria during a time of great famine. They recognized they had no option but to die. However, they had an idea and said, "Why just sit here until we die? If we say, 'Let's go into the city,' we will die there because the famine is in the city, but if we sit here, we will also die. So now, come on. Let's go to the Arameans' camp. If they let us live, we will live; if they kill us, we will die." And so they went to the Arameans' camp, and to their surprise, the Lord had caused the Arameans to flee in fear, leaving all kinds of treasure and provisions. The lepers hid what they found until their consciences caught up with them. They ultimately decided to go and tell the king's household the good news, so they too could reap the benefits!

This is a story of salvation. You are dead in your sins. Without Christ, you face hopelessness and death. You have a choice to sit and die in your sin, or get up and go discover the riches of grace, hope, love, and eternal life found in Jesus. To receive Jesus' grace, *you have to get up from the place of normalcy and go see what the Lord has for you.* When you believe what you have found in Jesus, you will become alive, made whole, and be healed. This good news is not just for you to receive but is for others as well. Go and tell others about these powerful riches found in Jesus alone.

Then they said to each other, "We're not doing what is right. Today is a day of good news. If we are silent and wait until morning light, our sin will catch up with us. Let's go tell the king's household." —2 Kings 7:9

Further Scripture: Mark 16:15; Romans 6:23; Ephesians 2:7

Day 273: 2 Kings 9—10

Don't Let Sin Remain

Elisha anointed Jehu as king of Israel. After killing King Joram, King Ahaziah, and Jezebel, King Jehu went on to kill the entire house of Ahab and all the Baal worshippers. Although King Jehu said he was zealous for the Lord and succeeded in killing and eliminating much of the evil, he never fully removed one sin—worshipping the golden calves. This sin remained in Israel.

Jesus came to set us free from the bondage of sin. He longs for you to surrender your whole life to Him. The Lord's grace covers you, and His love can't be separated from you. However, when you hang onto a pocket of sin, you miss out on the complete freedom in Christ. Because of Christ, there really is no sin worth hanging on to. What do you need to eliminate completely from your life today? Say, *"Lord, have it all."* Receive His grace, walk in the Spirit moment-by-moment, and you will not carry out the deeds of your flesh.

Jehu eliminated Baal worship from Israel, but he did not turn away from the sins that Jeroboam son of Nebat had caused Israel to commit—worshiping the gold calves that were in Bethel and Dan.
—2 Kings 10:28–29

Further Scripture: John 3:36; John 8:36; Galatians 5:1

Week 40, Day 274: 2 Kings 11—12

Waiting on the Lord's Timing

When Ahaziah's mother Athaliah discovered her son was dead, she killed all other heirs in line for the royal throne. Then she seized the throne for herself and served as queen of Judah for six years. However, a brave woman named Jehosheba secretly rescued and hid the young boy Joash, one of Ahaziah's sons. In the seventh year, the high priest Jehoiada revealed the secret that David's seed had survived—seven-year-old Joash was alive! They crowned and anointed Joash as king, and he took his rightful place on the throne. All the people rejoiced, and Athaliah was put to death.

For seven years, Joash remained hidden from the people of Judah. If he had not had this time in hiding, he may never have been crowned king of Judah. *Have you ever been through a season of hiddenness?* Maybe today, you know the Lord has called you to something, but you can sense the time has not yet come. You are in a place of hiding, a place of waiting, a quiet season. From the outside, no one may see or understand, but inside your heart, you know the Lord is preparing you for what lies ahead. Rest in Him. Don't force it. Don't push it. Trust God is at work in the hiddenness. As you wait, draw near to God, and He will draw near to you.

Joash was in hiding with Jehosheba in the Lord's temple six years while Athaliah ruled over the land. —2 Kings 11:3

Further Scripture: Ecclesiastes 3:11; Lamentations 3:25–27; Hebrews 6:12

Week 40, Day 275: 2 Kings 13—14
Awaken Dry Bones

Elisha was God's chosen prophet who had been given a double portion of the power that was within Elijah. Anointed for his calling, Elisha had God's great power within Him in miraculous ways. When Elisha passed away, his body was buried. In the spring of that year, the Israelites were burying a man but were caught off guard by a Moab raiding party, so they just threw the dead body into Elisha's tomb. When the dead body touched the bones of Elisha, the man was revived and stood up! The Lord had one more miracle that displayed His power and strength through the life and death of Elisha!

The Lord promises to wake up the things that are dead—to wake up the dry bones. As a follower of Christ, you have this same resurrection power inside you. What if someone bumped into you? Would they even know you are alive in Christ? Jesus came to bring *life* to all who will receive it. Today, live bursting with the love of Jesus and let it be contagious to those who bump into you as you live out your day. May today be a day of awakening the dry bones all around us!

Once, as the Israelites were burying a man, suddenly they saw a raiding party, so they threw the man into Elisha's tomb. When he touched Elisha's bones, the man revived and stood up!
—2 Kings 13:21

Further Scripture: Job 33:4; Ezekiel 37:5; John 5:21

October 3

Week 40, Day 276: 2 Kings 15—16

Defiling the Temple

Years before King Ahaz ruled Judah, the Lord instructed King Solomon on the specifics for His Temple—the permanent place for Yahweh's presence to dwell and where the people could go and worship Him. Even so, King Ahaz aligned himself with the king of Assyria and began to make changes to the Temple. He disregarded the previous instructions from the Lord. He removed side paneling, removed a reservoir, removed the Sabbath canopy, and removed the king's outer entrance. King Ahaz wanted to satisfy the king of Assyria more than Yahweh God.

When you seek to satisfy the world, you will begin changing things about yourself. The world will try to allure you, tempt you, and distract you from focusing on the Lord. You may slowly begin to remove parts of your life that represent Christ. The changes may seem small at first, but what you begin to do on the outside reflects the inside condition of your heart. If you remove things representing Christ, then you are most likely replacing them with things that are not of Christ. Today, ask yourself: *Are you living to satisfy the world's standards or walking in the ways pleasing to the Lord?*

To satisfy the king of Assyria, he removed from the Lord's temple the Sabbath canopy they had built in the palace, and he closed the outer entrance for the king. —2 Kings 16:18

Further Scripture: Psalm 84:10; Galatians 1:10; 1 Thessalonians 2:4

Week 40, Day 277: 2 Kings 17—18

Doing Evil in God's Sight

Israel became obstinate and did not believe in the Lord their God. They rejected His covenant, pursued worthless idols, abandoned His Word, worshipped heavenly hosts, served Baal, made cast images for themselves, and practiced divination, among other things. Ultimately, they devoted themselves to what was evil in the Lord's sight and provoked the Lord to anger. At last, the Lord had enough. In His anger, the Lord removed Israel from His presence. Only the tribe of Judah remained as the surviving seed for the coming Messiah.

Are you different from Israel? The people took their eyes completely off the Lord, His ways, His Word, His commands. They did whatever they wanted and found themselves back in bondage. *Are you any different?* Jesus came to set the captives free. Jesus came to bring you hope and a future. Jesus came to break you from bondage and give you freedom. Jesus came to offer you life and not death. *Where have you taken your eyes off the Lord?* Be honest with yourself and ask the Lord to reveal any area where you have gone astray. Surrender and confess it to the Lord. Then ask Him to set you free. He will bring you freedom just as He promises. He is such a faithful God!

They devoted themselves to do what was evil in the Lord's sight and provoked Him. Therefore, the Lord was very angry with Israel, and He removed them from His presence. Only the tribe of Judah remained.
—2 Kings 17:17–18

Further Scripture: Luke 4:18; Acts 26:18; 2 Corinthians 3:16–17

Week 40, Day 278: 2 Kings 19—20

God Gave Hezekiah a Second Chance

King Hezekiah became terminally ill. The prophet Isaiah told Hezekiah to get his affairs in order because he would not survive the illness. In this moment, Hezekiah turned to the Lord. He wept bitterly and asked the Lord to remember him and his faithful walk through life. Soon after this prayer, the Lord changed the course for Hezekiah's life. The word of the Lord came to Isaiah saying Hezekiah would be healed in three days. However, the Lord granted Hezekiah fifteen more years of life, allowing him to see victory in Assyria. The Lord heard Hezekiah's prayers and answered him.

Has there been a time in your life when you were hit with a difficult life circumstance and you sought the Lord in prayer? A surprise health report? A loss of a job? Unexpected news about your child? The Lord sees your tears. He hears your prayers. He is able to work in ways you can't imagine. Today, *seek the Lord in prayer*. He wants you to cry out to Him, and His ears are always open. No matter how big or little the need may be, if it is important to you, it's important to the Lord. He is there to lift you up and rescue you. The Lord came to redeem and is the God of second chances.

Then Hezekiah turned his face to the wall and prayed to the Lord,
"Please Lord, remember how I have walked before You faithfully and
wholeheartedly and have done what pleases You."
And Hezekiah wept bitterly. —2 Kings 20:2–3

Further Scripture: Psalm 66:17–18; 1 Peter 3:11b–12; 1 John 5:14

Week 40, Day 279: 2 Kings 21—22
The Beginning of Revival

Josiah was eight years old when he became king, and he reigned for thirty-one years. King Josiah did what was right in the Lord's sight and did not turn to the right or to the left. During Josiah's reign as king, as repairs were being made to the Temple, the Book of the Law was discovered and read in the presence of the king. When King Josiah heard the words of the Lord, he humbled himself and asked the Lord for help in understanding. Josiah longed to know more about the Lord's heart for His people, and his desire to follow the Book of the Law impacted an entire nation.

The Word of God is living and effective. It is used for teaching, rebuking, correcting, and training in righteousness so that you may be complete and equipped for *every* good work. The Word of God is a light to your feet and a lamp to your path. Most likely, you have the Word of God at your disposal wherever and whenever you want. *And yet, why is it so hard to read each day?* Today, open the Word of God and read His words. Be aware of the enemy's plans and schemes to keep you from reading the Word of God. Fight through the schemes and take time to open the Word of God. Your life will be transformed.

Go and inquire of the Lord for me, the people, and all Judah about the instruction in this book that has been found. For great is the Lord's wrath that is kindled against us because our ancestors have not obeyed the words of this book in order to do everything written about us. —2 Kings 22:13

Further Scripture: Psalm 119:105; 2 Timothy 3:16–17; Hebrews 4:12

Week 40, Day 280: 2 Kings 23
The Spirit of Revival

After Josiah read the Word of the Lord, it changed his life and prompted him to take action. He gathered all the elders, priests, prophets, and people from young to old, and he read to them all the words of the book of the covenant that had been found in the Temple. Then King Josiah made a covenant to follow the Lord and keep His commands, decrees, and statues with all his mind and all his heart. He vowed to carry out the words in the covenant, and all the people agreed! Following this commitment, King Josiah began removing, cleaning, burning, smashing, slaughtering, and tearing down anything that defiled God. The Word of God truly transformed this community!

It is time. It is time for revival in the nation, in the world, in your community, in your family, and in your life. Let the Word of God radically transform your life. As you read the Word and follow the Lord's way, think about what idols, images, or things in your life that need to be removed and torn down. Take action, and do the work. Purify yourself. May you live in the same boldness as King Josiah. *Do not hold back.* Start reviving your heart today through the Word of God, and take action!

In addition, Josiah removed the mediums, the spiritists, household idols, images, and all the detestable things that were seen in the land of Judah and in Jerusalem. He did this in order to carry out the words of the law that were written in the book that Hilkiah the priest found in the Lord's temple. Before him there was no king like him who turned to the Lord with all his mind and with all his heart and with all his strength according to all the law of Moses, and no one like him arose after him. —2 Kings 23:24–25

Further Scripture: Acts 28:31; 1 John 5:21; Revelation 21:27

Week 41, Day 281: 2 Kings 24—25

Temple Destruction

King Nebuchadnezzar of Babylon entered Jerusalem and destroyed everything—the Lord's Temple, the king's house, all the great houses, and the wall of Jerusalem. Everything the Lord instructed King Solomon to build during the Davidic covenant came to an end. *Everything.* Year after year, the kings had done what was evil in the Lord's eyes by welcoming activities into the Temple that were not of the Lord. As a result, everything man built ended in complete destruction, and the Jewish captives were exiled to live and serve in Babylon.

As a follower of Christ, holy and beloved, your body is the temple of the Lord. His presence abides inside you, and you are to present your bodies as a living sacrifice to Him. *What are you allowing into your temple?* The Lord says to dwell on whatever is true, honorable, just, pure, lovely, commendable, and of moral excellence. Because the Lord desires you to flourish, He instructs you to put to death the things that defile your temple, such as sexual immorality, impurity, lust, evil desire, and greed. Be aware of these things! Over time, if allowed in your temple, these activities will bring destruction in your life. In the moment, what you give up may seem like a sacrifice, but it is your act of worship to the Lord and is well worth the discipline. May the Lord bless you abundantly as you preserve your body, the temple of the Lord!

Indeed, this happened to Judah at the Lord's command to remove them from His sight. It was because of the sins of Manasseh, according to all he had done. —2 Kings 24:3

Further Scripture: Romans 12:1; 1 Corinthians 3:16–17; Colossians 3:5

October 9

Week 41, Day 282: 1 Chronicles 1
Christ's Genealogy

As the people of Israel returned to Jerusalem after exile in Babylon, they reconnected with their identity as the people of God's family. The genealogical review reminded them of their history and how God's hand had been on every single person through each generation. Each name in the lineage of Jesus, the Son of David, carries the significance of God's faithfulness, redemption, and calling. Whether they sought the Lord or rejected His ways, the Lord used their lives to carry on the seed of Christ.

Today, take a minute to reflect on your family heritage. As you reflect, you may feel a pit in your stomach, thinking of difficult times, or you may have all warm, cozy memories. Either way, the Lord used your family line to get you where you are today. The Lord is a God of restoration. The Lord is calling you to an identity in Him. As you trust Him, you are His. No matter what your family line may say, you are a child of God, and He is your Heavenly Father. He is writing your story. He has plans for your life and a purpose for *you*. Give thanks for the past and walk in your identity as God's chosen child.

Adam, Seth, Enosh, Kenan, Mahalalel, Jared, Enoch, Methuselah, Lamech, Noah, Noah's sons: Shem, Ham, and Japheth. —1 Chronicles 1:1–4

Further Scripture: John 1:12; 2 Corinthians 6:18; Galatians 3:26

Week 41, Day 283: 1 Chronicles 2

You Are Important

The list of names in the genealogy continues, remembering Israel's sons and Judah's descendants. Each name represents a family: a daughter, a son, a mother, a father. Each name represents a person in the Israelites' rich history. By listing the names, the chronicler confirmed the importance of reflecting on the families, making them known to the Israelites as they came out of exile. From Reuben to Perez to Caleb, each family and person pointed to the coming Messiah.

Just like each person recalled to the Israelites after their exile, *you too are important.* You may need to hear that today. You are a brother, a sister, a wife, a husband, a mother, a father. You build, you teach, you operate technology, you research, you do laundry, and you are important to the Lord and to His kingdom. Many have gone before you, playing a role in the kingdom of God. But *now* it's your time. Don't believe the lie that you are not important to the Lord. He created you. He loves you. He believes in you. So stand up tall and do the thing He called you to. The King, the Messiah, is coming back, and you have a role in ushering Him in as you live your life for Him and Him alone!

These were Israel's sons: Reuben, Simeon, Levi, Judah, Issachar, Zebulun, Dan, Joseph, Benjamin, Naphtali, Gad, and Asher.
—1 Chronicles 2:1–2

Further Scripture: Isaiah 43:1–2; Romans 12:11–12; Hebrews 9:28

Week 41, Day 284: 1 Chronicles 3
Preserving the Seed

Recalling the genealogy to the Israelites continues with David's descendants and Judah's kings. The names continue to point to the line of Christ and the seed preserved through the family of David and the tribe of Judah. Each person listed is a real person with a real story and real sin issues. However, they are not remembered by their sin but by preserving the seed of the Messiah.

You are not defined by your sin. Yes, the Lord hates sin, but Jesus came to free you from the bondage of sin and death and to give you life and a future. As you look at the family line of David, remember the seed of Jesus was preserved through the son of David. That is the key. God's hand was upon this family, just as the Lord's hand is upon you as His child. You may fall into sin. However, as you seek Jesus and turn away from sin, you receive His forgiveness. In Christ, you will find hope and freedom from sin. Don't dwell on the sin of your past; instead, allow the beautiful redemptive story of Jesus to shine through your life. God promises to work all things together for His good. He promises to bring beauty from ashes. *He promises redemption.* Let your name tell the story of redeeming love for His glory!

Six sons were born to David in Hebron, where he ruled seven years and six months, and he ruled in Jerusalem 33 years. These sons were born to him in Jerusalem: Shimea, Shobab, Nathan, and Solomon. These four were born to him by Bath-shua daughter of Ammiel. —1 Chronicles 3:4–5

Further Scripture: Ephesians 1:7–8; Philippians 3:13–14; 1 John 1:9

Week 41, Day 285: 1 Chronicles 4

The Prayer of Jabez

Jabez lived as an honorable man and prayed in faith as he called out to the God of Israel. In his prayer, Jabez asked the Lord to bless him and extend his borders. He asked for God's hand to be upon him to experience even more of the Lord's presence in his life. He asked for protection. Jabez talked to the Lord because he wanted to experience more of God in his life.

How do you pray? *Do you pray in faith and ask for more of the Lord's presence in your life?* Jabez's prayer isn't a formula. Rather, it is an honest man seeking more of the Lord's presence in his life. *Isn't that what you want?* Today, call out to the Lord. Ask Him to bless you and expand the borders in your life. Ask the Lord for protection. The Lord says He is your refuge and your stronghold. He will shelter you in His wings. The Lord says to call upon Him. He will answer you in His timing, so *trust him* as you cry out!

Jabez called out to the God of Israel: "If only You would bless me, extend my border, let Your hand be with me, and keep me from harm, so that I will not cause any pain." And God granted his request. —1 Chronicles 4:10

Further Scripture: Psalm 37:23; Isaiah 54:2; Jeremiah 33:3

Week 41, Day 286: 1 Chronicles 5
Cry Out in Battle

As the chronicler continued to remember the past generations, he wrote about Jacob's oldest son, Reuben, who lost his birthright after defiling his father's bed. Although he certainly sinned against God, Reuben's past did not define him, and the Lord didn't give up on him or his descendants. Later the sons of Reuben, Gad, and half of Manasseh waged war against the Hagrites, Jetur, Naphish and Nodab. During this battle, they received help from God because they cried out to Him. They found victory in the battle because they presented their requests to God and trusted Him.

Every day your spiritual enemy, the devil, wages war against you as you follow Jesus. *Do you ever wonder how to fight the battle?* Follow the example of the tribes of Reuben, Gad, and Manasseh, and *cry out to the Lord in battle.* Humble yourself before the Lord, admitting you don't have the strength to fight. Ask God to come to your side, and He will deliver you. He promises you will have victory in Him. Just go to Him. Don't let the sins of your past define you or keep you from asking the Lord for help. He loves you and nothing separates you from His great love. Allow Jesus to be Lord of your life, and He will give you victory in your battles.

They received help against these enemies because they cried out to God in battle, and the Hagrites and all their allies were handed over to them. He granted their request because they trusted in Him.
—1 Chronicles 5:20

Further Scripture: Psalm 20:7; Psalm 34:4; 1 Corinthians 15:57

Week 41, Day 287: 1 Chronicles 6

Territories and Assignments

As the chronicler continued reminding the Israelites of their past, the different roles of the Levites and Aaron's descendants were highlighted. Some were tabernacle service workers, some were priests, and some were musicians—each had a role. The chronicler reestablished truth for the Israelites about the different settlements for the Levites, assigning them to specific territories.

It is important to remember God's heartbeat is to point to the coming Messiah. Today, each follower of Christ has a unique role in specific territories. The Lord has given you a territory—a home, a workplace, a community, an organization. In your territory, you shine the light and love of Christ to those around you. In addition, He has called you to a unique role. So sing and make music, clean toilets, teach Scripture, cook, write the business plan, train up your children in the way they should go—ultimately, lead others to worship Jesus, the one true Savior and Son of God. Jesus says, *"Just worship Me."* Do the thing you do, in the place you do it, for the glory of God.

Their relatives, the Levites, were assigned to all the service of the tabernacle, God's temple. But Aaron and his sons did all the work of the most holy place. ... These were the places assigned to Aaron's sons from the Kohathite family for their settlements in their territory, because the first lot was for them. —1 Chronicles 6:48–49, 54

Further Scripture: Psalm 100:2–3; Romans 12:4; Ephesians 2:10

Week 42, Day 288: 1 Chronicles 7
A Warrior for Christ

The chronicler brings attention to the powerful number of warriors in the tribes of Issachar, Benjamin, and Asher as they continue to specifically list out the genealogy. The tribes trained several warriors in preparation for battle.

The Lord calls you, as a follower of Christ, as a warrior in the battle you face each day. The word *warrior* means "a person engaged or experienced in warfare; a soldier; a person who shows or has shown great vigor, courage, or aggressiveness; one who is brave." You can wake up each day saying, "*I am a warrior for the Lord! I am ready for battle.*" Remember, greater is He who is in you, than He who is in the world. Do not be afraid of what your days may hold because you are equipped with the armor of God, the power of God, and the grace of God. God clothes you in strength and subdues your enemies beneath you. Take heart, mighty warrior! No weapon formed against you will prosper. Today, walk in this powerful truth, and you will have victory in Jesus' name.

During David's reign, 22,600 descendants of Tola were recorded as warriors in their genealogies. —1 Chronicles 7:2

Further Scripture: Psalm 18:39; Isaiah 54:17; 1 John 4:4

Week 42, Day 289: 1 Chronicles 8
A Choice to Walk

As you read through Benjamin's descendants, you review who they were, who their fathers were, and where they came from. The tribe of Benjamin included King Saul, the first anointed king of Israel. However, the tribe of Judah anointed King David, which ultimately led to the throne of Jesus. Pause for a minute and think about the contrast between the tribe of Benjamin and the tribe of Judah. Think about David and Saul, both anointed as kings over God's people. King Saul chose to walk in evil ways, whereas King David walked in the ways of the Lord.

As anointed children of God, you have a choice to walk in the Spirit or walk in the flesh. Walking in the Spirit bears the fruit of the Spirit: love, joy, peace, patience, kindness, goodness, faithfulness, gentleness, and self-control. Walking in the flesh may lead to works of the flesh like lust, pride, idolatry, outbursts of anger, selfish ambition, envy, and drunkenness. *How are you walking?* The Lord says to remain in Him. As you spend time with Christ, praying and reading God's Word, you will begin to bear the fruit of the Spirit. Ultimately, the world will know you are a follower of Christ by your love as you remain in Christ. The Lord promises when you walk in the Spirit, you will not give way to the temptations of the flesh.

Ner fathered Kish, Kish fathered Saul, and Saul fathered Jonathan, Malchishua, Abinadab, and Esh-baal. —1 Chronicles 8:33

Further Scripture: Galatians 5:19–21a, 22–23a; 1 John 2:6

Week 42, Day 290: 1 Chronicles 9
Embrace Your Role

The kingdoms of Judah and Israel were no longer divided. They returned to Jerusalem after the seventy-year exile in Babylon to rebuild the temple. The first to return to live in towns on their own property were the Israelites, the priests, the Levites, and the temple servants. The chronicler outlines each role used to rebuild the temple—a distinct calling and act of obedience for this time in history.

As a follower of Christ in the kingdom of God, you have a specific role. In His body, He has chosen some to be apostles, teachers, evangelists, shepherds, and prophets for the training up of the saints for the work of the ministry. Each role serves one another as they work together in unity to build up the body of Christ. Today, *embrace the role you have been asked to do with humility*. Serve one another—no matter the task and no matter the role. Whether you are seen or unseen, work with all your heart as though working for the Lord, not for people. When you embrace what you have been asked to do for the Lord with a selfless attitude, you will experience the Lord's presence in your life and abundant joy and peace.

The first to live in their towns on their own property again were Israelites, priests, Levites, and temple servants. —1 Chronicles 9:2

Further Scripture: Romans 15:25; Ephesians 4:11–12; Colossians 3:23

Week 42, Day 291: 1 Chronicles 10
Saul's Eulogy

In just a few sentences, the chronicler summarizes King Saul's life for the people of Israel. It's like they wrote a eulogy of Saul's life.

As you read this summary of Saul's life, think about what your eulogy would be. If your life ended tomorrow, how would people describe you in a few sentences? Are you living your life the way you hope to be remembered? Live your life with no regrets. Don't hold back. Don't wait for tomorrow. Be who the Lord created you to be. Go and do the thing on your heart you've wanted to do but just haven't yet. Reach out to that friend. Forgive that person. Have that party. Go after that career change. Stop the busy schedule, and spend your day in solitude with Jesus. Just do it! As you do, trust in the Lord with all your heart, and follow Him. Let go of the fear, and live in faith. Walk humbly with your God. Jesus will hold you in His loving hands. Go for it!

Saul died for his unfaithfulness to the Lord because he did not keep the Lord's word. He even consulted a medium for guidance, but he did not inquire of the Lord. So the Lord put him to death and turned the kingdom over to David son of Jesse. —1 Chronicles 10:13–14

Further Scripture: Psalm 118:24; Psalm 119:73–74; Micah 6:8

Week 42, Day 292: 1 Chronicles 11—12

Being a Mighty Man

When David ruled as king, not only was he anointed, but he also surrounded himself with thirty mighty men. These men allowed David to grow more powerful in his calling as king. These mighty men stood apart from others as formidable warriors. They overcame the odds by faith and their commitment to endure tiredness. For example, Benaiah killed a lion in the snow, and Jashobeam wielded his spear against three hundred, killing them at one time! These mighty men were committed to take the initiative, show loyalty, and selflessly serve their king, regardless of the cost. For instance, three men went out to the frontlines to get water for a thirsty King David, risking their lives for his needs.

Like the mighty men, you are called to full devotion to the Lord, the King of kings. The Lord doesn't ask you to follow Him because of a tradition or because it will get you something. Rather, *you follow Jesus out of a wholehearted love for Him.* He asks you to deny yourself, pick up your cross, and follow Him. Love Jesus with all your heart, soul, and mind. You may look different from the crowd. You may stand alone. You may have to overcome great odds. You may grow weary. But … the Lord promises you can do anything through Christ who gives you strength.

The following were the chiefs of David's warriors who, together with all Israel, strongly supported him in his reign to make him king according to the Lord's word about Israel. —1 Chronicles 11:10

Further Scripture: 1 Kings 8:61; Matthew 16:24; Philippians 4:13

Week 42, Day 293: 1 Chronicles 13—14

Face Your Enemy

David faced his enemy the Philistines with confidence that the Lord had established him as the king over Israel. Even though David heard the Philistines had searched for him, he faced them boldly. Then David inquired of the Lord about going to war with the Philistines. The Lord said, "Go, and I will hand them over to you."

Like David, God has established you. He made you, called you, equipped you, and empowered you to face your enemy. Fear may say to back down, go hide, or let someone else face it, but confident faith in the Lord speaks truth into your soul. As a child of God, you are more than able to face your enemy. Ask the Lord to replace each lie with a truth from His Word. You are more than able because He will abundantly do more than you can even dream or imagine. The same power that raised Jesus from the dead is in you. You are perfectly and wonderfully made. In Jesus, there is victory. Pray at all times as you walk this out with confidence in the Lord. He will hand your enemy over to you in Jesus' mighty name!

When the Philistines heard that David had been anointed king over all Israel, they all went in search of David; when David heard of this, he went out to face them. —1 Chronicles 14:8

Further Scripture: Proverbs 16:7; Acts 4:13; Romans 8:11

Week 42, Day 294: 1 Chronicles 15–16
David Danced before the Lord

Three months after David's first attempt to move the Ark of the Covenant to Jerusalem, he attempted the move again. This time David inquired of the Lord and prepared a place for the Ark. As the people walked through the streets, they danced, celebrated, and worshipped the Lord. At the same time, Michal, David's wife and Saul's daughter, sat near her window and looked down on King David celebrating in the streets. As they moved the Ark, she despised David in her heart.

The presence of God moves when His people seek Him. You can either jump in and be a part of it or sit on the sidelines. Where are you? Do you judge those walking with the Lord in the fullness of joy? Do you watch others enjoy their lives with Jesus as they walk in faith, while you drown in fear and bitterness? It's never too late to make the choice to come to Jesus and enjoy His presence. Jesus loves you. Let go of control. Let go of fear. Let go of pride. As you release these things, allow Him to fill you up with His great love, peace, and joy. Walk in humility and seek the Lord. When you seek Him, you will find Him, so seek Him with all your heart.

As the ark of the covenant of the Lord was entering the city of David, Saul's daughter Michal looked down from the window and saw King David dancing and celebrating, and she despised him in her heart.
—1 Chronicles 15:29

Further Scripture: Psalm 16:11; Jeremiah 29:13; John 3:17

Week 43, Day 295: 1 Chronicles 17—18
Go and Sit

David desired to build a permanent home for the Lord to dwell in. However, through a word given to the prophet, Nathan, God shared a different plan for David and for who would build His permanent dwelling place. After King David heard the word, he *went and sat in the Lord's presence* where he thanked and worshipped the Lord. Then David petitioned the Lord for further fulfillment of His promises.

When you hear from the Lord, however He speaks to you, take the time to *go and sit* in His presence. Maybe you have a favorite chair or a prayer closet. Maybe you need to sit in your car a little longer before walking into the house or office. Maybe you need to go for a walk alone. Wherever the place, abide and rest in Him. Today, if you have a burden, a decision to make, or the Lord has redirected the desires of your heart, *go and sit* in the Lord's presence. As you sit, give thanks to the Lord, praise His name, and then ask Him to fulfill His promises in your life.

Then King David went in, sat in the Lord's presence, and said, Who am I, Lord God, and what is my house that You have brought me this far?
—1 Chronicles 17:16

Further Scripture: Psalm 103:1–2; Mark 6:31; John 15:5

Week 43, Day 296: 1 Chronicles 19—20
Not Alone in the Battle

The Arameans lined up in battle formation in front of Joab, the commander of the Israelite army. And then Joab noticed the Ammonites were lined up in battle behind him as well. He chose some men to fight the Arameans in front and placed the rest of the forces under the command of his brother to engage the Ammonites coming from behind the army. He told his brother, "Be strong! If the battle gets too much for me, *then you'll be my help,* and if the battle is too much for you, then *I'll help you!*" The Lord brought them victory in this battle.

As believers in Christ, the Lord promises you will face spiritual battles. Through these battles, you may feel exhausted or even angry with the Lord and feel as though you have no strength to keep going. In these moments, remember you are never alone. The Lord is always with you, and you have brothers and sisters in Christ to help you fight the battle, to pray for you, to strengthen you with words of encouragement, and to remind you of Truth. Whatever you face today, humble yourself and reach out to a friend. Share with them if the battle is too much for you alone, and *ask for help.* Be strong in the Lord, and trust He will bring you victory.

"If the Arameans are too strong for me," Joab said, "then you'll be my help. However, if the Ammonites are too strong for you, I'll help you. Be strong! We must prove ourselves strong for our people and for the cities of our God. May the Lord's will be done." —1 Chronicles 19:12–13

Further Scripture: Isaiah 43:2; Galatians 6:10; Philippians 2:4

Week 43, Day 297: 1 Chronicles 21—22
The Price of Pride

David was victorious in battle and accumulated more troops. During this season of success, Satan tempted him with the desire to count the people of Israel. The Lord never commanded David to count the people, and it was evil in His eyes. Although God's great mercies ultimately saved Israel, the sin of pride still impacted the nation, and seventy thousand Israelite men died. After this, David continued serving the Lord in humility and obedience because of God's forgiving love and mercy.

Pride often presents itself as a hidden, private sin. It can show up in different ways—too proud to ask for help, too good to do certain tasks, being critical of others, disregarding the advice of others, or being pre-occupied with your physical appearance. Just as David's pride affected and almost destroyed a nation, your pride has the ability to greatly impact the lives of others. However, there is still hope. As you walk with Jesus, He desires for you to make every effort to live humbly and unselfishly. *Ask the Lord if you have any prideful areas in your heart.* Then confess this sin and ask for forgiveness. As you allow His grace and mercy to infiltrate your life, the Lord will create in you a clean heart filled with grace and love for others.

Satan stood up against Israel and incited David to count the people of Israel. So David said to Joab and the commanders of the troops, "Go and count Israel from Beer-sheba to Dan and bring a report to me so I can know their number." ... David said to God, "I have sinned greatly because I have done this thing. Now, please take away Your servant's guilt, for I've been very foolish." —1 Chronicles 21:1–2, 8

Further Scripture: Philippians 2:3; James 4:6; 1 John 1:9

Week 43, Day 298: 1 Chronicles 23—24

The Power of a Plan

King David outlined the Levite's specific assignments and roles for the temple, a permanent home for the presence of the Lord. The Levites received new assignments because transporting the tabernacle was no longer needed. In the temple, they would assist the sons of Aaron with the service. Specifically, it was important to have regular temple music. Therefore, every morning and evening, they were instructed to stand and give thanks and praise to the Lord.

As New Testament believers, the Lord's presence is with you always. He promises to never leave you. The Lord delights when you praise and give Him thanks. He tells you, "In everything give thanks." Today, be intentional! Make it a priority to stand up in the morning and give thanks and praise to the Lord! Then do it again in the evening. Perhaps before you eat dinner, take five minutes to stand up and tell the Lord why you are thankful for the day and give Him praise! Sometimes life can get mundane. Sometimes life is just plain hard. But through it all, the Lord's presence remains with you. So *stop, stand up, and give Him praise!* Today is going to be a great day in the presence of the Lord!

They are also to stand every morning to give thanks and praise to the Lord, and likewise in the evening. —1 Chronicles 23:30

Further Scripture: Psalm 9:1; Psalm 95:2–3; Matthew 28:20b

Week 43, Day 299: 1 Chronicles 25—26
Receiving God's Blessing

The chronicler remembered Obed-edom, recalling how God had *blessed him*. Obed-edom, a gatekeeper by profession, joined the musicians as they carried the Ark of the Covenant to Jerusalem. This gatekeeper/musician had eight sons, and the chronicler recorded sixty-two *capable men* as descending from Obed-edom.

Children are a gift from the Lord, a heritage, and a reward. The Lord delights in the concept of family, and as followers of Christ, He calls you His son or daughter. Perhaps the concept of family stirs up difficult emotions, and you feel pain or recall hurt. Today, ask the Lord to begin to heal this area of your life and bring about reconciliation. On the other hand, perhaps you have children, and you need to pause today and thank the Lord for the gift of children. Maybe you need to ask the Lord for fresh wisdom in parenting and in training them up in the Word of God. Through all the emotions the idea of family and children bring, you are called to give thanks and rejoice. *The Lord sees you and will bless you as you depend upon Him* entirely for the needs of your children and even for your deepest pain. He is working, even when you can't see Him. His love is everlasting.

Obed-edom also had sons: Shemaiah the firstborn, Jehozabad the second, Joah the third, Sachar the fourth, Nethanel the fifth, Ammiel the sixth, Issachar the seventh, and Peullethai the eighth, for God blessed him.
—1 Chronicles 26:4–5

Further Scripture: Psalm 127:3–5; Matthew 5:3; Romans 12:18

Week 43, Day 300: 1 Chronicles 27—28

Passing on the Plans of the Temple

King David gathered the leaders, commanders, officials in charge of all the property and cattle, the court officials, the fighting men, and the brave warriors. When they were all together, King David rose and humbly shared his heart. He talked honestly and vulnerably. He explained how it was on his heart to build the temple, but God said He had a different plan. Therefore, David yielded to the Lord and His plans for the temple.

Have you ever been so burdened *in your heart* to do something and yet the Lord suddenly redirected your plans? You may have been passionately moving along in one direction, and then you have a "but God said to me" moment like David. Therefore you yielded to God's new plan and accepted it. It may not have made any sense. It may have even seemed goofy to those on the outside. But you knew the Lord was redirecting you, and you couldn't delay responding to His leading and guidance. You dropped the pride. You stopped worrying what others might think. And you obediently followed His voice. This may even be what you need to do today. Remember, He will not fail you when you follow Him. Trust Him with all your heart, and don't depend on your own understanding. He will direct your path as you walk humbly, depending on the Lord.

Then King David rose to his feet and said, "Listen to me, my brothers and my people. It was in my heart to build a house as a resting place for the ark of the Lord's covenant and as a footstool for our God. I had made preparations to build, but God said to me, 'You are not to build a house for My name because you are a man of war and have shed blood.'"
—1 Chronicles 28:2–3

Further Scripture: Proverbs 3:5–6; Proverbs 16:9; Romans 12:2

Week 43, Day 301: 1 Chronicles 29
Finding Delight in the Lord

Before the temple building began, King David spoke to the assembly and explained the task was great because it was for the Lord, not man. King David provided for the expenses as best he could but also approached the leaders and asked them to set money aside as well. As people who worshipped and delighted in the Lord, they answered David's plea for resources. Then the people rejoiced and worshipped the Lord together because of their willingness to give with a whole heart.

Every good and perfect gift comes from the Lord. One way God calls you to worship Him is through the giving of your resources. But remember, giving to the Lord is not meant to be a drag. God doesn't want you to give because of tradition, obligation, or peer pressure. The Lord desires for you to give with a cheerful heart. In the Greek, this means "hilarious giving." In other words, it means to give up of yourself even beyond the point it makes sense, and yet you give out of obedience to the Lord. If the Spirit leads you to give a specific amount and it seems *hilarious*, trust the Lord because it will make sense in His economy. God will grant you abundant grace, and you will have everything you need for the work He has called you to! *Is the Lord asking you to give hilariously for His work today?* Respond in obedience as an act of worship.

Moreover, because of my delight in the house of my God, I now give my personal treasures of gold and silver for the house of my God over and above all that I've provided for the holy house ... Now who will volunteer to consecrate himself to the Lord today? —1 Chronicles 29:3, 5

Further Scripture: 1 Chronicles 29:6, 9; Psalm 37:4; 2 Corinthians 9:7–8

Week 44, Day 302: 2 Chronicles 1—2

Grant Wisdom and Knowledge

In preparing the temple, God had to first prepare Solomon. The chronicler describes Solomon as a leader and a king—a man not competent out of his own power but rather a man the Lord highly exalted and was with. When the Lord gave Solomon the opportunity to request one thing, Solomon asked for wisdom. And with wisdom from the Lord, he also received wealth, riches, and glory.

The New Testament describes wisdom from the Lord as pure, peace-loving, gentle, compliant, full of mercy and good fruits, and without favoritism or hypocrisy. As a follower of Christ, Paul wrote you are to pay attention to how you walk, not as unwise but as wise because the days you live in are hard. *How will today be different from yesterday if in every situation you pause and ask the Lord for wisdom?* You are promised that when you call upon the Lord, He will answer you and tell you great things you do not know. Today, pause in every situation and seek the Lord for wisdom, believe He will hear you, and look for His answer. Fear the Lord because He wants to do great things in your life today!

Now grant me wisdom and knowledge so that I may lead these people, for who can judge this great people of Yours? —2 Chronicles 1:10

Further Scripture: Jeremiah 33:3; Ephesians 5:15–16; James 3:17

Week 44, Day 303: 2 Chronicles 3—4
Solomon's Obedience to Start the Plans

After Solomon's coronation as king, he didn't waste any time getting started on the temple. Early in the fourth year of his reign, he completed the foundation—the first step in the building project. King Solomon believed God would establish the plans and provide the strength necessary to walk it out in faith. The Lord remained faithful, and Solomon remained obedient to the plans given by the Lord.

God calls you to live obediently as He leads you. Is there anything you know God has asked you to do, but you are just blowing it off? It could be sending a letter, giving to a person in need, seeking reconciliation, or even cleaning your house or car. *The Lord desires to see your faithfulness even in the small things entrusted to you.* So today, stop procrastinating, write it down, ask the Lord for wisdom, and then do it! Just as Solomon started with the foundation of the temple, put the first "block" into whatever the Lord has asked you to do. The Lord will be faithful as you walk obediently. Just get started!

Then Solomon began to build the Lord's temple in Jerusalem on Mount Moriah where the Lord had appeared to his father David, at the site David had prepared on the threshing floor of Ornan the Jebusite. He began to build on the second day of the second month in the fourth year of his reign. These are Solomon's foundations for building God's temple.
—2 Chronicles 3:1–3

Further Scripture: Psalm 119:60; Matthew 25:21; Romans 1:5

Week 44, Day 304: 2 Chronicles 5—6
Praising God in One Voice

The construction for the temple was completed, and the priests carried the Ark of the Covenant to its proper place in the inner sanctuary. Once in place, King Solomon, along with all the priests and Levitical musicians, regardless of their division or role, *gathered to worship the Lord in one voice.* At this point, the Lord's glory came and filled the temple as a great cloud. The people united together and focused on God alone.

Those who had been divided came together with one voice. Unity happened. God's glory came. *Did you catch it?* Did you see what brings God glory? *Unity in the body of Christ.* What will it take for the church to stop arguing over differences and become *one?* The Lord instructs believers to walk in humility and gentleness, with patience, accepting each other in love, diligently keeping unity of the spirit with the bonds of peace. That peace is Jesus Christ. Worship the Lord in unity because of the love of Christ. Focus on the Lord, not on man. When you have *one* voice, the Lord will reveal His glory. And then others will want to know the love binding you together. Gather together as *one* voice, and expect God's glory!

The trumpeters and singers joined together to praise and thank the Lord with one voice. They raised their voices, accompanied by trumpets, cymbals, and musical instruments, in praise to the Lord: For He is good; His faithful love endures forever. The temple, the Lord's temple, was filled with a cloud.
—2 Chronicles 5:13

Further Scripture: John 17:23; Romans 15:6–7; Ephesians 4:1–3

Week 44, Day 305: 2 Chronicles 7—8

If My People …

All King Solomon desired to do for the Lord's temple and his own palace succeeded. After the dedication ceremonies, the Lord responded to Solomon at night, confirming everything Solomon had prayed. The Lord told Solomon that *even if* God's covenant people turn away from Him, if they then *humble themselves, pray and seek His face, and turn from their evil ways*, God would hear them from heaven, forgive their sin, and heal their land.

The principles in this promise from the Lord still hold true today. The Lord remains a forgiving and healing God to the person with a humbled, repentant heart who seeks His face and turns from their wicked ways. The world desperately needs the Lord's gracious, redeeming love. With this in mind, take a moment to pray: "*May we, as God's people, humble ourselves, pray, seek the face of the Lord, and turn from our evil ways. And may God hear our prayers from heaven, forgive our sin and heal our land.*" May you begin with humbling yourself, praying, seeking the face of the Lord, and turning from your evil ways. The time is now.

And My people who are called by My name humble themselves, pray and seek My face, and turn from their evil ways, then I will hear from heaven, forgive their sin, and heal their land. —2 Chronicles 7:14

Further Scripture: Proverbs 8:17; Psalm 34:14; 1 Peter 5:6

Week 44, Day 306: 2 Chronicles 9—10

Decision Time

Rehoboam took over as king of Israel after Solomon's forty-year reign. With a new king in place, the people requested the harsh service and heavy yoke be lightened. King Rehoboam took three days to seek counsel in making this decision. First he sought the advice of the elders who served his father. Then he consulted the younger men, his peers. In the end, he listened to the younger men and made a poor decision, which divided the nation of Israel in two.

When you have a decision to make, what do you do? Remember, slow down, take your time, and seek the Lord. He promises to be your helper as you delight in Him day and night. Oftentimes, the Lord will lead you to seek counsel. However, be careful who you turn to for counsel. Find someone with a pure heart who faithfully serves the Lord. Some people will offer you advice, but they may have selfish or prideful motives. Others may just go along with whatever you say, not really offering sound advice. *Seek the Lord for discernment as you listen to counsel and make your decision.* In all things, the Lord promises to work all things together for the good of those who trust Him. He hears you when you cry for help, and He will never leave you.

---

*Then the king answered them harshly. King Rehoboam rejected the elders' advice and spoke to them according to the young men's advice, saying, "My father made your yoke heavy, but I will add to it; my father disciplined you with whips, but I, with barbed whips." —*2 Chronicles 10:13–14

Further Scripture: Psalm 1:1–2; Proverbs 11:14; 1 John 4:1

Week 44, Day 307: 2 Chronicles 11–12

Don't Stop at Just a Little

When King Rehoboam and the leaders heard the Lord was abandoning them because they were unfaithful and had forsaken the law, they humbled themselves before Him. However, they did not pray, seek God's face, or turn from their wicked ways as the Lord had previously instructed His people. Therefore the Lord granted them just a *little deliverance*. Later the chronicler recorded that Rehoboam did what was evil. He may have humbled himself for a bit, but he never fully devoted himself to the Lord, turning his heart from evil. As a result, King Rehoboam faced the consequences for his sin.

God sees everything, and He knows your heart. He asks you to confess *all* your sin. And He promised to forgive *all* of it. Don't go halfway or you will only experience a *little deliverance* and will likely fall back into your old ways. The Lord says pray and seek Him with *all* your heart. Give the Lord your heart, your temptations, your fears, your joys, and your dreams. Surrender all of it to Him. Trust Him. Turn away from the things not from the Lord. Begin to walk with Jesus, and He will make your path straight, leading you through full deliverance and complete freedom in Christ.

When the Lord saw that they had humbled themselves, the Lord's message came to Shemaiah: "They have humbled themselves; I will not destroy them but will grant them a little deliverance. My wrath will not be poured out on Jerusalem through Shishak." —2 Chronicles 12:7

Further Scripture: 2 Chronicles 7:14; Proverbs 28:13; Romans 10:9

Week 44, Day 308: 2 Chronicles 13—14

God Fights for You

King Asa of Judah did what was good and right in the sight of the Lord. Even when the Cushite army, which was double the size of King Asa's army, came against Judah, Asa remained confident in the Lord. Asa walked in faith, marching out against his enemy and lining up in battle formation. At that moment, he cried out to the Lord: "There is no one besides You to help the mighty and those without strength. Help us, Lord, for *we depend on You*." The Lord brought King Asa's army complete victory in the battle, plus a bonus of provision for the people's needs!

What battle do you need the Lord to fight for you today? Do you feel weak or unsure about how today will turn out? Take a moment and intentionally depend upon the Lord. Humble yourself, submit to His ways, and turn from evil. Believe that even in your weakness, the Lord is strong with you. He will fight your battle. It may require you to walk out in faith and step up to the battle line—but believe the Lord *will show up*. In God, you have victory. In God, you are a conqueror. In God, you are not alone. God will even trample your enemies and bring you *life* in abundance. Today, do not be afraid of the battle before you. Walk it out in faith, for the Lord is mighty within you!

Then Asa cried out to the Lord his God: "Lord, there is no one besides You to help the mighty and those without strength. Help us, Lord our God, for we depend on You, and in Your name we have come against this large army. Yahweh, You are our God. Do not let a mere mortal hinder You."
—2 Chronicles 14:11

Further Scripture: Deuteronomy 20:4; Psalm 44:5; 1 Corinthians 15:57

Week 45, Day 309: 2 Chronicles 15—16

Yahweh with You

Over time, the people abandoned the Lord's ways, filling the temple with idols. However, when King Asa heard the Word of the Lord through the prophet Azariah, he courageously removed the idols from the whole land of Judah and Benjamin. King Asa cleaned up the temple and even gathered the people to seek the Lord with all their minds and hearts. King Asa lived boldly for the Lord before all the people, and they recognized *Yahweh was with him.*

Ask yourself whether or not people recognize Jesus is with you. When King Asa cleaned up the temple, the people recognized *Yahweh was with him.* It may be time to clean up an area of your life so you too reflect Jesus. Today, look at your life and "clean your temple" where needed. Start with just one area the Lord puts on your heart. Gossip? Materialism? Addictions? Sports teams? Rid your life of any idols interfering with your reflection of Jesus. The time to love the Lord with *all* of your heart, soul, and mind, authentically reflecting Jesus, is *now.* If you want to see change in your community, it can begin with shining the love of Jesus to those around you. May they want the Jesus who is *with you.*

Then he gathered all Judah and Benjamin, as well as those from the tribes of Ephraim, Manasseh, and Simeon who had settled among them, for they had defected to him from Israel in great numbers when they saw that Yahweh his God was with him. —2 Chronicles 15:9

Further Scripture: Deuteronomy 32:21; Isaiah 42:6; Acts 13:47

Week 45, Day 310: 2 Chronicles 17—18

Hearing the Word of the Lord

King Ahab of Israel disguised himself during the battle in Ramoth-gil-ead. In contrast, King Jehoshaphat of Judah clothed himself with his royal robes. King Jehoshaphat walked out his calling with confidence in the Lord, not himself. When the enemies attacked, King Jehoshaphat cried out to the Lord for help, and God drew the enemy away, saving King Jehoshaphat. On the other hand, King Ahab, in his disguised identity, was killed when an unintentional arrow hit a weakness in his armor.

In fear, King Ahab attempted to manipulate a situation. In confidence, King Jehosephat walked by faith in the Lord. As you face your own battles, you have a choice: *take control and manipulate* or *have faith in the Lord and walk with integrity*. Remember, you are called as a chosen child of the King. You are loved. You are part of a royal priesthood. You don't need to hide or even blend into your surroundings. Walk confidently in Christ. King Jehoshaphat studied God's Word and drew strength from the truth. As a believer, God calls you to live on His bread alone to fight the battles. Don't try to be who you are not. Let go of control and walk in your identity in Christ. God is fighting your battles!

But the king of Israel said to Jehoshaphat, "I will disguise myself and go into battle, but you wear your royal attire." So the king of Israel disguised himself, and they went into battle. —2 Chronicles 18:29

Further Scripture: Matthew 4:4; Ephesians 3:12; 1 Peter 2:9

Week 45, Day 311: 2 Chronicles 19—20

Jehoshaphat's Prayer

A vast number of Moabites, Ammonites, and Meunites came together to fight against King Jehoshaphat. Facing the battle afraid, King Jehoshaphat sought the Lord, proclaiming a fast for all of Judah. *King Jehoshaphat did not know what to do; he only knew to seek the Lord.* So the people praised the Lord, they remembered His promises, and they believed He would fight their battle. The Lord answered them, saying, "Tomorrow, go down against them ... you do not have to fight this battle. Position yourselves, stand still, and see the salvation of the Lord." The people went out and believed in Yahweh their God. And the Lord brought them victory in the battle.

Are you afraid of something today? Take a deep breath and seek the Lord. Have a radical trust that says, "I do not know what to do, but I look to You, God." Believe the Lord will provide. Believe the Lord is faithful. Believe the Lord will guide you. Believe the Lord will turn your enemy around. Just as the Lord instructed Jehoshaphat in battle, today, you need to get up, go face your battle, and believe in the Lord your God. He says, "Be still. I will fight for you." Give thanks to the Lord for His faithful love that endures forever.

Our God, will You not judge them? For we are powerless before this vast number that comes to fight against us. We do not know what to do, but we look to You. —2 Chronicles 20:12

Further Scripture: 2 Chronicles 20:20; Psalm 46:10; Psalm 136:1

Week 45, Day 312: 2 Chronicles 21—22

God Is the Keeper of Promises

Judah's leadership style changed following King Jehoshaphat's reign. Jehosaphat's son, Jehoram, succeeded as king after strengthening his position by killing his six brothers. Just as the prophet Elijah prophesied, King Jehoram was struck by an intestinal disease because he did not walk in the ways of the Lord like his father had. Jehoram died without honor to no one's regret.

As a follower of Christ, Jesus commands you to go and make disciples. He encourages you to invest into people's lives, depositing the love of Christ. Consequently, when the Lord calls you home, the love of Christ you invested into others will be carried on long after your own life. Think about this: if you died tomorrow, would anyone regret it? Would they miss the love of Jesus alive in you? God's grace is abundant. Jesus poured out His love for you, just as you are. Believe you are worthy to receive His love. And as you receive Christ's love into your own life by faith, go deposit Jesus' love into someone else. The love of Jesus can impact someone for eternity.

But his people did not hold a fire in his honor like the fire in honor of his fathers. Jehoram was 32 years old when he became king; he reigned eight years in Jerusalem. He died to no one's regret and was buried in the city of David but not in the tombs of the kings. —2 Chronicles 21:19–20

Further Scripture: Matthew 28:19–20; 1 Timothy 1:16; 1 John 4:19

Week 45, Day 313: 2 Chronicles 23—24
Joash Repairs the Temple

When Joash became king, the Lord burdened his heart with the task to renovate the temple. King Joash gathered the Levites, instructed them to collect money, and told them to do so quickly. However, the Levites did not hurry. Therefore Joash took a different approach. He made a chest and positioned it outside the gate of the Lord's temple. In response, the people of Judah and Jerusalem gave generously and obediently. Money was collected daily, enabling the temple's complete restoration.

When God calls you to something, He will provide. Keep in mind, you may have to press in and continue seeking the Lord for His plan and His timing. You never know exactly how the Lord will move in the hearts of His people. When plans don't go the way you imagined or in your expected time frame, don't give up. Don't get frustrated. Press in and seek the Lord for wisdom in the situation. Be open minded, willing to make an adjustment. Sometimes the Lord will use frustrating moments to get to the sweet spot of God's will. Seek the Lord and your plans will succeed. Remain focused on God's will through a situation, and it will work out as *He* planned.

So he gathered the priests and Levites and said, "Go out to the cities of Judah and collect money from all Israel to repair the temple of your God as needed year by year, and do it quickly." However, the Levites did not hurry.
—2 Chronicles 24:5

Further Scripture: Psalm 84:11; Psalm 105:4; Proverbs 16:3

Week 45, Day 314: 2 Chronicles 25—27

Becoming Desensitized to God's Word

The Lord made King Uzziah of Judah very powerful, and his fame spread as far as Egypt. King Uzziah tore down walls, built cities, found victory in battle, and led a mighty army. A marvelous and strong leadership evolved into King Uzziah becoming arrogant. Consequently, he acted unfaithfully against God, which led to his own destruction. King Uzziah stopped depending on the Lord as he became strong in himself. His leadership crumbled, ultimately leading to his death.

From the moment you said yes to Jesus as your Savior and Lord, you were saved through faith, not by any works of your own. As you go through life with your eyes on Christ, your strength, success, and accomplishments come from the Lord alone. Although some people trust in the things of this world, as a follower of Christ, *you trust only in the name of the Lord your God.* The Lord says if you remain humble, He will lift you up in due time. Therefore, you do not need to exalt yourself. Don't even waste time giving yourself credit. Honor the Lord and give thanks for His great faithfulness, strength, and might! No matter how powerful you become from the world's perspective, may the Lord receive all the glory!

He made skillfully designed devices in Jerusalem to shoot arrows and catapult large stones for use on the towers and on the corners. So his fame spread even to distant places, for he was marvelously helped until he became strong. But when he became strong, he grew arrogant and it led to his own destruction. He acted unfaithfully against the Lord his God by going into the Lord's sanctuary to burn incense on the incense altar.
—2 Chronicles 26:15–16

Further Scripture: Proverbs 16:5; Ephesians 2:8–9; 1 Peter 5:6

Week 45, Day 315: 2 Chronicles 28—29
From Evil Leadership to Godly

After the ungodly reign of King Ahaz, his son Hezekiah took over the throne. In contrast to his father, Hezekiah began turning things around for the Lord. In the first month in the first year of his reign, twenty-five-year-old Hezekiah didn't hesitate or waste time doing what was right in the Lord's sight, just as his ancestor David had done. King Hezekiah followed the desire the Lord placed on his heart to make a covenant with Yahweh and began cleansing the Temple. He repaired the broken things and removed anything impure from the holy place. After this, King Hezekiah and those around him sang praises with rejoicing, bowing down in worship to the Lord. A sudden revival occurred in Jerusalem, and it was good!

Is it time to turn things around in your life? Your past and the generations of sin before you do not define who you are. Is it on your heart to repair, heal, or remove the "junk" from your life? It can happen. Allow the love of Jesus to cleanse you from all unrighteousness. His grace covers all, and His mercy is new day by day. Surround yourself with others to love and support you through this time. You will rejoice again. You will make music again. You will live in the freedom of Christ's love. *The hard work and effort to restore all things will be worth it.* If it's in your heart to turn around, then start walking it out in faith.

It is in my heart now to make a covenant with Yahweh, the God of Israel so that His burning anger may turn away from us. My sons, don't be negligent now, for the Lord has chosen you to stand in His presence, to serve Him, and to be His ministers and burners of incense. —2 Chronicles 29:10–11

Further Scripture: Titus 3:3–5; 1 Peter 2:1–3; 1 John 1:9

Week 46, Day 316: 2 Chronicles 30—31
The Call for Revival

King Hezekiah sent word throughout all Israel and Judah for the people to gather at the Lord's Temple in Jerusalem to observe the Passover of Yahweh, the God of Israel, which hadn't been observed in quite some time. He wrote letters and sent couriers to spread the message: "*It is time to return to Yahweh, the God of Abraham, Isaac, and Israel, so that He may return to those of you who remain.*" Upon hearing the message, some laughed and mocked the couriers, but others humbled themselves and traveled to Jerusalem. God's power united them all, and King Hezekiah was the tool through which the Lord's power worked.

Sometimes you may need to walk obediently as the Lord's messenger in someone's life, understanding that God's power goes before you. Today, take a minute to ask the Lord if there is someone in your life who needs to *return to the Lord.* Don't worry. If they chose not to listen, or if they laugh and mock you, they are rejecting Jesus, not you. However, you may hear a humble response and witness them turn their heart back to the Lord. The Lord's mercy covers all those who return to Him. So go send that text, write that email, or pick up the phone and call! *Be the tool that can help change begin in someone's life and* allow God's grace to flow.

So the couriers went throughout Israel and Judah with letters from the hand of the king and his officials, and according to the king's command, saying, "Israelites, return to Yahweh, the God of Abraham, Isaac, and Israel so that He may return to those of you who remain, who have escaped from the grasp of the kings of Assyria." —2 Chronicles 30:6

Further Scripture: Jeremiah 15:19; Joel 2:13; 1 Corinthians 15:1–3

Week 46, Day 317: 2 Chronicles 32—33
God Is Your Warrior

After King Hezekiah's faithfulness in leading the people to return to Yahweh, Sennacherib, king of Assyria, entered Judah with the intention to break into the fortified cities. King Hezekiah saw the enemy approaching, recognized he was in battle, and immediately sought counsel. Then he gathered the people together and encouraged them: "Be strong and courageous … Sennacherib has only human strength, but we have Yahweh our God to help us and to fight our battles." The Lord brought the victory and saved King Hezekiah along with all Jerusalem, giving them rest on every side.

Many times, after a season of great faithfulness to the Lord, the enemy comes in to steal, kill, and destroy. Be aware of the battle raging around you as you live your life boldly for the Lord. But do not be afraid. Just as the Lord said to Moses, Joshua, David, and Hezekiah as they led the people, the Lord tells you to be ready for battle. Be strengthened by the Lord. Put on the full armor of God so you can stand against the tactics of the devil. Pray in the Spirit at all times. Stay alert. The Lord your God is with you to fight your battle, so continue to speak boldly about the mystery of the Gospel. Others only have human strength, but you have the Lord on your side. Walk by faith and do not fear.

"Be strong and courageous! Don't be afraid or discouraged before the king of Assyria or before the large army that is with him, for there are more with us than with him. He has only human strength, but we have Yahweh our God to help us and to fight our battles." So the people relied on the words of King Hezekiah of Judah. —2 Chronicles 32:7–8

Further Scripture: Deuteronomy 31:7–8; Joshua 1:7; Ephesians 6:10–11

Week 46, Day 318: 2 Chronicles 34—36
Doing Evil in God's Sight

The people of Israel multiplied their unfaithful deeds, imitated all the detestable practices of the nations around them, and defiled the Lord's temple. Because of God's compassion, He offered them opportunities to repent, but they kept ridiculing God's messengers, despising His words, and scoffing at His prophets. Finally the Lord sent Nebuchadnezzar to carry the people from Jerusalem to exile in Babylon for seventy years. Later the Lord used Cyrus, the pagan king of Persia, to issue a decree for the Israelites to return to their homeland and rebuild the temple of the Lord. The Lord allowed yet another opportunity for His people to return to His presence, fulfilling His promises.

The Lord longs for you to be near Him. He is the God of second, third, and fourth chances. He will never give up on pursuing you. His love is wide. His love is deep. His love is high. You may feel like you have been banned from God's presence. You may feel like you have lost your way. You may feel like there is no way back to the Lord. But today, rest in knowing there is nowhere to escape from His Spirit. He desires for you to return to Him. *It is time to seek Him with all your heart.* He is your good Father, and He loves you.

For He had compassion on His people and on His dwelling place. But they kept ridiculing God's messengers, despising His words, and scoffing at His prophets, until the Lord's wrath was so stirred up against His people that there was no remedy. —2 Chronicles 36:15–16

Further Scripture: Psalm 139:7–10; Jeremiah 29:13–14; Ephesians 3:17–18

Week 46, Day 319: Ezra 1—2

The Release of the Captives

Nothing is impossible for God. While the Israelites were captive in Babylon, the Lord put it on the heart of Cyrus, the pagan king of Persia, to issue a proclamation for God's people to return to Jerusalem and rebuild the house of the Lord. The Lord's promise given to Abraham continued to be fulfilled.

No matter what your situation looks like, remember God is a promise keeper. Even in hopeless situations, God remains faithful. He used the power of a pagan leader to allow the Israelites to return to their homeland, fulfilling His promises. God can use anyone because He is an all-knowing, all-powerful, omnipresent God. If He says it in His Word, He will do it. Today if you feel like giving up, *hold on to hope.* Hold fast to the hope found in Christ. Ask the Lord to help you during this time of need. Do not grow anxious or weary; rather rest in God's promises. The Lord will not let you down.

The Lord put it into the mind of King Cyrus to issue a proclamation throughout his entire kingdom and to put it in writing.... .
"Whoever is among His people, may his God be with him, and may he go to Jerusalem in Judah and build the house of the Lord, the God of Israel, the God who is in Jerusalem." —Ezra 1:1–3

Further Scripture: Genesis 12:2; Deuteronomy 7:9; Hebrews 10:23

Week 46, Day 320: Ezra 3—5

Rebuilding the Temple

After seventy years of captivity, the people returned to Jerusalem to rebuild the Temple. When the new foundation was completed, the people praised the Lord with shouts of joy and thanksgiving: "For He is good; His faithful love to Israel endures forever." However, while some praised the Lord, the older men who remembered the past foundation wept loudly as they recalled and grieved what Israel had done, what God had to do, and all that had been lost.

God restores all things in your life when you come to Him. He laid the foundation of the earth, and as you follow Him, He is your foundation and solid rock. There may be seasons when you must rebuild your foundation. You may be coming out of bondage or leaving a season of bitterness, a season of hopelessness, or even a season of discipline. As you rebuild your foundation in the Lord, you will praise Him as you find joy for new beginnings and what lies ahead; but you may also grieve what happened in the past. Continue to recall His promises of yes and amen. *He is good and His faithful love endures forever.* The Lord is mighty to save, gives strength to the weak, and fights your every battle. When the world seems like slippery sand, may Christ alone be your firm foundation. In Him, you will not be shaken.

They sang with praise and thanksgiving to the Lord: "For He is good; His faithful love to Israel endures forever." Then all the people gave a great shout of praise to the Lord because the foundation of the Lord's house had been laid. But many of the older priests, Levites, and family leaders, who had seen the first temple, wept loudly when they saw the foundation of this house, but many others shouted joyfully. —Ezra 3:11–12

Further Scripture: Psalm 62:6; Matthew 16:18; 2 Corinthians 1:20

Week 46, Day 321: Ezra 6—8

Ezra Returns to Jerusalem

About eighty years after Zerubbabel and Jeshua led a group of exiled Israelites back to Jerusalem, Ezra returned with a different Israelite group. Before their return journey, Ezra proclaimed a fast for all to humble themselves before the Lord, asking for a safe journey for the travelers and their possessions. This group traveled without a protective infantry or cavalry, seeking the powerful hand of the Lord for protection. Along the journey, the Lord strengthened them and protected them from potential enemies and any ambush. The Lord answered their prayers for the return journey to Jerusalem!

The Lord is enough for the journey He is leading you on. Whether you are returning to Him, following Him in a new calling, or pressing on in perseverance, do not fear and do not tremble. Lay your worries and your concerns at His feet. Consider fasting. Trust that the Lord will protect you and strengthen you. The Lord will cause your enemies to fall by your side. Press on, seek the Lord, and walk in humility as you go along your journey! He is with you and for you. He is your light and salvation. Rest in His faithful promises today. The Lord sees you and is with you!

We set out from the Ahava River on the twelfth day of the first month to go to Jerusalem. We were strengthened by our God, and He protected us from the power of the enemy and from ambush along the way. So we arrived at Jerusalem and rested there for three days. —Ezra 8:31–32

Further Scripture: Psalm 27:1–3; 2 Thessalonians 3:3; 2 Timothy 4:18

Week 46, Day 322: Ezra 9—10

Confession and Repentance

Ezra became aware of sin in Jerusalem: the people of Israel, the priests, the Levites, even the leaders and officials, had intermarried and been unfaithful to the Lord. Ezra was devastated over Israel's sinful ways. In response, he prayed, confessed, and wept in humility before the Lord. As the people witnessed Ezra's brokenness, they joined him in confession and repentance. They brought their brokenness and hidden sins before the Lord. The Lord used Ezra to lead the people forward with a plan to change their lifestyles, and they received God's grace and strength.

The Lord promises healing when you come before Him in humility and brokenness. If you are hiding a sin, most likely you feel the weight of your disobedience. It sits on your shoulders or forms a pit in your stomach. No sin is hidden from the Lord. Go ahead and let go of it. Tell the Lord everything in humility and brokenness. *Then take action and turn away from your old ways.* God promises that when you release your sin to Him, you will find mercy and forgiveness. The Lord removes your guilt, your shame, and your sin as far as the east is from the west. He wants you to walk in freedom. He loves you. Just come before Him today.

While Ezra prayed and confessed, weeping and falling facedown before the house of God, an extremely large assembly of Israelite men, women, and children gathered around him. The people also wept bitterly.
Then Shecaniah son of Jehiel, an Elamite, responded to Ezra:
"We have been unfaithful to our God by marrying foreign women from the surrounding peoples, but there is still hope for Israel in spite of this.... .
Get up, for this matter is your responsibility, and we support you.
Be strong and take action!" —Ezra 10:1–2, 4

Further Scripture: Psalm 32:3–5; Proverbs 28:13; 1 John 1:9

Week 47, Day 323: Nehemiah 1—2
God Will Grant You Success

Nehemiah wept and grieved over the destruction of Jerusalem. The walls were broken down and the gates burned. After Nehemiah spent time mourning, fasting, and praying before the God of heaven, the Lord led him before the king. The king asked Nehemiah: "What is your request?" First Nehemiah prayed. And although Nehemiah was fearful, he boldly requested to be sent to Judah to rebuild the city. Something that seemed impossible happened, as it pleased the king to send his cupbearer, Nehemiah, to go to Jerusalem!

Do you weep for the state of your nation? Or maybe destruction has hit closer to home, and you grieve for your marriage or the relationships in your family. As you grieve, seek the Lord and follow Nehemiah's example. He was only a cupbearer in a seemingly unpowerful position, and he was fearful. Nevertheless, he humbled himself, prayed, and sought the Lord. The Lord made the impossible, possible. As you seek the Lord regarding the destruction around you, *expect Him to show up with an answer*. He promises to hear your prayers. And then, as He opens up the doors, press on in confident obedience. The Lord will strengthen you.

When I heard these words, I sat down and wept. I mourned for a number of days, fasting and praying before the God of heaven. —Nehemiah 1:4

Further Scripture: Psalm 5:3; Nehemiah 2:8b; 1 John 5:14

Week 47, Day 324: Nehemiah 3—4

Be Serious! Be Alert!

Nehemiah and all the people followed the Lord and worked together to rebuild the city's wall. But then *opposition from the enemy came.* Enemies plotted together to fight against Jerusalem and brought confusion and discouragement to the people. At this point, Nehemiah led the people in prayer to God. They were not afraid of the enemy. They remembered God called them to rebuild the wall, and Nehemiah encouraged them: "Do not be afraid!" The Lord gave them wisdom for a plan to stay on guard day and night, and they trusted He would fight for them.

As you walk obediently with Jesus, the enemy will come your way, devising plans to discourage and confuse you. You may think: *This is too hard—am I really following the Lord?* Be firm in your calling. Remember when the Lord confirmed the work of your hands. Stand strong in Him and remain alert. The Lord will fight for you and will give you wisdom. The Lord will protect you in battle when you feel surrounded by enemies. The Lord promises He is greater in you, than the one who is in the world. You can do this! You will not be destroyed.

After I made an inspection, I stood up and said to the nobles, the officials, and the rest of the people, "Don't be afraid of them. Remember the great and awe-inspiring Lord, and fight for your countrymen, your sons and daughters, your wives and homes." —Nehemiah 4:14

Further Scripture: Acts 20:28; 2 Corinthians 2:11; 1 Peter 5:8–9

Week 47, Day 325: Nehemiah 5—6
Experiencing Opposition

Nehemiah and the builders pressed on in their calling to rebuild the wall. The fifth attempt to harm and discourage Nehemiah came when rumors were spread. The enemy continued to intimidate and dispirit the builders, so the work on the wall would not be finished. Nehemiah remained strong in the Lord. He stayed focused on the task, and the Lord granted him wisdom and discernment not to give in to the enemy's threats. After fifty-two days, the Israelites completed the wall. This intimidated their enemies, who lost confidence. In the end, the Israelites' enemies recognized it was the Lord God who built the wall.

Where is the enemy attempting to discourage you as you do what the Lord has called? Pursuing a unified marriage? Giving generously from your finances? Discipling a new believer? As you walk with the Lord, in His power, *the enemy will come after you.* Stay focused. Don't turn to the left or the right. Don't look back. Don't compromise. Seek the Lord for discernment of good and evil. If you feel like you can't bear up under the pressure, remember that your strength comes from the Lord God Almighty. *He will fight for you.* You will complete all the Lord has called you to, and others will see it was the Lord's doing, not your own. To Him be the glory forever and ever. Amen!

Then I replied to him, "There is nothing to these rumors you are spreading; you are inventing them in your own mind." For they were all trying to intimidate us, saying, "They will become discouraged in the work, and it will never be finished." But now, my God, strengthen me.
—Nehemiah 6:8–9

Further Scripture: Nehemiah 6:15–16; Psalm 31:13–15; Proverbs 4:26–27

Week 47, Day 326: Nehemiah 7—8
Public Reading of the Law

After Nehemiah rebuilt the wall, he gathered the people together and opened the Book of the Law of Moses the Lord gave Israel. The people stood and listened to the reading of the Word. Certain Levites translated and explained the Word, so the people could understand it. Nehemiah encouraged the people to celebrate all they learned from God's Word. Indeed, the joy of the Lord was their strength! This joy motivated the people to not merely listen to the Word of the Lord but to obey it as well.

Why is it so hard to open the Word of God and actually read it? You walk by it, you see it sitting on the bookshelf, you carry it in your backpack or purse all day long. You even have it on your phone … but you get distracted. You neglect to open it and actually read it. Today, open the Word of God and read a verse or two. The Israelites were strengthened with joy by reading the Word, and it motivated them to action. If you are feeling down, lonely, nervous, unmotivated, or in need of guidance, *open the Word of God.* Allow God's truth to settle in your heart. The joy of the Lord will be your strength!

Ezra opened the book in full view of all the people, since he was elevated above everyone. As he opened it, all the people stood up. Ezra praised the Lord, the great God, and with their hands uplifted all the people said, "Amen, Amen!" Then they bowed down and worshiped the Lord with their faces to the ground. —Nehemiah 8:5–6

Further Scripture: Nehemiah 8:10; Psalm 19:8; Jeremiah 15:16

Week 47, Day 327: Nehemiah 9
The Grace of God

The Israelites assembled, fasted, wore sackcloth, and put dust on their heads as a sign of mourning for their sins and spiritual condition. Then they prayed and praised the Lord. They spent time remembering God's faithfulness to the covenant He made with Abraham. They confessed their disobedience and recognized the Lord's compassion. He rescued and delivered them. He never abandoned them because He kept His gracious covenant. As a remnant, they made a binding agreement to follow the Lord.

The Lord will never abandon you. He will never leave you. God is your deliverer and your rescuer. He is a compassionate God. The Lord hears you when you cry out in distress. Maybe you feel abandoned by someone—a parent, sibling, or friend. Maybe even by God. However, unlike the others, *the truth is God will never abandon you.* He promises He will be with you always; nothing will ever separate you from His great love. Nothing. God's love is a free gift you receive by saying, "Yes, Lord, I receive Your grace." No binding agreement necessary. Today, accept His free gift; believe His promises.

You warned them to turn back to Your law, but they acted arrogantly and would not obey Your commands. They sinned against Your ordinances, which a person will live by if he does them. They stubbornly resisted, stiffened their necks, and would not obey. You were patient with them for many years, and Your Spirit warned them through Your prophets, but they would not listen. Therefore, You handed them over to the surrounding peoples. However, in Your abundant compassion, You did not destroy them or abandon them, for You are a gracious and compassionate God.
—Nehemiah 9:29–31

Further Scripture: Deuteronomy 31:8; Romans 8:38–39; Ephesians 2:8–9

Week 47, Day 328: Nehemiah 10
Continuing the House of the Lord

The Israelites submitted to Yahweh and made the decision to walk in His ways. They committed to separate themselves from others in the area because they were children of God, followers of Yahweh. It's one thing to say, "We love the Lord and read His Word," but they needed to *live their lives differently from those who did not follow God.* The Israelites vowed to obey and follow God's Word through marriage, honoring the Sabbath, and supporting the house of the Lord with their firstfruits.

If you truly love the Lord your God with all your heart, soul, and mind, then your behavior, your actions, and the way you spend your time, resources, and talents will be transformed. As a New Testament Christian, your faith is not about a list of laws and rules. Rather, it's a matter of daily yielding your heart to the Lord and receiving His grace and power that transforms you into His image. *Does your life resemble Christ or the world?* If you remain in the world, then you will resemble the world. But as you remain in Christ and walk in the Spirit, you will bear much fruit: love, joy peace, patience, kindness, goodness, faithfulness, gentleness, and self-control. As the world sees the fruit of the Spirit displayed in your life, they will know something is different about you. That difference is Jesus empowering you!

The rest of the people—the priests, Levites, gatekeepers, singers, and temple servants, along with their wives, sons, and daughters, everyone who is able to understand and who has separated themselves from the surrounding peoples to obey the law of God—join with their noble brothers and commit themselves with a sworn oath to follow the law of God given through God's servant Moses and to carefully obey all the commands, ordinances, and statutes of Yahweh our Lord. —Nehemiah 10:28–29

Further Scripture: John 15:4; 2 Corinthians 3:18; Philippians 1:27

Week 47, Day 329: Nehemiah 11
Nehemiah's Leadership

The Israelites returned to Jerusalem, the Holy City. They rebuilt the wall and the city itself. Again they worshipped Yahweh and submitted to His ways. They even sacrificed their land and firstfruits to Him. Now it was time to embrace where the Lord brought them by getting settled and structured in order to bring about sustainability as a nation. Nehemiah remained a strong leader the people followed to walk out God's plan and purpose for the nation of Israel.

There's a time for everything. Settling means commitment, which can be hard. Have you fully embraced the season you are in? In order for a house to feel more like *your home, you must settle in.* Unpack boxes. Paint the walls. Hang up pictures. Host a party for friends. Are you attending a new church? Maybe it's time to introduce yourself to the pastor, go to the membership class, offer to help in the nursery, or serve as a parking attendant. When you settle in somewhere, sustainability will likely occur. And that's a good thing! It means you have committed to the change. Change is not something to fear if you know it's from the Lord. Embrace the season the Lord has you in, and as you do, His peace will sustain you.

Now the leaders of the people stayed in Jerusalem, and the rest of the people cast lots for one out of ten to come and live in Jerusalem, the holy city, while the other nine-tenths remained in their towns. —Nehemiah 11:1

Further Scripture: Proverbs 16:3; Jeremiah 17:7; Luke 9:62

Week 48, Day 330: Nehemiah 12

The Joy of Jerusalem

Nehemiah led the people in a joy-filled dedication of the wall around Jerusalem. They had come out of exile, worked together, and rebuilt the wall of Jerusalem. It was time to celebrate! They gathered together as purified people and gave thanks with singing and the sound of trumpets.

Every day, you wake up to a new day and the opportunity to dedicate your life to the Lord as a living sacrifice. So praise the Lord! The Lord gives you life! The Lord gives you hope! The Lord gives you great joy and strength! The Lord offers the free gift of salvation and eternal life to all who believe in Him by faith! Perhaps you have a new baby, a new home, a new job, or a new work project. Dedicate your new season to the Lord. Sing a new song to Him. Blow a trumpet or pick up a guitar, and make a joyful noise to the Lord. And if others hear you as you dedicate your life to the Lord ... so what? Let them hear and wonder, *What is that joyful noise of praise?*

On that day they offered great sacrifices and rejoiced because God had given them great joy. The women and children also celebrated, and Jerusalem's rejoicing was heard far away. —Nehemiah 12:43

Further Scripture: 2 Samuel 7:29; Psalm 98:4–6; Romans 12:1–2

Week 48, Day 331: Nehemiah 13
The Surprise Ending of Nehemiah

After the dedication of the wall, Nehemiah went back to assist King Artaxerxes in Babylon, later returning to the Israelites. When Nehemiah left for Babylon, the people were praising the Lord and devoted to His ways. However, during Nehemiah's absence, the people gave in to temptation, turned away from the ways of the Lord, and walked in disobedience to their God. Once again, Nehemiah brought hope. He sought the Lord and prayed without ceasing on behalf of the people. *The Lord used Nehemiah to rekindle the flame for the Lord inside the people, and they turned their hearts back to Him.*

Just like a blazing fire will go out if left unattended, believers, if left alone, will most likely lose their passion and purity for the Lord. As you follow Christ, you are to remain diligent, be fervent in spirit, and serve the Lord. Just as iron sharpens iron, people sharpen each other. Continue to abide in the Lord and in His Word. Spend time with other believers. Stretch your faith. *What do you need to do today to stoke your fire for the Lord?* God longs for you to keep the fire inside you ablaze so that the world will know of His great love.

While all this was happening, I was not in Jerusalem, because I had returned to King Artaxerxes of Babylon in the thirty-second year of his reign. It was only later that I asked the king for a leave of absence so I could return to Jerusalem. Then I discovered the evil that Eliashib had done on behalf of Tobiah by providing him a room in the courts of God's house. I was greatly displeased and threw all of Tobiah's household possessions out of the room. —Nehemiah 13:6–8

Further Scripture: Proverbs 27:17; Romans 12:11; 2 Timothy 1:6

Week 48, Day 332: Esther 1—2
Finding the King's Favor

Queen Vashti refused to do as King Ahasuerus ordered. Consequently, she was removed as the queen. The search for a new queen began. After several months of beauty treatments, the king loved the unlikely candidate, Esther, an orphan given the Hebrew name Hadassah at birth. Her uncle, Mordecai, adopted her and watched over her, even from the palace gate. Esther won more favor and approval from the king than any other young woman. She had the king's attention and respect. So, when Mordecai overheard two men plotting to assassinate the king, he told Esther to tell the king, thus saving the king's life.

The Lord uses the most unlikely people, at the most unlikely times, to do His will. You may wonder why you are in the season you are in. You may feel as though you are not adequate for a job or position. You may question the timing. But take a deep breath. Receive this season as a gift with a purpose from the Lord. God has a reason, and if you are willing to yield to Him and His plans, He will use you for great purposes in His time. Don't question, try to figure out, or manipulate the situation. Simply trust the Lord, walk in integrity, and do the next right thing. God puts people in place for a specific time and purpose. Just take one step at a time, and do not worry. *Walk it out.*

When Mordecai learned of the plot, he reported it to Queen Esther, and she told the king on Mordecai's behalf. When the report was investigated and verified, both men were hanged on the gallows. This event was recorded in the Historical Record in the king's presence. —Esther 2:22–23

Further Scripture: Ecclesiastes 3:1; Lamentations 3:25–26; Habakkuk 2:3

Week 48, Day 333: Esther 3—4
Called for Such a Time as This

King Ahasuerus promoted Haman the Agagite in rank and even gave him the king's signet ring, enabling Haman to enforce decisions. Esther's uncle, Mordecai, refused to bow down to Haman as ordered, which enraged Haman. Therefore, Haman ordered all Jewish people to be destroyed. Mordecai heard this decree and brought it to Esther's attention. Mordecai encouraged Esther to go before the king and personally plead with him to save her people. Even though this action would put her own life at risk, Esther recognized her strategic position as queen was *for such a time as this*. She courageously agreed to go before the king in an effort to save her people, saying, "If I perish, I perish."

You may have an opportunity to stand up for the Gospel, risking your reputation, financial or promotion opportunities, friendships, or perhaps even your life. You can choose to be quiet or take a bold, courageous stance for Jesus, with an Esther mindset saying, "If I perish, I perish." As a believer, you are called to deny yourself, pick up your cross, and follow Jesus. *Sometimes that means doing the difficult thing.* Regardless of the cost, *trust God.* Live in such a way you are willing to let go of your life for God. *For such a time as this*, the Lord has placed you where you are today. Remember, God is with you. God is for you. He is worthy of it all.

"If you keep silent at this time, liberation and deliverance will come to the Jewish people from another place, but you and your father's house will be destroyed. Who knows, perhaps you have come to your royal position for such a time as this." Esther sent this reply to Mordecai: "Go and assemble all the Jews who can be found in Susa and fast for me. Don't eat or drink for three days, day or night. I and my female servants will also fast in the same way. After that, I will go to the king even if it is against the law. If I perish, I perish." —Esther 4:14–16

Further Scripture: Matthew 16:24; Acts 20:24; Romans 8:31

Week 48, Day 334: Esther 5—6

Pride before the Fall

Mordecai saved King Ahasuerus's life after overhearing an assassination plot at the King's Gate. And yet Mordecai neither sought nor received recognition for his life-saving actions. Mordecai chose to walk in humility and integrity. Haman, on the other hand, always looked out for his own interest. When the king asked Haman how to honor someone, Haman assumed it was himself the king wished to honor and replied with an extensive plan. Haman walked in pride with the expectation of reward for himself. Haman's plan for honor backfired as the king at last honored Mordecai with honor and dignity throughout the city square.

As a follower of Christ, you are not to look out for your own interest or think of yourself more highly than others. Keep in mind, *the Lord despises the proud but gives grace to the humble*. If you know you have done something worthy of recognition, it is best not to "toot your own horn." God sees you. He knows every move you make. You will receive honor from Him. As you walk in humility, He will exalt you. Today, make the choice to walk poor in spirit and see the Lord move in your life!

Haman entered, and the king asked him, "What should be done for the man the king wants to honor?" Haman thought to himself, "Who is it the king would want to honor more than me?" —Esther 6:6

Further Scripture: Proverbs 27:2; Philippians 2:3; James 4:6

Week 48, Day 335: Esther 7—8

Hasten with the Message

Queen Esther sat down at the feast with the king and Haman. For the third time, the king said to the queen, "Whatever you ask will be given to you. Whatever you seek, even to half the kingdom will be done for you." This time, Queen Esther spoke directly to the point and asked for two things—for her life to be spared and for her people to be spared. The Lord moved the king to grant Esther all she requested and even more. The Jewish people were saved. Esther was saved. And Esther's uncle, Mordecai, even received a place of honor in the palace. The time was right, and Esther received the answer for which she had prayed and fasted.

God can still do the impossible today. The Lord moves as the "Esthers" of this generation rise up in boldness, courage, and dependence on God alone. Esther didn't depend on her good looks. She didn't depend on her position. She fasted and prayed and then asked an entire people group to join her, all while depending on a faithful God. God does the impossible when you have faith, even faith as small as a mustard seed. Pray precise and direct prayers, fast, seek the Lord, and wait for His timing. You may not know how big God can move until you take a leap of faith. Take courage and don't be afraid. *Go ahead and take that step of faith that makes you say, "But what if...?"* Have faith because the Lord is with you!

Queen Esther answered, "If I have obtained your approval, my king, and if the king is pleased, spare my life—this is my request; and spare my people—this is my desire." —Esther 7:3

Further Scripture: Matthew 14:27–29; Matthew 17:20; John 14:14

Week 48, Day 336: Esther 9—10

The Deliverance of the Jews

Once again Esther went before the king asking for favor. She asked that the Jewish people be given one more day to kill their enemies and hang Haman's sons. The king gave orders for this to be done. Mordecai recorded these events and ordered the people near and far to celebrate the fourteenth and fifteenth days of the month Adar every year because, "During those days the Jews got rid of their enemies." That month, sorrow turned into rejoicing and mourning turned into a holiday. It was to be two days of feasting, rejoicing, and of sending gifts to one another and to the poor.

How great it is to celebrate! You celebrate the birth of Christ at Christmas and His death and resurrection at Easter. *But what if you celebrated a special day in your relationship with Jesus?* The day you said *yes* to Jesus and went from death to life? Perhaps the day you broke free from the bondage of unforgiveness, pain, or bitterness? As a follower of Christ, you can celebrate these moments in your spiritual journey just as much as a birthday or anniversary. The Lord promises to turn your mourning to dancing and ashes to beauty. Celebrating provides a time to look back and remember how the Lord has moved in your life. Today, think of a day to celebrate in your own walk with the Lord, and then throw a party, spend time in worship and praise to the Lord, or give a gift to someone who needs to know Jesus loves them!

He ordered them to celebrate the fourteenth and fifteenth days of the month Adar every year because during those days the Jews got rid of their enemies. That was the month when their sorrow was turned into rejoicing and their mourning into a holiday. They were to be days of feasting, rejoicing, and of sending gifts to one another and the poor. —Esther 9:21–22

Further Scripture: Psalm 30:11–12; Isaiah 61:3; Luke 15:22–24

Week 49, Day 337: Acts 1
The Holy Spirit Promised

After Jesus' death and Resurrection, He appeared to the disciples for forty days before His ascension to heaven. During this time, He instructed the disciples on things concerning the kingdom of God. Jesus promised the disciples they would *receive power when the Holy Spirit came upon them.* He also gave them the final instruction to be His *witnesses in Jerusalem, in all Judea and Samaria, and throughout the entire world.* After stating this, Jesus was taken up to heaven, and the disciples returned to Jerusalem united in prayer.

Because Jesus has not yet returned, His promise and final instruction to the disciples still remains true for believers today. Your purpose as a believer is to bear witness of Jesus *through the power of the Holy Spirit,* not in your own strength, but as you receive power from the Holy Spirit. Whether you are in the grocery store, at school, hanging out with family, or in a country across the world and far from home, your instruction is to be a witness for Jesus. You have nothing to fear. The same power that raised Jesus from the dead lives in you. So go forth in power. Let your light shine before all men, bearing witness that Jesus is the way, the truth, and the life!

But you will receive power when the Holy Spirit has come on you, and you will be My witnesses in Jerusalem, in all Judea and Samaria, and to the ends of the earth. —Acts 1:8

Further Scripture: Matthew 28:18–20; John 14:6; Romans 8:11

Week 49, Day 338: Acts 2
What Must We Do?

Peter's audience came to believe that Jesus was the Messiah and Lord—Israel's hope for salvation. Upon realizing this, they were deeply convicted and asked Peter, "What must we do?" Peter responded, "Repent and be baptized in the name of Jesus Christ for the forgiveness of your sins and you will receive the gift of the Holy Spirit." As they accepted Peter's message, the Holy Spirit came upon them, and they devoted themselves to the apostles' teaching, fellowship, breaking bread, and prayer. They saw the Lord work in supernatural ways, and the Lord added to their numbers daily.

Without conviction, things are just mediocre—conviction brings deep belief, passion, and devotion that are contagious. Do you have conviction that Jesus is Lord and Messiah of your life? Do your *daily actions and words reflect your conviction?* It's one thing to believe in Jesus, but it's another thing to reflect this belief. Are you more devoted to social media updates or a specific TV program than to reading God's Word, praying, and making time for fellowship with other believers? Live your life with a conviction for Jesus and expect the Holy Spirit's presence and power as you walk it out in faith. With conviction, lives will change.

When they heard this, they came under deep conviction and said to Peter and the rest of the apostles: "Brothers, what must we do?" "Repent," Peter said to them, "and be baptized, each of you, in the name of Jesus Christ for the forgiveness of your sins, and you will receive the gift of the Holy Spirit. For the promise is for you and for your children, and for all who are far off, as many as the Lord our God will call." —Acts 2:37–39

Further Scripture: Acts 2:42; Ephesians 3:19–20; 1 Thessalonians 1:5

December 5

The Power of His Name

While walking up to the Temple complex to pray, Peter and John saw a lame man. They didn't offer the man silver or gold, but they spoke in the name of Jesus Christ and told him, "Get up and walk!" At once, as they took his right hand and raised him up, his feet and ankles became strong! He jumped up, stood, started to walk, and then leapt and praised God! As others witnessed this healing miracle, Peter addressed the people, giving all glory to Jesus. The lame man could walk because of faith in Jesus' name.

If you have faith in Jesus, then the same power that raised Jesus from the dead is inside you. Therefore, you can walk in the authority of Jesus Christ. *There is power in His name.* Jesus said whatever you ask in His name will be given to you. As you pray, the Lord will give you opportunities to walk out His power. Walking in Jesus' authority doesn't have to be weird or complicated. Keep it simple and say, "In the name of Jesus Christ, get up and walk by faith!" All the glory will go to Jesus' name, not to yourself. What are you doing with the authority of Jesus you have been given? Start walking it out and anything can happen!

But Peter said, "I don't have silver or gold, but what I have, I give you: In the name of Jesus Christ the Nazarene, get up and walk!"
—Acts 3:6

Further Scripture: John 14:13; Acts 3:16; Philippians 2:9–11

December 6

Week 49, Day 340: Acts 4
Have You Spent Time with Jesus?

The rulers, elders, and scribes assembled in Jerusalem questioned Peter and John. They asked, "By what power or in what name have you done this?" Peter didn't answer in his own strength or wisdom; rather, he responded by the power of the Holy Spirit. The religious leaders observed Peter's boldness and realized Peter *had been with Jesus.* They had nothing to say in response.

Have you ever worried about what you will say when people question you about your belief in Jesus? You do not need to worry or fear. Through the power of the Holy Spirit inside you, you are promised you have all authority to bear witness to others about Jesus Christ. He will equip you. Even in your weakness, His grace is strong. When people see you, would they recognize *you have you been with Jesus?* When you spend time with Jesus, God promises your life will be transformed. So today, spend time with Jesus, rest in His promises, and give thanks for the Holy Spirit who is alive in you. Like Peter, after spending time with Jesus, you will be ready for whatever comes your way through the power of the Holy Spirit. Walk in faith and don't be afraid to open your mouth! The Lord will give you the words you need.

When they observed the boldness of Peter and John and realized that they were uneducated and untrained men, they were amazed and recognized that they had been with Jesus. —Acts 4:13

Further Scripture: Luke 21:14–15; John 15:4; Acts 4:7–8

Week 49, Day 341: Acts 5
Wanting to Look Good before Others

Ananias and his wife Sapphira sold a piece of property. They deceivingly held back a portion of the proceeds before bringing the money to the apostles. Not only did they lie to the apostles, but they also lied to God. Because of their hypocrisy, both Ananias and Sapphira were immediately struck dead. In contrast, Peter and the apostles pressed on teaching and speaking in Jesus' name and in His authority. They saw people healed and transformed in Jesus' name. Even so, because of their bold conviction, they were put in jail and flogged. Through it all, the Lord sustained them. *They obeyed God rather than man.* They lived with passion and rejoiced even through their sufferings because they suffered in Jesus' name!

As a believer, are you like Ananias and Sapphira, with deceitful ways and a heart far from Christ? Or are you like Peter and the apostles, ready to lose your life for the sake of Christ, no matter the cost? *It's time to stop pretending to follow Christ wholeheartedly while secretly seeking to please man.* Choose to live with integrity and obedience to the Lord. There are no secrets with God. He knows all. Even if you lose your life, you will gain life in Christ. How will you choose to live today?

But Peter and the apostles replied, "We must obey God rather than men."
—Acts 5:29

Further Scripture: Matthew 10:39; Mark 7:6; Luke 6:46

Week 49, Day 342: Acts 6
Choosing Men to Serve

As the number of believers grew, people recognized the widows were being overlooked and weren't receiving their daily distributions. The twelve apostles decided it would be best for them to continue in prayer and teaching. Therefore, they developed a plan to raise up seven men of good reputation, full of the Spirit and wisdom, to appoint over this responsibility. When they established these men, the preaching of God continued to flourish, and the number of disciples multiplied greatly.

The Lord designed the body of Christ to be one body with many parts, each with a different function. The Lord desires His body to work together. One person does not need to take care of every detail. Stop trying to do everything by yourself. If you feel spread thin, ask the Lord for wisdom in the situation. Look for the "Stephens" around you—someone you can rely on with a good reputation, full of the Spirit and wisdom. Then follow through in obedient faith to the plan the Lord gives you. Yes, it may mean letting go of control; *but what if in your obedience to let go, it enables others to thrive?* As this happens, you will also flourish for the Lord. It may take some faith, but the Lord promises to walk with you each step of the way!

Then the Twelve summoned the whole company of the disciples and said, "It would not be right for us to give up preaching about God to handle financial matters. Therefore, brothers, select from among you seven men of good reputation, full of the Spirit and wisdom, whom we can appoint to this duty. But we will devote ourselves to prayer and to the preaching ministry." —Acts 6:2–4

Further Scripture: Romans 12:4–5; 1 Corinthians 7:17; Ephesians 2:10

Week 49, Day 343: Acts 7
The Testimony of Stephen

The high priest and the Sanhedrin questioned Stephen, a man full of faith and the Holy Spirit. He spoke before them, boldly recalling how God had been at work since early times. Stephen focused on God's presence and power in the land, the Law, and the temple, even though the people had made these things their idols rather than tools the Lord used to point to His glory. Stephen's message enraged his audience, and eventually Stephen was stoned to death. Stephen died as the first martyr for the Gospel.

The Lord put a message on Stephen's heart, and he spoke it clearly to the Sanhedrin. What do you do with his message? Are you focused more on the land, the Law, and the temple as idols? The world can distract and persuade your thoughts and heart. However, Christ has promised you strength through times of weakness and joy through times of persecution. Sit and rest on the truths of Jesus, not just the history or the law. Pray at all times and give thanks. *Don't resist the Holy Spirit.* Rather, walk in Spirit and truth, living out the fullness of Christ and all He has for you!

You stiff-necked people with uncircumcised hearts and ears! You are always resisting the Holy Spirit; as your ancestors did, so do you.
—Acts 7:51

Further Scripture: 1 Corinthians 2:14; Ephesians 4:30–31; 1 Thessalonians 5:17–21

Week 50, Day 344: Acts 8
Walking in the Spirit Immediately

While Phillip was traveling, an angel of the Lord spoke to him, telling him to get up and go south on the desert road. *Immediately*, Philip went and saw an Ethiopian man in a chariot. The Spirit told Philip to join the chariot, and again, Philip did as the Spirit instructed. The Ethiopian man was reading a passage from the prophet Isaiah and was confused. As the two men sat in the chariot, Philip explained the Scripture in question and went on to share the good news of Jesus. The Ethiopian man heard, believed, and received Jesus as Lord and then was baptized. This man's life changed forever because Philip listened and obeyed the voice of the Lord *immediately*.

The Lord intends for His believers to listen to the Holy Spirit and obey Him *immediately*. When you hear something from the Spirit, act on it! Don't analyze or question what you hear, but walk in obedience. Just go, just do, just give, just listen, and receive whatever you hear! If it does not contradict Scripture, then trust it's from the Lord. Will you be obedient to listen and obey? What's holding you back? Go and do what the Spirit is telling you today, even if it means walking along a desert road … the Lord will be with you! He will faithfully lead you to each next step. Have fun because it will lead to a great adventure with Jesus!

An angel of the Lord spoke to Phillip: "Get up and go south to the road that goes down from Jerusalem to Gaza." (That is the desert road.) So he got up and went. There was an Ethiopian man, a eunuch and high official of Candace, the Queen of the Ethiopians, who was in charge of her entire treasury. He had come to worship in Jerusalem and was sitting in his chariot on his way home, reading the prophet Isaiah aloud. The Spirit told Phillip, "Go and join that chariot." —Acts 8:26–29

Further Scripture: Isaiah 30:21; Matthew 7:24; James 1:22

Week 50, Day 345: Acts 9
The Power of One

Saul traveled on the road to Damascus with a mission to find followers of Christ and bring them back to Jerusalem as prisoners. However, a flash of heavenly light blocked his way, and Jesus spoke directly to Saul, telling him where to go next. Saul was blinded by this encounter and was unable to see for three days. Ananias, a disciple of Jesus, listened to the Lord's instructions and obediently went to visit Saul in Damascus. The Lord used Ananias to remove the scales from Saul's eyes in Jesus' name. Saul was now a believer and was baptized by Ananias. From that point on, Saul spent time with the disciples in Damascus and proclaimed Jesus as the Son of God in the synagogues.

Saul's life powerfully reflects the words of the hymn "Amazing Grace": "I once was blind, but now I see, was lost but now am found." You may think you have the most messed up, sinful, disobedient past and no one would ever accept you or see anything in you. You may even believe your life is just fine all on your own without a Savior. But then, you haven't met Jesus. Jesus forgives your sins, not because you earned it or deserve it but because He loves you and offers you the free gift of grace, love, hope, and His peace that passes all understanding. You just have to receive it. It's truly *amazing grace.* If you have never said yes to Jesus, take a minute today and receive Him into your life. If you are a believer in Christ, tell someone your story about going from blindness to sight. There is power in the great love and amazing grace of Jesus!

So Ananias left and entered the house. Then he placed his hands on him and said, "Brother Saul, the Lord Jesus, who appeared to you on the road you were traveling, has sent me so that you can regain your sight and be filled with the Holy Spirit." —Acts 9:17

Further Scripture: Romans 11:6; Ephesians 2:8–9; 1 Peter 2:9

Week 50, Day 346: Acts 10
Breaking the Norm

Cornelius, a Gentile centurion from Caesarea, saw an angel from God in a vision giving him directions to send men to Joppa and call for Simon (Peter). In Joppa, Simon Peter, one of Jesus' disciples, also had a vision from the Lord; however, he didn't understand it. Upon being called on by Cornelius's men, Peter traveled to Cornelius's home. Confident in what he heard from the Lord, Cornelius expected Peter to come and deliver a message. He even gathered his relatives and close friends to listen to Peter. God then clarified and confirmed in Peter's heart that he, a Jew, was to share the Gospel with this Gentile man and his family. They all received the Gospel, the Holy Spirit fell on them, and they were baptized.

Have you ever had a dream or vision but then ignored it because it didn't make sense to you? Remember, the Lord speaks to His people through dreams and visions to proclaim His glory and lead others to the Gospel. *Next time you have a dream or vision, ask the Lord for clarity and wisdom.* If the Lord gives you insight, then act immediately and expectantly in His authority. If you don't have the meaning to a dream or vision, ask a trusted friend and continue to press in and pray through it. Then, as God reveals the meaning, act on it expectantly! Peter and Cornelius trusted the Lord through their visions, and the Gospel went forth in a powerful new way to the Gentiles! Be the type of person to walk out God's authority, expecting Him to show up!

Therefore I immediately sent for you, and you did the right thing in coming. So we are all present before God, to hear everything you have been commanded by the Lord. —Acts 10:33

Further Scripture: Jeremiah 33:3; Joel 2:28; Acts 10:34–35

Week 50, Day 347: Acts 11
Even to the Gentiles

After Cornelius and his family accepted the Gospel message, Peter had to defend these Gentile conversions to the other apostles and brothers throughout Judea. He testified about his vision from the Lord and the witness of the Holy Spirit's moving. Peter understood it was hard to believe but asked his Jewish friends, "How can we possibly hinder God?" After hearing Peter's explanation, they were silent, and then they gave glory to the Lord for granting eternal life even to the Gentiles. The Gospel went beyond the Jewish people for the first time, and the Lord was praised for it.

Have you ever heard of God moving in such an unbelievable way that you couldn't believe it? *Anything is possible with the Lord!* The Gospel message is for anyone and everyone all around this world. Therefore the Lord will use the impossible—dreams and visions, signs and wonders—to draw people to His name and His love. May you believe this and desire this in your own life! Do not judge others, live in disbelief, or hinder God. The Gospel, God's power, and His authority are for anyone who hungers and thirsts for hope. May you be part of a generation who believes this powerful truth and walks it out!

"Therefore, if God gave them the same gift that He also gave us when we believed on the Lord Jesus Christ, how could I possibly hinder God?" When they heard this they became silent. Then they glorified God, saying, "So God has granted repentance resulting in life even to the Gentiles!"
—Acts 11:17–18

Further Scripture: Matthew 19:26; Luke 18:16; James 5:9

Week 50, Day 348: Acts 12
The Result of Earnest Prayer

King Herod attacked some who belonged to the church, killing James and arresting Peter with the intention of executing him. While Peter sat chained in prison, many gathered and earnestly prayed for the Lord to spare Peter's life. Suddenly one night, an angel of the Lord appeared to Peter telling him, "Get up!" Peter's chains fell off, and the angel escorted him out of prison to the outside of the city. The Lord answered the people's prayers and miraculously freed Peter! The people, although asking the Lord for Peter's freedom, were still astounded when Peter showed up at their door.

The Lord promises to answer your prayers. Prayer is communicating with God—talking with Him like a friend. The more you know God, the more natural praying becomes. Earnest prayer means *praying with passion, steadfastness, intensity, and intentionality.* Are you waiting for a brother to come back to Christ? Are you asking the Lord for a marriage to be restored? Are you seeking the Lord for a job? Consider earnestly seeking the Lord in prayer with tears and intensity—even gathering friends regularly to join you. When you do this, don't be surprised when God answers your prayer! He will show up, and His will will be done.

So Peter was kept in prison, but prayer was being made earnestly to God for him by the church. —Acts 12:5

Further Scripture: Psalm 34:15; Colossians 4:2–3; James 5:16

Week 50, Day 349: Acts 13
Barnabas and Saul Set Apart for God's Work

As the church in Antioch ministered, the Holy Spirit led the leaders to set Saul and Barnabas apart for the work God had called them to. Earlier when Paul encountered Jesus on the road to Damascus, the Lord told Ananias that Paul would be His chosen instrument to take His name to the Gentiles, kings, and the Israelites. Now was the time. After the church leaders fasted, prayed, and laid hands on Paul and Barnabas, they sent them off on their first missionary journey.

There may have been a time in your life you felt the call to be a worship leader, a pastor, an overseas missionary, or used in ministry in some other way. You may still be waiting for that moment to come. Remember, you can't force this to just happen. Press on in prayer, seek the Lord, and walk through any doors the Lord leads you through, gaining wisdom along the way. *The Lord will open the door at the right time.* When the Lord leads you into a new season of ministry, follow the example of the early church: the Holy Spirit spoke to the leaders, and they fasted, prayed, and laid on hands as a sendoff. Praise the Lord for His promise to call people into new places of influence for His kingdom as they patiently wait upon Him.

As they were ministering to the Lord and fasting, the Holy Spirit said, "Set apart for Me Barnabas and Saul for the work I have called them to." Then after they had fasted, prayed, and laid hands on them, they sent them off. —Acts 13:2–3

Further Scripture: Isaiah 6:8; Isaiah 43:1; Acts 9:15

Week 50, Day 350: Acts 14
Paul and Barnabas Pass through Troubles

Paul and Barnabas traveled from city to city as the Lord led them on their first missionary journey. They even returned to Lystra, Iconium, and Antioch to strengthen the disciples by encouraging them to continue in their faith. Paul and Barnabas shared that, as believers in the kingdom of God, *they would pass through many troubles*. Paul and Barnabas experienced hardship and persecution themselves, along with joy and spiritual growth, as they shared the Gospel. God gave them grace and strengthened them along the way.

The same is true for you as you seek first the kingdom of God. Will you have hardship and persecution? Yes. But be courageous and press on in hope. God has overcome the world. Have faith. *God is bigger than any hardship you may endure.* As you share the Gospel, keep Jesus as the focus, and you will be strengthened by His sufficient grace. The mission from God is to go out with His power and His authority, proclaiming His name. In doing so, you put yourself on the front lines, whether at the corporate office, on the mission field, in your neighborhood, or in your own family. Be a voice for Jesus, trusting He will strengthen you through any troubles.

After they had evangelized that town and made many disciples,
they returned to Lystra, to Iconium, and to Antioch, strengthening the
disciples by encouraging them to continue in the faith and by telling them,
"It is necessary to pass through many troubles on our way into the kingdom
of God." —Acts 14:21–22

Further Scripture: John 16:33; Acts 14:26–27; 2 Corinthians 11:28–31

Week 51, Day 351: Acts 15
Unity and Reconciliation

When Paul and Barnabas returned from their first missionary journey, a debate began as the two men testified in detail about Gentile conversions. The main issue of the debate centered on whether Gentile Christians needed to be circumcised in order to be considered believers, in accordance with the customs of Moses. *Seeking to bring unity* to the believers, the apostles and elders gathered in Jerusalem at what was called the Jerusalem Council. After much discussion, Peter stated, "On the contrary, we believe we are saved through the grace of the Lord Jesus in the same way they are." Then James pointed out the Old Testament prophet writings: "All of humanity, even the Gentiles, are called by God's name." The Jerusalem Counscil concluded they would not cause difficulties for the Gentiles who turned to God.

What is the greatest witness of Jesus Christ that believers can offer the world? *Unity among believers.* Jesus said the world would know God sent His Son when the world sees unity. Therefore, if an argument exists with another believer, seek reconciliation. Don't just sweep it under the rug and hope it goes away. Ask the Lord how to walk in humility through the disagreement. Gather together and talk it out. Seek the Holy Spirit for wisdom and help to reconcile. Focus on Jesus, who came to bring peace. *Today, ask the Holy Spirit if there is anything preventing you from unity with a brother or sister in Christ.* Now, go walk it out in obedience.

On the contrary, we believe we are saved through the grace of the Lord Jesus in the same way they are. —Acts 15:11

Further Scripture: John 17:23; Acts 15:17–18; 1 Corinthians 1:10

Week 51, Day 352: Acts 16
Paul's Macedonian Call

As Paul, Silas, and a young disciple named Timothy began the second missionary journey, the Holy Spirit prevented them from sharing the Gospel message in Asia. Then the Holy Spirit did not allow them into Bithynia. As they spent the night in Troas, a vision came to Paul directing him to go to Macedonia. After Paul saw the vision, the men immediately set off for Macedonia with intentions to share the Gospel. Sure enough, after two closed doors, the Lord at last brought them to a businesswoman named Lydia. She and her entire household were saved! God had the best plan of all!

Do you ever feel as though you've hit one closed door just to run right into another closed door? You may feel frustrated, confused, and discouraged. During these times, keep trusting the Lord. *Trust that He knows the door has closed.* Trust that He is aware of your frustration. Remember, God promises He has plans for you. Press on. The Lord will strengthen you as you wait upon Him. Listen to the Holy Spirit guiding you. God's plan remains the best plan for you and is worth the journey. So keep walking at God's pace, to God's place, and you will receive the peace and joy found only in Him! Don't give up!

They went through the region of Phrygia and Galatia and were prevented by the Holy Spirit from speaking the message in Asia. When they came to Mysia, they tried to go into Bithynia, but the Spirit of Jesus did not allow them. —Acts 16:6–7

Further Scripture: Proverbs 3:5–6; Jeremiah 29:11; Acts 16:9–10

Week 51, Day 353: Acts 17

Keep It Simple

Paul reasoned with, explained, and showed the message of Jesus through the Scriptures, proclaiming Jesus as the Messiah throughout his second missionary journey. Some were persuaded to believe. But many, especially Jewish people, became jealous and formed mobs to threaten Paul. They even followed Paul from Thessalonica to Berea to agitate and disturb his ministry. But Paul wasn't alone in his travels. During this difficult time, he relied on Timothy and Silas to stay behind and deal with the opposition in Berea, which allowed Paul to further the Gospel and travel on to Athens.

Building friendships and remaining in community with others is especially important when you endure times of suffering or persecution. In those times, you may need someone to stand by your side and help fight the battle, either through prayer or to help speak for you. *Do not isolate yourself.* If you feel alone with no one to turn to, pray and ask the Lord to bring someone with whom to share your burdens. Remember, as a child of God, you are a part of the family of God. You are not alone.

But when the Jews from Thessalonica found out that God's message had been proclaimed by Paul at Berea, they came there too, agitating and disturbing the crowds. Then the brothers immediately sent Paul away to go to the sea, but Silas and Timothy stayed on there. —Acts 17:13–14

Further Scripture: 1 Corinthians 12:26; Galatians 6:2; 2 Timothy 3:12

Week 51, Day 354: Acts 18
Founding the Corinthian Church

While Paul traveled on his second missionary journey, he left Athens and traveled to Corinth. Paul reasoned and preached the message testifying about Jesus the Messiah in the synagogues to both Jews and Gentiles. He began to receive resistance from the Jews. So Paul continued preaching but focused on the Gentiles, among whom he found a fruitful harvest. During this time, the Lord spoke a confirming word to Paul through a vision one night. He reminded Paul of His promise: *"Don't be afraid, keep on speaking, and don't be silent. For I am with you, and no one will lay a hand on you to hurt you."* And so, Paul pressed on, teaching the Word of God in Corinth for a year and a half.

Like Paul, you may be going along in your job, your routine, and your responsibilities, wherever the Lord has you, and you may face some resistance. Or at times, you may find favor. But at some point, it is so encouraging to receive a confirming word from the Lord. The Lord speaks through dreams and visions, through His Scriptures, and even through a word from a friend during a prayer time. Today, this promise from the Lord may be just for you: *"Don't be afraid, keep on speaking, and don't be silent. For I am with you, and no one will lay a hand on you to hurt you."* Walk in the Lord's authority and believe with all your heart that you don't need to be afraid. God is with you!

Then the Lord said to Paul in a night vision, "Don't be afraid, but keep on speaking and don't be silent. For I am with you, and no one will lay a hand on you to hurt you, because I have many people in this city." And he stayed there a year and six months, teaching the word of God among them.
—Acts 18:9–11

Further Scripture: Psalm 90:17; Psalm 138:7; Isaiah 41:10

Week 51, Day 355: Acts 19
The Holy Spirit inside You

Paul traveled to Ephesus and found some disciples there. They believed in Jesus as the Way, but when Paul asked them if they had received the Holy Spirit, they replied, "We haven't even heard that there is a Holy Spirit." Paul explained the Holy Spirit to them, laid hands on them, and prayed for them.

You may have received Jesus as your Lord and Savior. You prayed, "*Yes!* Lord, I believe You are the way, the truth and the life! I receive You, Jesus, into my life." *However, did you know, when you received Jesus, He promised to send the Holy Spirit to live inside you? You have the Holy Spirit inside you!* Jesus referred to the Holy Spirit as the counselor who will guide you in all truth. As you walk with the Spirit, you display the fruit of the Spirit. The Spirit also empowers you with gifts: supernatural power to equip the saints for the work of the ministry. Walking in the power of the Holy Spirit leads to an adventure with Jesus beyond what you can imagine! Do not think you are alone in this Christian journey. You have the power of the Holy Spirit inside you. Please do not end up saying, "I haven't heard there is a Holy Spirit." Wake up to the Holy Spirit empowering your life!

"No," they told him, "we haven't even heard that there is a Holy Spirit." —Acts 19:2

Further Scripture: John 14:16–17; John 16:13; Romans 8:9

December 22

Week 51, Day 356: Acts 20

Paul's Final Journey toward Jerusalem

After spending three years in Ephesus, Paul sensed the Lord had a new season awaiting him back in Jerusalem, possibly one of chains and afflictions. However, before leaving, he imparted a word of encouragement, truth to both Jews and Greeks, and a warning to stand firm as believers in Jesus. His heart ached to say goodbye to these believers he loved. Even so, he chose to entrust them to the Lord and moved on to a new season of ministry.

Have you ever had to leave people you love and thought, *What do I say to these people to whom I feel so connected and who desire to stay strong in the Lord?* Maybe you moved away, departed from the mission field, or even sent your child off to college. Paul gave a good example of how to leave loved ones by imparting last minute words of wisdom, love, and grace. First, remind them about the love of Jesus and His message of grace, which is able to build up and give hope. Second, remind them to be on guard because the enemy prowls around seeking to destroy their faith and bring discouragement. Last, remind them to stay alert. As you leave, you must ultimately trust the Holy Spirit to carry them. It's not easy to say goodbye, but when God calls you into a new season, know He will be faithful.

Therefore, be on the alert, remembering that night and day for three years I did not stop warning each one of you with tears. And now I commit you to God and to the message of His grace, which is able to build you up and to give you an inheritance among all who are sanctified. —Acts 20:31–32

Further Scripture: 1 Corinthians 16:13; Hebrews 10:38–39; 1 Peter 5:8

Week 51, Day 357: Acts 21
The Lord's Will Be Done

As Paul journeyed back to Jerusalem, he stopped in Tyre and stayed with disciples who warned him through the Spirit not to go to Jerusalem. Even so, Paul continued traveling toward Jerusalem, stopping in Ptolemais. While staying the night with fellow believers, Paul met a prophet named Agabus who delivered a message to him about Jews in Jerusalem binding him up. After hearing this, the locals begged Paul not to travel farther. Nevertheless, confident in his calling to go back to Jerusalem and risk his life for Christ, Paul replied to them, "For I am ready not only to be bound but also to die in Jerusalem for the name of the Lord Jesus." Upon hearing this, the people stopped talking and simply said, "The Lord's will be done."

Have you ever prayed, "May the Lord's will be done"? It's a prayer of humility, surrender, and trust in God. It's trusting the Lord, *even if* the healing doesn't come, *even if* you lose the job, *even if* you endure hardship; you keep the faith to glorify the name of Jesus! Paul came to the point of complete surrender, *even if* it cost him his life. When Jesus suffered and came to the end of His life in pain, He cried out to the Father, "Not My will, but Yours, be done." *As you ask for the Lord's will to be done and surrender your life in such a way, remember through the pain and the suffering, God will strengthen you.* His hope will remain forever.

Then Paul replied, "What are you doing, weeping and breaking my heart? For I am ready not only to be bound but also to die in Jerusalem for the name of the Lord Jesus." Since he would not be persuaded, we stopped talking and simply said, "The Lord's will be done!" —Acts 21:13–14

Further Scripture: Luke 22:42; 2 Corinthians 12:10; Philippians 3:7–8

Week 52, Day 358: Acts 22

Facing the Crowd with His Testimony

Paul asked the Roman commander to allow him to speak to the mob pressing in around him before being taken to the barracks in Jerusalem. Paul addressed the crowd in the Hebrew language and shared his encounter with Jesus, testifying of his complete transformation and new calling in life. The people listened and yet still considered Paul a disgrace and wanted him killed. They were about to beat him when the commander discovered Paul was a Roman citizen from birth. This unique fact released Paul, even while the Sanhedrin continued discussing what to do with him.

Do you remember the moment you believed in Jesus as your Lord and Savior and how God transformed your life? As a believer, be ready to share your testimony. The world wants to hear tangible testimonies of God's power. *How will others know about Jesus or even want to know Jesus if they don't hear about the goodness of His love and transforming power working in your own life?* Don't be afraid to share. God will equip you in that moment and give you words to say. If you feel ashamed of your life before Christ, remember, God promises to work all things together for good. Trust Him to redeem your past and use your testimony to encourage and comfort others. It's time to find your voice and share your journey with others!

Then he said, "The God of our fathers has appointed you to know His will, to see the Righteous One, and to hear the sound of His voice. For you will be a witness for Him to all people of what you have seen and heard."
—Acts 22:14–15

Further Scripture: Matthew 10:18–20; Luke 8:39; 2 Corinthians 1:3–4

Week 52, Day 359: Acts 23

The Beginning of Paul's Journey to Rome

As Paul continued facing attacks in Jerusalem, waiting for the Sanhedrin to decide what to do with him, the Lord showed up one night saying: "Have courage! For as you testified about Me in Jerusalem, so you must also testify in Rome." Even while Paul faced death, the Lord spoke life into him, giving him a mission to testify in Rome. From Paul's viewpoint, it seemed impossible for him to survive his current situation and travel to Rome. But God provided an unpredictable plan, removing Paul from his enemies in Jerusalem and escorting him safely to Caesarea.

God instructs you to live your life fully surrendered, denying yourself and following after Jesus. But how do you press on when there seems to be no way? Doors are closing, you have no money in your checking account, and there seems to be no way you will ever make it to where you thought the Lord called you. *Press on, friend, with a clear conscience.* Believe in your calling. Resist any pride rising up within you, and walk in humility. Fully surrender everything to the Lord. Fully trust in God's promised provision and protection. Anything is possible with God. Anything. So keep walking. Don't give up. God is about to do something unpredictable in order to fulfill His promise for your life. Have courage!

The following night, the Lord stood by him and said,
"Have courage! For as you have testified about Me in Jerusalem,
so you must also testify in Rome." —Acts 23:11

Further Scripture: Joshua 21:45; Isaiah 43:16–19; Matthew 16:24

Week 52, Day 360: Acts 24
The Jews Try to Kill Paul

Paul had been waiting in Caesarea for five days when a lawyer named Tertullus brought false accusations against him in front of Governor Felix. Tertullus called Paul a plague, an agitator among the Jews throughout the Roman world, a ringleader of the sect of the Nazarenes, and even accused him of desecrating the temple. During his defense, Paul explained his faithfulness in worshipping the Way, his hope found in God, and his offering of charitable gifts. Paul lived with a clear conscience, not hiding anything. So when false accusations came, Paul didn't worry. He continued walking faithfully before the Lord His God, allowing God's will to be done and trusting Him along the way.

As you live fully surrendered to the Lord, choose to live with a clear conscience. Remember, nothing is hidden from God. He sees all. Eventually, the truth will be revealed. It is better to suffer for doing good than for doing evil. Therefore, ask the Lord for strength to walk with integrity and resist the enemy's temptations to deceive others. *Desire to live in such freedom that when accusations come, you don't have to defend yourself or even worry.* The Lord's peace will cover you as you choose to walk in this way as a testimony of God's grace.

And I have a hope in God, which these men themselves also accept, that there is going to be a resurrection, both of the righteous and the unrighteous. I always do my best to have a clear conscience toward God and men.
—Acts 24:15–16

Further Scripture: Proverbs 11:3; 1 Peter 3:16–17; 1 Timothy 1:18–19

Week 52, Day 361: Acts 25
Paul's Defense before Governor Festus

Governor Felix kept Paul in prison for two years. Then Porcius Festus succeeded Felix in office. Just three days after Festus took office as the new governor, the chief priests presented Paul's case again, hoping to move Paul's case along. However, their plan failed. When Paul sat before Festus, he spoke with authority from the Holy Spirit and *in good conscience, said, "I have done nothing wrong."* Eventually, Paul's case came before King Agrippa in Caesarea. Governor Festus explained to the king that he believed Paul had done nothing wrong and didn't deserve death.

How do you live such a life where you would be able to stand before authorities and say, "I have done nothing wrong"? It's not with arrogance but rather with a confident authority in Jesus. In Christ, you are fully righteous. You are a new creation, and the old is gone. This truth sets you free—*you are made new in Christ.* Don't walk in your flesh with pride, arrogance, anger, lust, or selfishness, things that lead to guilt and perverse ways. Instead, choose to walk in the Spirit with peace, gentleness, kindness, patience, self-control, and love. As you receive Christ and walk in His Spirit, *you leave no room for false accusations* because you have complete freedom in Christ!

Now I realized that he had not done anything deserving of death, but when he himself appealed to the Emperor, I decided to send him.
—Acts 25:25

Further Scripture: Acts 25:10; Romans 8:5–9; 2 Corinthians 5:21

Week 52, Day 362: Acts 26
Paul's Defense before King Agrippa

Paul testified before King Agrippa, once again sharing his testimony from the Damascus road when the Lord shined a great light on him, talked with him, and gave Paul his calling for life. Paul continued to share the Gospel message with King Agrippa, even to the point the king thought Paul had gone crazy. Paul testified with a *confident authority from the Lord*. He believed so strongly in the testimony of Jesus Christ that he boldly asked the king to believe in Jesus.

Have you ever shared your heart, your testimony, and your journey with someone and then said, "I wish you would just believe in Him"? Because Jesus changed your life, you desire for Him to change those you love. Most likely, you have people in your life with whom you have shared the Gospel, loving them and showing them kindness. Yet they chose not to believe. You may even want to shake them into believing, but you can't force it. That's not your role. Only the Holy Spirit can touch hearts to cause a genuine repentance and belief in Jesus. As a believer, *continue to pray, continue to go, and continue to share Jesus' love as He leads you*. Never lose hope. You are planting seeds. God will move in your midst as you walk in love for His name and for His glory.

"I wish before God," replied Paul, "that whether easily or with difficulty, not only you but all who listen to me today might become as I am—except for these chains." —Acts 26:29

Further Scripture: Zechariah 4:6; Acts 26:17–18; 1 Corinthians 3:6

Week 52, Day 363: Acts 27
Take Courage

Just as the Lord promised, King Agrippa ordered Paul to Rome so he could appeal to Caesar. Paul, along with Luke, other prisoners, and a centurion named Julius, sailed from Caesarea to Rome. The ship encountered unpredicted troubles as the wind tossed it back and forth on the sea. Some winds were light but others were typhoon-like and eventually shipwrecked the boat along the island of Malta. The passengers became discouraged and frustrated. However, even in the darkest night as the storm raged on, the Lord showed up to Paul, promising all on board would survive. The Lord spoke through Paul to the passengers, telling them to take courage and not be afraid because God was with them.

Do you ever feel as though you are sinking or surrounded by darkness for days on end? Like the weary passengers, do you feel all hope is lost? Today, you may need to hear this promise from the Lord—*the Lord is with you.* Take courage, friend. In Christ, you have hope. The Lord loves you and is mighty to save. *Sometimes the hardest part of life may not be walking by faith but waiting in faith.* As you experience times in life when you don't know your next step or darkness encircles you, call upon the name of the Lord. Take authority over the darkness. Jesus promises you victory in Him. He promises His Word is a lamp to your feet and a light to your path. If you don't know the next step to take today, open the Word of God. He promises to give you direction. Take a deep breath and trust Him.

For many days neither sun nor stars appeared, and the severe storm kept raging. Finally all hope that we would be saved was disappearing. . . . "Now I urge you to take courage, because there will be no loss of any of your lives, but only of the ship." —Acts 27:20, 22

Further Scripture: Isaiah 41:10; Habakkuk 3:17–19; Zephaniah 3:17

Week 52, Day 364: Acts 28
Be on Alert and Stand Firm

Paul and all the ship's passengers safely reached the shore of an island called Malta, just as the Lord had promised. The locals greeted the ship's passengers with kindness. While Paul helped to build a fire, a viper attacked him. The people thought he would swell up and drop dead, but Paul shook the snake off into the fire. He suffered no harm from the snake attack. His strength and good health shocked the people, and because of this, they respected him.

Even on the small island of Malta, Paul was attacked. No matter where you go, as you walk with authority in the Lord, in His strength, and for His glory, the enemy will prowl around you. The attacks will come. However, the Lord is with you in battle. He is your rock. He is your shelter. He will fight for you. *Do not be afraid, but be on the alert.* In every circumstance, submit to the Lord, resist the devil, and he will flee from you. Put on the full armor, so when the enemy comes, you will stand strong against his tactics. No weapon formed against you will prosper, friend. So press on, walking with Jesus. He is mighty within you! As you stand firm, people will see Jesus in you.

However, he shook the creature off into the fire and suffered no harm.
They expected that he would swell up or suddenly drop dead. But after they
waited a long time and saw nothing unusual happen to him, they changed
their minds and said he was a god. —Acts 28:5–6

Further Scripture: Luke 10:19; 1 Peter 5:8; Ephesians 6:11–12

Week 52, Day 365: Psalm 119
reviveDAILY in the Word

You have read the Word day after day and night after night. The Word was in the beginning, became flesh, and dwelt among you. The Word is Jesus. He is the living water your dry soul longs for. He says come to Him with a broken heart and a contrite spirit. He doesn't instruct you to come as an unblemished jar, rather come as dusty broken pieces.

Allow God's Word to mold you, shape you, and transform you. Come broken before the Lord. Come in humility. Come as you are. May His faithful love be water for your thirsty soul day after day and year after year. *May the Word revive you daily.*

"My soul cleaves to the dust; revive me according to Your word."
—Psalm 119:25

Further Scripture: Psalm 117:1–2; Mark 14:3; John 1:14

About Laura Kim Martin and Time to Revive

From the time Laura Kim Martin was a little girl growing up in Minnesota, she has sensed the Lord's calling to ministry. Her desire has always been to serve the Lord and tell the lost about Jesus Christ. A communication studies graduate of Taylor University (Indiana), Laura married Kyle Lance Martin, and together, they founded the Dallas-based ministry Time to Revive in 2010. As a couple, they surrendered their lives for the sake of the Gospel, reaching the lost, and encouraging the Church. With her heart for prayer and full dependence on the Lord, Laura began writing a weekly prayer and encouragement devotional, *Along the Journey.*

Through years of living out surrendered faith and trust in the Lord, Laura has tasted and seen that God is good. She has walked through trials and unknowns and personally witnessed God's faithfulness in the miracle moments of her own life, believing God through the impossible. She's received the love of Christ and freedom found in resting in His presence, while walking in His grace and Truth. Laura joyfully walks with Jesus through the power of His Holy Spirit and listens to His voice. Now, she shares the lessons the Lord has written on her own heart, encouraging others to press on in their personal faith journeys with Jesus.

When not writing or opening up her home with her heart for hospitality in Richardson, Texas, Laura relishes time with Kyle and their four kids: Maya, Nadia, Selah, and Jude. Whether spending time outside or getting involved in activities that bring her kids joy, she loves seeing her family laugh and play well. Laura also enjoys exploring new coffee shops with friends, shopping for meaningful gifts for others, and sitting in her comfy chair at home where she can spend intimate time with the Lord.

Follow Laura Kim Martin:
www.laurakimmartin.com
ⓕ Facebook: Laura Kim Martin
ⓖ Instagram: @laurakimmartin

time torevive

Time to Revive (TTR) equips the believers to get ready for the return of Christ. TTR partners with the church in communities, bringing believers together across denominational lines and inspiring them to obey the Great Commission to go in the power of the Holy Spirit and make disciples. Through hands-on training, the TTR team empowers the saints to leave familiar church walls and walk by faith to share the Gospel in authentic and life-changing ways.

www.timetorevive.com
info@timetorevive.com
https://www.facebook.com/timetorevive

If you have enjoyed this devotional and would like to dig even deeper into studying the Word of God, we invite you to register online to reviveSCHOOL.org. reviveSCHOOL is a two-year interactive Bible study that teaches through the Bible daily from Genesis to Revelation. Teaching and study are focused on seeing the Complete Portrait of the Messiah in all 66 books of the Bible. Additional resources include a 29-minute video teaching for each lesson, daily teaching notes, study guide questions, and a painting that summarizes each book of the Bible.

www.reviveSCHOOL.org
info@reviveSCHOOL.org

Reading Plans for *revive*DAILY

I don't know about you, but I love to check boxes off after I complete something. Therefore, I have included these reading plans for *Year 1* and *Year 2* of *revive*DAILY. You can look ahead at what is coming as well as check off the boxes as you read daily through the Bible. Keep in mind, however, that reading and studying through the Bible is not a sprint race. It's more like a marathon. Give yourself grace on this journey as you daily spend time with Jesus and in the Word of God.

Remember, you can find additional study resources, including a daily video teaching for each daily reading, at www.reviveschool.org.

Enjoy the journey!

YEAR 1

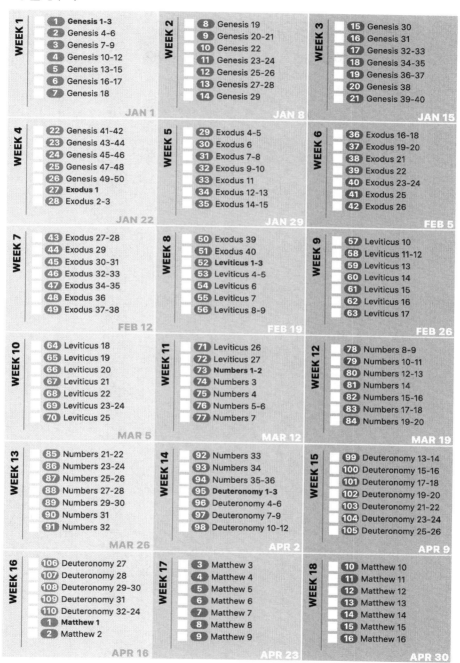

WEEK 1
- 1 **Genesis 1-3**
- 2 Genesis 4-6
- 3 Genesis 7-9
- 4 Genesis 10-12
- 5 Genesis 13-15
- 6 Genesis 16-17
- 7 Genesis 18

JAN 1

WEEK 2
- 8 Genesis 19
- 9 Genesis 20-21
- 10 Genesis 22
- 11 Genesis 23-24
- 12 Genesis 25-26
- 13 Genesis 27-28
- 14 Genesis 29

JAN 8

WEEK 3
- 15 Genesis 30
- 16 Genesis 31
- 17 Genesis 32-33
- 18 Genesis 34-35
- 19 Genesis 36-37
- 20 Genesis 38
- 21 Genesis 39-40

JAN 15

WEEK 4
- 22 Genesis 41-42
- 23 Genesis 43-44
- 24 Genesis 45-46
- 25 Genesis 47-48
- 26 Genesis 49-50
- 27 **Exodus 1**
- 28 Exodus 2-3

JAN 22

WEEK 5
- 29 Exodus 4-5
- 30 Exodus 6
- 31 Exodus 7-8
- 32 Exodus 9-10
- 33 Exodus 11
- 34 Exodus 12-13
- 35 Exodus 14-15

JAN 29

WEEK 6
- 36 Exodus 16-18
- 37 Exodus 19-20
- 38 Exodus 21
- 39 Exodus 22
- 40 Exodus 23-24
- 41 Exodus 25
- 42 Exodus 26

FEB 5

WEEK 7
- 43 Exodus 27-28
- 44 Exodus 29
- 45 Exodus 30-31
- 46 Exodus 32-33
- 47 Exodus 34-35
- 48 Exodus 36
- 49 Exodus 37-38

FEB 12

WEEK 8
- 50 Exodus 39
- 51 Exodus 40
- 52 **Leviticus 1-3**
- 53 Leviticus 4-5
- 54 Leviticus 6
- 55 Leviticus 7
- 56 Leviticus 8-9

FEB 19

WEEK 9
- 57 Leviticus 10
- 58 Leviticus 11-12
- 59 Leviticus 13
- 60 Leviticus 14
- 61 Leviticus 15
- 62 Leviticus 16
- 63 Leviticus 17

FEB 26

WEEK 10
- 64 Leviticus 18
- 65 Leviticus 19
- 66 Leviticus 20
- 67 Leviticus 21
- 68 Leviticus 22
- 69 Leviticus 23-24
- 70 Leviticus 25

MAR 5

WEEK 11
- 71 Leviticus 26
- 72 Leviticus 27
- 73 **Numbers 1-2**
- 74 Numbers 3
- 75 Numbers 4
- 76 Numbers 5-6
- 77 Numbers 7

MAR 12

WEEK 12
- 78 Numbers 8-9
- 79 Numbers 10-11
- 80 Numbers 12-13
- 81 Numbers 14
- 82 Numbers 15-16
- 83 Numbers 17-18
- 84 Numbers 19-20

MAR 19

WEEK 13
- 85 Numbers 21-22
- 86 Numbers 23-24
- 87 Numbers 25-26
- 88 Numbers 27-28
- 89 Numbers 29-30
- 90 Numbers 31
- 91 Numbers 32

MAR 26

WEEK 14
- 92 Numbers 33
- 93 Numbers 34
- 94 Numbers 35-36
- 95 **Deuteronomy 1-3**
- 96 Deuteronomy 4-6
- 97 Deuteronomy 7-9
- 98 Deuteronomy 10-12

APR 2

WEEK 15
- 99 Deuteronomy 13-14
- 100 Deuteronomy 15-16
- 101 Deuteronomy 17-18
- 102 Deuteronomy 19-20
- 103 Deuteronomy 21-22
- 104 Deuteronomy 23-24
- 105 Deuteronomy 25-26

APR 9

WEEK 16
- 106 Deuteronomy 27
- 107 Deuteronomy 28
- 108 Deuteronomy 29-30
- 109 Deuteronomy 31
- 110 Deuteronomy 32-24
- 1 **Matthew 1**
- 2 Matthew 2

APR 16

WEEK 17
- 3 Matthew 3
- 4 Matthew 4
- 5 Matthew 5
- 6 Matthew 6
- 7 Matthew 7
- 8 Matthew 8
- 9 Matthew 9

APR 23

WEEK 18
- 10 Matthew 10
- 11 Matthew 11
- 12 Matthew 12
- 13 Matthew 13
- 14 Matthew 14
- 15 Matthew 15
- 16 Matthew 16

APR 30

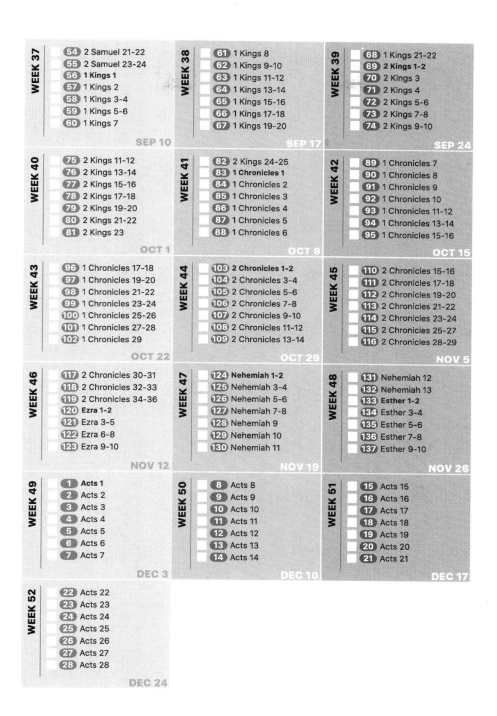

WEEK 37
- 54 2 Samuel 21-22
- 55 2 Samuel 23-24
- 56 **1 Kings 1**
- 57 1 Kings 2
- 58 1 Kings 3-4
- 59 1 Kings 5-6
- 60 1 Kings 7

SEP 10

WEEK 38
- 61 1 Kings 8
- 62 1 Kings 9-10
- 63 1 Kings 11-12
- 64 1 Kings 13-14
- 65 1 Kings 15-16
- 66 1 Kings 17-18
- 67 1 Kings 19-20

SEP 17

WEEK 39
- 68 1 Kings 21-22
- 69 **2 Kings 1-2**
- 70 2 Kings 3
- 71 2 Kings 4
- 72 2 Kings 5-6
- 73 2 Kings 7-8
- 74 2 Kings 9-10

SEP 24

WEEK 40
- 75 2 Kings 11-12
- 76 2 Kings 13-14
- 77 2 Kings 15-16
- 78 2 Kings 17-18
- 79 2 Kings 19-20
- 80 2 Kings 21-22
- 81 2 Kings 23

OCT 1

WEEK 41
- 82 2 Kings 24-25
- 83 **1 Chronicles 1**
- 84 1 Chronicles 2
- 85 1 Chronicles 3
- 86 1 Chronicles 4
- 87 1 Chronicles 5
- 88 1 Chronicles 6

OCT 8

WEEK 42
- 89 1 Chronicles 7
- 90 1 Chronicles 8
- 91 1 Chronicles 9
- 92 1 Chronicles 10
- 93 1 Chronicles 11-12
- 94 1 Chronicles 13-14
- 95 1 Chronicles 15-16

OCT 15

WEEK 43
- 96 1 Chronicles 17-18
- 97 1 Chronicles 19-20
- 98 1 Chronicles 21-22
- 99 1 Chronicles 23-24
- 100 1 Chronicles 25-26
- 101 1 Chronicles 27-28
- 102 1 Chronicles 29

OCT 22

WEEK 44
- 103 **2 Chronicles 1-2**
- 104 2 Chronicles 3-4
- 105 2 Chronicles 5-6
- 106 2 Chronicles 7-8
- 107 2 Chronicles 9-10
- 108 2 Chronicles 11-12
- 109 2 Chronicles 13-14

OCT 29

WEEK 45
- 110 2 Chronicles 15-16
- 111 2 Chronicles 17-18
- 112 2 Chronicles 19-20
- 113 2 Chronicles 21-22
- 114 2 Chronicles 23-24
- 115 2 Chronicles 25-27
- 116 2 Chronicles 28-29

NOV 5

WEEK 46
- 117 2 Chronicles 30-31
- 118 2 Chronicles 32-33
- 119 2 Chronicles 34-36
- 120 **Ezra 1-2**
- 121 Ezra 3-5
- 122 Ezra 6-8
- 123 Ezra 9-10

NOV 12

WEEK 47
- 124 **Nehemiah 1-2**
- 125 Nehemiah 3-4
- 126 Nehemiah 5-6
- 127 Nehemiah 7-8
- 128 Nehemiah 9
- 129 Nehemiah 10
- 130 Nehemiah 11

NOV 19

WEEK 48
- 131 Nehemiah 12
- 132 Nehemiah 13
- 133 **Esther 1-2**
- 134 Esther 3-4
- 135 Esther 5-6
- 136 Esther 7-8
- 137 Esther 9-10

NOV 26

WEEK 49
- 1 **Acts 1**
- 2 Acts 2
- 3 Acts 3
- 4 Acts 4
- 5 Acts 5
- 6 Acts 6
- 7 Acts 7

DEC 3

WEEK 50
- 8 Acts 8
- 9 Acts 9
- 10 Acts 10
- 11 Acts 11
- 12 Acts 12
- 13 Acts 13
- 14 Acts 14

DEC 10

WEEK 51
- 15 Acts 15
- 16 Acts 16
- 17 Acts 17
- 18 Acts 18
- 19 Acts 19
- 20 Acts 20
- 21 Acts 21

DEC 17

WEEK 52
- 22 Acts 22
- 23 Acts 23
- 24 Acts 24
- 25 Acts 25
- 26 Acts 26
- 27 Acts 27
- 28 Acts 28

DEC 24

Year 2

392

WEEK 19
- 6 Romans 6
- 7 Romans 7
- 8 Romans 8
- 9 Romans 9
- 10 Romans 10
- 11 Romans 11
- 12 Romans 12

MAY 7

WEEK 20
- 13 Romans 13
- 14 Romans 14
- 15 Romans 15
- 16 Romans 16
- 17 **1 Corinthians 1**
- 18 1 Corinthians 2
- 19 1 Corinthians 3

MAY 14

WEEK 21
- 20 1 Corinthians 4
- 21 1 Corinthians 5
- 22 1 Corinthians 6
- 23 1 Corinthians 7
- 24 1 Corinthians 8
- 25 1 Corinthians 9
- 26 1 Corinthians 10

MAY 21

WEEK 22
- 27 1 Corinthians 11
- 28 1 Corinthians 12
- 29 1 Corinthians 13
- 30 1 Corinthians 14
- 31 1 Corinthians 15
- 32 1 Corinthians 16
- 33 **2 Corinthians 1**

MAY 28

WEEK 23
- 34 2 Corinthians 2
- 35 2 Corinthians 3
- 36 2 Corinthians 4
- 37 2 Corinthians 5
- 38 2 Corinthians 6
- 39 2 Corinthians 7
- 40 2 Corinthians 8

JUN 4

WEEK 24
- 41 2 Corinthians 9
- 42 2 Corinthians 10
- 43 2 Corinthians 11
- 44 2 Corinthians 12
- 45 2 Corinthians 13
- 46 **Galations 1**
- 47 Galations 2

JUN 11

WEEK 25
- 48 Galations 3
- 49 Galations 4
- 50 Galations 5
- 51 Galations 6
- 52 **Ephesians 1**
- 53 Ephesians 2
- 54 Ephesians 3

JUN 18

WEEK 26
- 55 Ephesians 4
- 56 Ephesians 5
- 57 Ephesians 6
- 58 **Philippians 1**
- 59 Philippians 2
- 60 Philippians 3
- 61 Philippians 4

JUN 25

WEEK 27
- 62 **Colossians 1**
- 63 Colossians 2
- 64 Colossians 3
- 65 Colossians 4
- 66 **1 Thessalonians 1**
- 67 1 Thessalonians 2
- 68 1 Thessalonians 3

JUL 2

WEEK 28
- 69 1 Thessalonians 4
- 70 1 Thessalonians 5
- 71 **2 Thessalonians 1**
- 72 2 Thessalonians 2
- 73 2 Thessalonians 3
- 74 **1 Timothy 1**
- 75 1 Timothy 2

JUL 9

WEEK 29
- 76 1 Timothy 3
- 77 1 Timothy 4
- 78 1 Timothy 5
- 79 1 Timothy 6
- 80 **2 Timothy 1**
- 81 2 Timothy 2
- 82 2 Timothy 3

JUL 16

WEEK 30
- 83 2 Timothy 4
- 84 **Titus 1**
- 85 Titus 2
- 86 Titus 3
- 87 **Philemon 1**
- 1 **Isaiah 1-2**
- 2 Isaiah 3-4

JUL 23

WEEK 31
- 3 Isaiah 5-6
- 4 Isaiah 7-8
- 5 Isaiah 9-10
- 6 Isaiah 11-13
- 7 Isaiah 14-16
- 8 Isaiah 17-18
- 9 Isaiah 19-20

JUL 30

WEEK 32
- 10 Isaiah 21-22
- 11 Isaiah 23-25
- 12 Isaiah 26-27
- 13 Isaiah 28-29
- 14 Isaiah 30-31
- 15 Isaiah 32-33
- 16 Isaiah 34-36

AUG 6

WEEK 33
- 17 Isaiah 37-38
- 18 Isaiah 39-40
- 19 Isaiah 41-42
- 20 Isaiah 43-44
- 21 Isaiah 45-46
- 22 Isaiah 47-49
- 23 Isaiah 50-52

AUG 13

WEEK 34
- 24 Isaiah 53-55
- 25 Isaiah 56-58
- 26 Isaiah 59-61
- 27 Isaiah 62-64
- 28 Isaiah 65-66
- 29 **Jeremiah 1-2**
- 30 Jeremiah 3-5

AUG 20

WEEK 35
- 31 Jeremiah 6-8
- 32 Jeremiah 9-11
- 33 Jeremiah 12-14
- 34 Jeremiah 15-17
- 35 Jeremiah 18-19
- 36 Jeremiah 20-21
- 37 Jeremiah 22-23

AUG 27

WEEK 36
- 38 Jeremiah 24-26
- 39 Jeremiah 27-29
- 40 Jeremiah 30-31
- 41 Jeremiah 32-33
- 42 Jeremiah 34-36
- 43 Jeremiah 37-39
- 44 Jeremiah 40-42

SEP 3

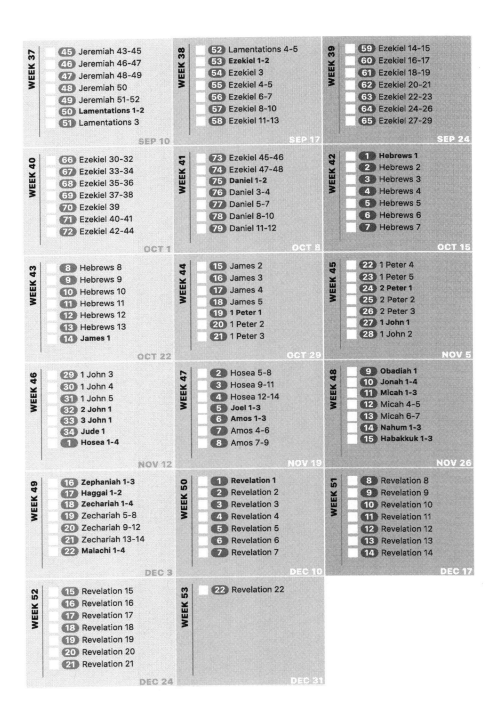

WEEK 37
- 45 Jeremiah 43-45
- 46 Jeremiah 46-47
- 47 Jeremiah 48-49
- 48 Jeremiah 50
- 49 Jeremiah 51-52
- 50 **Lamentations 1-2**
- 51 Lamentations 3

SEP 10

WEEK 38
- 52 Lamentations 4-5
- 53 **Ezekiel 1-2**
- 54 Ezekiel 3
- 55 Ezekiel 4-5
- 56 Ezekiel 6-7
- 57 Ezekiel 8-10
- 58 Ezekiel 11-13

SEP 17

WEEK 39
- 59 Ezekiel 14-15
- 60 Ezekiel 16-17
- 61 Ezekiel 18-19
- 62 Ezekiel 20-21
- 63 Ezekiel 22-23
- 64 Ezekiel 24-26
- 65 Ezekiel 27-29

SEP 24

WEEK 40
- 66 Ezekiel 30-32
- 67 Ezekiel 33-34
- 68 Ezekiel 35-36
- 69 Ezekiel 37-38
- 70 Ezekiel 39
- 71 Ezekiel 40-41
- 72 Ezekiel 42-44

OCT 1

WEEK 41
- 73 Ezekiel 45-46
- 74 Ezekiel 47-48
- 75 **Daniel 1-2**
- 76 Daniel 3-4
- 77 Daniel 5-7
- 78 Daniel 8-10
- 79 Daniel 11-12

OCT 8

WEEK 42
- 1 **Hebrews 1**
- 2 Hebrews 2
- 3 Hebrews 3
- 4 Hebrews 4
- 5 Hebrews 5
- 6 Hebrews 6
- 7 Hebrews 7

OCT 15

WEEK 43
- 8 Hebrews 8
- 9 Hebrews 9
- 10 Hebrews 10
- 11 Hebrews 11
- 12 Hebrews 12
- 13 Hebrews 13
- 14 **James 1**

OCT 22

WEEK 44
- 15 James 2
- 16 James 3
- 17 James 4
- 18 James 5
- 19 **1 Peter 1**
- 20 1 Peter 2
- 21 1 Peter 3

OCT 29

WEEK 45
- 22 1 Peter 4
- 23 1 Peter 5
- 24 **2 Peter 1**
- 25 2 Peter 2
- 26 2 Peter 3
- 27 **1 John 1**
- 28 1 John 2

NOV 5

WEEK 46
- 29 1 John 3
- 30 1 John 4
- 31 1 John 5
- 32 **2 John 1**
- 33 **3 John 1**
- 34 **Jude 1**
- 1 **Hosea 1-4**

NOV 12

WEEK 47
- 2 Hosea 5-8
- 3 Hosea 9-11
- 4 Hosea 12-14
- 5 **Joel 1-3**
- 6 **Amos 1-3**
- 7 Amos 4-6
- 8 Amos 7-9

NOV 19

WEEK 48
- 9 **Obadiah 1**
- 10 **Jonah 1-4**
- 11 **Micah 1-3**
- 12 Micah 4-5
- 13 Micah 6-7
- 14 **Nahum 1-3**
- 15 **Habakkuk 1-3**

NOV 26

WEEK 49
- 16 **Zephaniah 1-3**
- 17 **Haggai 1-2**
- 18 **Zechariah 1-4**
- 19 Zechariah 5-8
- 20 Zechariah 9-12
- 21 Zechariah 13-14
- 22 **Malachi 1-4**

DEC 3

WEEK 50
- 1 **Revelation 1**
- 2 Revelation 2
- 3 Revelation 3
- 4 Revelation 4
- 5 Revelation 5
- 6 Revelation 6
- 7 Revelation 7

DEC 10

WEEK 51
- 8 Revelation 8
- 9 Revelation 9
- 10 Revelation 10
- 11 Revelation 11
- 12 Revelation 12
- 13 Revelation 13
- 14 Revelation 14

DEC 17

WEEK 52
- 15 Revelation 15
- 16 Revelation 16
- 17 Revelation 17
- 18 Revelation 18
- 19 Revelation 19
- 20 Revelation 20
- 21 Revelation 21

DEC 24

WEEK 53
- 22 Revelation 22

DEC 31

Hey friend,

Happy New Year's and congrats! I hope you have enjoyed reading *revive*DAILY as you read through the Word of God! You are halfway through reading the Bible in its entirety! Well done! You have one more year to finish reading all the way through to Revelation. I pray you press on to continue to grow deeper and stronger in the Lord so that your roots grow deep and you continue to bear much fruit. The Lord will give you strength! Press on, dear friend!

I am the vine; you are the branches. The one who remains in Me and I in him produces much fruit, because you can do nothing without Me.
—John 15:5

---

*revive*DAILY*: Year Two* will be available for purchase anywhere books are sold.

Made in the USA
Middletown, DE
05 August 2021